SATHER CLASSICAL LECTURES
Volume Thirty-nine

LYSIAS AND THE *CORPUS LYSIACUM*

LYSIAS AND THE *CORPUS LYSIACUM*

by K. J. DOVER

UNIVERSITY OF CALIFORNIA PRESS
BERKELEY AND LOS ANGELES 1968

UNIVERSITY OF CALIFORNIA PRESS
BERKELEY AND LOS ANGELES, CALIFORNIA

CAMBRIDGE UNIVERSITY PRESS
LONDON, ENGLAND

ISBN:978-0520-30214-3 (pbk. : alk. paper).
© 1968 BY THE REGENTS OF THE UNIVERSITY OF CALIFORNIA
LIBRARY OF CONGRESS CATALOG CARD NUMBER: 68-63337

Preface

THE ARGUMENT of this book is that of the six lectures which it was my privilege to give as Sather Professor of Classical Literature in the University of California during the winter quarter of 1966/67. The order of presentation remains unchanged, but the argument has been amplified by digressions, references, tables and lists which were not suitable for oral delivery.

I have addressed myself to one question only: to what extent, and by what means, is it possible to isolate the work of Lysias himself within the very large number of speeches ascribed to him at any time from the fourth century B.C. to the present day? To the best of my ability I have resisted the temptation to discuss problems which do not seem to me to bear upon that question, and it will be obvious to the reader that my concern has been more with methods than with positive results. This explains what might otherwise seem an oddly selective bibliography; I sometimes cite an inferior work which has been devoted to the problems of ascription and has (rightly or wrongly) influenced our thinking on that subject, while I may pass over in silence a distinguished work which begs the question—that is to say, which treats as axiomatic a particular answer to the question which my own book is designed to pose. My preoccupation with method also accounts for the fact that I discuss only a limited number of the linguistic phenomena relevant to ascription; I examine a few phenomena in detail, refer briefly to others, and leave still more for future investigation. A growing feeling that many books on

Classical subjects are much too long has made it easier for me to be brief.

Readers who believe that all problems of ascription have been solved, or are on the point of being solved, by putting the appropriate questions to computers will be disappointed at my cautious attitude to the mechanisation of literary history. This is a matter which is apt to arouse strong emotions, and a scholar feels at times that whatever he says he will be labelled either a Philistine or a Luddite. I can only say that I regard emotional reactions as inappropriate. Problems peculiar to Attic forensic oratory, combined with the brevity of most of the speeches ascribed to Lysias, have so far precluded the formulation of useful questions which can be better answered by computers than by people. Mechanisation brings with it disadvantages as well as advantages; but nothing that I say or believe entails a judgment on the present usefulness of the computer in the study of other literary genres or its potential usefulness, at any unforeseeable time from tomorrow onwards, in the study of the *corpus Lysiacum*.

Readers who hope that I am about to offer them firmer grounds than have yet been offered for asserting that certain speeches are by Lysias and certain others are not will find that the opposite is the case. My whole argument is to the effect that confidence which has seemed justified is unjustified and that the question of ascription is less easily answered than has commonly been allowed.

Working at Berkeley was a most memorable experience for me, and I am deeply grateful for the unfailing kindness and helpfulness of Professor and Mrs. W. K. Pritchett and of colleagues, office staff, friends and neighbours.

University of St. Andrews　　　　　　　　　　　K. J. DOVER
April, 1967

Abbreviations

REFERENCE TO speeches ascribed to Lysias is by large Roman numerals, normally without the addition of "Lys." Small Roman numerals are used for other authors.

Authors' names are in general abbreviated as in the ninth edition of Liddell and Scott, but some of them are hellenised (e.g., "Kallim.," not "Call.") and others are expanded (e.g., "Dem.," not "D.," for Demosthenes). References follow the system of Liddell and Scott except that fragments of the orators are numbered as in the most recent Teubner editions, except where "BS" (= Baiter and Sauppe) is added; testimonia on rhetoricians, as well as quotations from Gorgias and Alkidamas, are numbered as in Radermacher's *Artium Scriptores*. Fragments of Kallimachos are numbered as in Pfeiffer's edition. References to Dionysios of Halikarnassos are by volume, page and line of the Usener-Radermacher edition of his *Scripta Minora*.

Reference is made to editions of Lysias by the editor's name only, and to the following modern works by the author's name only:

Blass, F., *Die attische Beredsamkeit*, Leipzig, vol. i (2nd ed.), 1887; ii (1st ed.), 1874; iii.1 (2nd ed.), 1893; iii.2 (1st ed.), 1880.
Bruns, I., *Das literarische Porträt der Griechen*, Berlin, 1896.
Büchler, O., *Die Unterscheidung der redenden Personen bei Lysias*, Heidelberg, 1936.
Cloché, P., *La Restauration démocratique à Athènes en 403 av. J.-C.*, Paris, 1915.

Darkow, Angela C., *The Spurious Speeches in the Lysianic Corpus*, Bryn Mawr, 1917.
Devries, W. L., *Ethopoiia*, Baltimore, 1892.
Dover, K. J., *Greek Word Order*, Cambridge, 1960.
Francken, C. W., *Commentationes Lysiacae*, Utrecht, 1865.
Hollingsworth, J. E., *Antithesis in the Attic Orators from Antiphon to Isaeus*, Menasha, 1915.
Kennedy, G., *The Art of Persuasion in Greece*, Princeton and London, 1963.
Lämmli, F., *Das attische Prozessverfahren in seiner Wirkung auf die Gerichtsrede*, Paderborn, 1938.
MacDowell, D. M. (ed.), *Andokides, On the Mysteries*, Oxford, 1962.
Lavency, M., *Aspects de la logographie judiciaire attique*, Louvain, 1964.
Navarre, O., *Essai sur la rhétorique grecque avant Aristote*, 1900.
Pilz, W., *Der Rhetor im attischen Staat*, Basel, 1924.

Contents

	Abbreviations	vii
I	Corpus and Corpusculum	1
II	Kallimachos and the Booksellers	23
III	Chronology	28
IV	Ideology and Political Association	47
V	Genre and Ethos	57
VI	Crude Stylometry	94
VII	Refined Stylometry	115
VIII	Client and Consultant	148
IX	Orator, Rhetorician and Reader	175
	Index	197

I

Corpus and Corpusculum

THE STARTING point of my enquiry is a twelfth-century manuscript, and the end of the enquiry will necessarily involve us in assessing some aspects of Athenian society. This, in my view, is to take things in the right order. Objects which we can see and touch and smell are the data of history: all else is construction. The historian's task, whether he is a historian of language, literature, politics or any other aspect of human behaviour, is to explain completely why a given object exists here and now, and to ensure that his explanation does not conflict with the explanation which he gives of the existence of any other object.

The manuscript Palatinus 88 consists entirely of speeches, and its contents may be divided into three extremely unequal parts:

(1) Two speeches of Lysias, one forensic and the other epideictic; two of Alkidamas, two of Antisthenes and one of Demades.

(2) Twenty-nine speeches of Lysias. As we see from the table of contents written by the copyist himself, there were originally thirty; but damage to the manuscript has removed one speech and portions of four others.[1]

(3) Gorgias's *Helen*.

[1] The table of contents will be found most conveniently in the preface to Hude's and Albini's editions.

Part 1, an oratorical anthology, is of the same character as the latter part of the early Paleologan manuscript, Burneianus 95. The two Lysian speeches, *On the Killing of Eratosthenes* and the *Epitaphios*, appear in similar contexts, divorced from the bulk of Lysias, not only in Paleologan manuscripts but also earlier; the *Epitaphios*, for example, is to be found in Coislinianus 249 (of the tenth or eleventh century), in company with the three surviving speeches of Aischines, the *Helen* of Gorgias and much of Synesios. The *Epitaphios* earned its place in anthologies: it is a splendid piece of formal rhetoric, and if anyone proved to my satisfaction that Lysias did not write it my evaluation of it would no more be altered than my admiration for *Prometheus Bound* would be diminished by proof that it is not the work of Aischylos. It is not so easy to see why the speech *On the Killing of Eratosthenes* should appear in an anthology. It is lively and interesting, but not exceptional, and I am tempted to suggest that an anthologist of late antiquity selected it under a misapprehension—having intended, or having been instructed, to copy out one of the most famous and remarkable of all the speeches ascribed to Lysias: XII, in which the orator himself charged a different and more important Eratosthenes with the killing of his brother Polemarchos.

Part 2 of Palatinus 88, with its thirty speeches, gives us a small fraction of the total number of speeches to which the name of Lysias was attached in the Hellenistic period; that much is plain from the explicit references made to many speeches in Dionysios of Halikarnassos, Harpokration and other Hellenistic sources. I therefore call Part 2 of Palatinus 88 the "corpusculum," and I assign the name "Corpus G" to the larger body of Lysias's work from which it was extracted.

Part 3 we may dismiss as an "addendum," drawn from an anthology related to the source of part of Burneianus 95. Addenda of this kind are a common phenomenon not only in Paleologan manuscripts (cf. the addition of the Lysian *Epitaphios* as a tailpiece to Demosthenes in Vaticanus gr. 69) but also much earlier: Coislinianus 249, which begins with a collection of essays by Synesios, also ends with one more essay of his.

Modern reference to the speeches by numbers is based on the Palatinus in its present condition. Thus the speech *On the Killing of Eratosthenes* and the *Epitaphios*, although separated from the corpusculum, are numbered I and II, and the speeches of the corpusculum are numbered from III to XXXI (leaving no number free for the *Prosecution of Nikides*, which has perished from the Palatinus). It has become editorial practice to allocate the numbers XXXII, XXXIII and XXXIV respectively to the extensive citations made by Dionysios from the *Prosecution of Diogeiton*, the *Olympikos* and the political speech *Against the Proposal of Phormisios*, and XXXV to the *Erotikos* attributed to Lysias in Plato's *Phaedrus*. This system of reference has its unsatisfactory aspects, but it is far too late now to make any significant departure from existing practice. I therefore use the numbers III–XXXI when referring to speeches of the corpusculum, and I and XXXII for *On the Killing of Eratosthenes* and the *Prosecution of Diogeiton*, but I refer to the others by name. I also refer by name to fragmentary speeches discovered since Thalheim's edition.

We can say for certain that the criterion of selection which produced the corpusculum was not chronological; very few of the speeches can be dated with exactitude, most can be dated only by making arbitrary assumptions about the interval of time between the proceedings which they represent and the upper termini which they mention, and some cannot be dated at all. It is doubtful whether anyone in ancient and medieval times even attempted so unprofitable an exercise as making a selection from an orator's work on a purely chronological basis. For good measure, it should be added that those speeches in the corpusculum which can be dated with certainty or probability are not in chronological order; X is one of the latest, XII the second earliest, XX the earliest, while VI and XXX are both datable between X and XII.

We can also see at a glance that the corpusculum is not a portion of a corpus which was ordered alphabetically; contrast the survival of the "alphabetic" plays of Euripides and the collections of dramatic hypotheses ordered alphabetically. Unlike chronological order, alphabetic order would have been a possibility—as we see from the order in which the lost speeches have been arranged in modern editions ever since Taylor. Sometimes, the names of both adversaries can be discovered from the text of a speech (e.g., Dem. xxxvii.52). When the title of a speech as given in the Palatinus is vague or wrong, the name of either or both of the adversaries, or of some person involved, can usually be discovered; XVII is a case in point, for a title incorporating "The Estate of Eraton" could be substituted for the nonsensical δημοσίων ἀδικημάτων.[2] There is also little doubt that in many cases a name not mentioned in the text of a speech was once discoverable from documents which were incorporated in the speech when it was first put into circulation but were subsequently omitted;[3] it is presumably from such documents that the authors of hypotheses to Demosthenes discovered that Pamphilos's partner in Dem. lvi was named Dareios and the speaker of Dem. lvii Euxitheos (where mere inference from the text would have suggested "Thoukritides," the name of the speaker's paternal grandfather [§20]).[4] The text of Deinarchos's speech against Proxenos, as known to Dionysios (i.301.1 ff.), had the charge attached to it (προσκειμένην). It was also possible to discover a speaker's name by cross reference; confrontation of Dem. xxii.2 with xxiv.7 and xxiv.64 shows us that Diodoros was the prosecutor of Androtion in xxii, and I imagine that it was passages in a speech now lost which justified the authors of the Demosthenic hypotheses in naming Euthykles as the prosecutor of Aristokrates (Dem. xxiii) and concluding from §42 of the speech *On Halonnesos*

[2] But disagreement was possible; the author of *P. Oxy.* 2537 (cf. p. 11) interpreted IX.5 as meaning that the speaker's name was Kallikrates, whereas modern belief (upheld by careful reading of the text) is that his name was Polyainos.

[3] Although some documents in Demosthenic speeches are transparent forgeries, there is no reason why documents should not have been included in the written version of a speech whenever it seemed likely that the reader would be helped to follow the argument thereby: X.15–20, for example, would be unintelligible without its documents, and And. i greatly impaired.

[4] It is an odd coincidence that Sopatros (Rh. Gr. iv.316) knew or believed "Euxitheos" to be the name of the Mytilenean defendant in Ant. v.

(Dem. vii) that Hegesippos delivered that speech (cf. Hyper. i [col. 2]. 1).[5]

Where the names of both adversaries were known, the same speech could have been placed at either of two points in a collection ordered alphabetically, in the absence of any generally accepted convention, and there was obviously no such convention. The speech on the estate of Nikias's brother (XVIII) is cited by Galen (xviii.2, p. 657) as κατὰ Πολιούχου—which is inaccurate, though πρὸς Πολίοχον (cf. XVIII.12) would have been acceptable —and Is. iii is cited by Harpokration (239.19 and 260.15 f.) indifferently as *On the Estate of Pyrrhos* and *Prosecution of Nikodemos*. Where the name of neither adversary was known, a speech might still be placed in alphabetical order by using a conventional title— for instance, by including ὑπὲρ τοῦ ἀδυνάτου under α. There is some slight evidence that an alphabetic principle was on occasion applied. *P. Ryl.* 489, a leaf from a papyrus codex of the third or fourth century A.D., has the end of speech I and the beginning of one entitled *In Defence of Eryximachos, Who Remained in the City*. Since "remaining in the city" (*sc.*, under the rule of the Thirty) could not be the subject of a charge after the sworn amnesty of 403, however prejudice against it might be exploited (e.g., XVIII.19),[6] it is probable that this speech, like XXV, belongs to a δοκιμασία.[7] Generically, therefore, it is absolutely remote from the speech which precedes it, and it cannot be chronologically connected, for there is no pointer to the date of the death of the adulterer Eratosthenes. Three possibilities remain. First, *P. Ryl.* 489 may be a fragment of a book which differed from the other known ancient medieval texts of the orators in that its contents followed the alphabetic order of the titles. Secondly, the two speeches may have been "thematically" connected—as, by political association between Euphiletos (the killer of Eratosthenes) and Eryximachos —and a passage in the speech for Eryximachos may have revealed

[5] Cf. the use made by Dion. Hal. i.313.15–314.4 of the references to Menekles in Dem. xxxix.2 and xl.9.

[6] XIII, the prosecution of Agoratos, was pretty certainly in contravention of the amnesty; cf. Cloché, 338.

[7] Cf. Cloché, 396 f.

this association (cf. p. 9). Thirdly, the order may exemplify some other principle, or lack of principle, which we have yet to consider.

Those plays of Aischylos, Sophokles and Aristophanes which survive were selected in late antiquity for their literary and educational value, and the order in which they are placed in the earliest medieval texts shows no regard for chronology or for the alphabet. The same is true of the "select" plays of Euripides. There is no reason *a priori* why a corpusculum of an orator's work should not be formed on this principle; but when we compare the corpusculum of Lysias with what information we have about the lost speeches, I find it difficult to imagine that anyone making a selection of forensic speeches with some regard for historical interest, literary quality and educational value could have included VIII (which is not forensic, and is allusive to the point of incoherence), XX (which is crude and ill organised), and two précis, XI and XV, while excluding the speeches against Aischines the Socratic (Ath. 611E, Harp. 61.13 *al.*) and Hippotherses (*P. Oxy.* 1606; cf. p. 34), speeches for Iphikrates (Dion. Hal. i.20.15–22.9) and the speech on the estate of Androkleidas (Dion. Hal. i.98.18 ff.).

The corpusculum differs at first sight in one striking respect from the surviving speeches of Antiphon and Isaios. All six of Antiphon are concerned with homicide (three normal forensic cases and three imaginary). Of the nineteen lost speeches of Antiphon, eleven are shown by their titles not to have been homicide cases, the citations suggest that a further three were not, and we have no clear indication of the genre of the remaining five. There is thus a strong possibility that what survived from the corpus of Antiphon was one complete division, the homicide cases (cf. Blass, i.107). We may compare the survival of the victory odes of Pindar when his paeans, dithyrambs and all other genres were lost. The eleven speeches of Isaios which survive as a corpusculum in the codex Burneianus 95 all concern inheritance. Of the lost speeches, at least six concerned inheritance, adoption or wardship, twenty-three did not, and the subject of sixteen is unknown. These data suggest that what survives of Isaios was one division out of two or more devoted to inheritance and related matters (cf. Blass, *ibid.*). Compare the "Philippics" of Demosthenes—not the four speeches to which we now attach the term, but what were called his Φιλιππικοὶ λόγοι in Roman times, i–xiii (excluding xii, the *Letter of Philip*) according to Didymos and i–xi according to the author of the anonymous hypotheses (Dem. vii, which is the sixth speech in Parisinus 2934, has the subscription τόμος ᾱ Φιλιππικῶν λόγων ζ).

We now have to consider whether the complete corpusculum of Lysias may not be (*a*) several divisions of his work, to the exclusion of most of the original divisions, or (*b*) a selection from divisions made in such a way that their original sequence in the corpus can still be discerned.

It is no surprise that XI and XV come where they do, for XI is a précis of X and XV of XIV (cf. p. 166).

III and IV are both cases of malicious wounding, heard before the Areopagus.

V, VI and VII all concern religious offences: V, most of which is lost, was a defence against a charge of ἱεροσυλία (if the title is to be trusted); VI is one of the speeches against which Andokides' *On the Mysteries* was a defence; VII, on the alleged removal of a sacred olive tree, was heard before the Areopagus.

XVII, XVIII and XIX all concern, in different ways, confiscation of property by the state: in XVII the speaker claims, as a creditor, a share of confiscated property, and XVIII and XIX are pleas against confiscation.

XXV and XXVI belong to δοκιμασίαι. The title of XXV in the Palatinus, δήμου καταλύσεως ἀπολογία, finds no support in the text of the speech (of which the end, however, is missing); δοκιμασία on appeal from Council to law court (cf. 'Αθ.π. 55.2) is suggested by §10: ὑμᾶς οὖν χρὴ ἐκ τούτων δοκιμάζειν τοὺς πολίτας (cf. Blass, i.360,510 f.).

XXVII, XXVIII and XXIX are all attempts to secure the condemnation of men who are alleged to have embezzled public money and taken bribes; XXIX arises directly out of XXVIII.

Among the remainder, some are of so unusual a type that we

should not expect to find a whole division of any corpus assigned to that type;⁸ and others, though not necessarily of a rare type, we can imagine to have lacked company in the corpus of Lysias. We can (with some degree of hesitation, which we shall soon see to be more than justified) assign to these categories VIII, which is not part of a lawsuit (for no word in it is addressed to a jury) but an attack by an unidentified individual on his former associates and a formal declaration (§18) of his severance from them; X, a prosecution for slander; XIV, a prosecution for military desertion; XXII, a prosecution of grain dealers for price-fixing; XXIII, a rebuttal of a παραγραφή (cf. Blass, i.618 f.); XXIV, a defence of a cripple who has been denounced (perhaps at a δοκιμασία [cf. Aischin i.104; Blass, i.633 f.], but possibly by εἰσαγγελία [cf. p. 189]) as not entitled to the maintenance which the state pays him; and XXX, which can easily be mistaken (and was so mistaken by the author of the titles in the Palatinus) for a complaint brought against an elected official at his εὔθυναι, although careful reading of the text (note §§4 f. ~ 8) shows that it must fall under a different type of proceedings against officials (cf. Blass, i.463).

We are left with seven speeches which are separated from those with which we would expect to find them keeping company.

IX is a defence of a man accused as a debtor to the state (§§3, 21) since he has failed to pay a fine imposed on him (§6). We might have expected to find this with XXVII–XXIX.

XII and XIII accuse Eratosthenes and Agoratos respectively of murder, and thus seem to belong with III and IV. Unlike III and IV, however, they are addressed to a jury (ὦ ἄνδρες δικασταί), not to the Areopagus. Neither is a δίκη φόνου. Eratosthenes was one of the Thirty Tyrants, who were entitled to present themselves for εὔθυναι after the democratic restoration ('Αθ.π. 39.6), and XII is most easily interpreted as a complaint made in that connection.⁹ In

---

⁸ Pindar's "*Nemean* 10" was included among the Nemean victory odes although it celebrates a victory in an Argive festival and has nothing to do with Nemea; but it had to be put somewhere. It appears from Kallim. fr. 441 that the victory odes of Simonides were classified by types of athletic events, not by festivals.

⁹ Cf. Cloché, 266 f., 309 ff.; Blass, i.361 and 540 f. antedate the discovery of the London fragments of 'Αθ. π.

XIII it appears that Agoratos has been subjected to ἀπαγωγὴ ἐπ' αὐτοφώρῳ (§§ 85 f.)—possibly, by stretching the law a long way, as a κακοῦργος, like the Mytilenean accused of the murder of Herodes (Ant. v.9)—but the formulation of the charge against him is uncertain.[10]

XVI is composed for a man who has drawn by lot membership of the incoming Council and is undergoing scrutiny by the outgoing Council (§§ 1, 3, 8 f.: cf. 'Αθ.π. 45.3). XXXI is an attack on a man in the same situation (§§ 1 f., 24, 31, 34). We would have expected to find XVI and XXXI together and with XXV–XXVI; but XXXI, as the last item of the corpusculum, may be an addendum to a selection or simply copied from an intact manuscript into a mutilated one, and as such it could be of any character.[11]

The nature of the charges against the defendants in XX and XXI is not clear, but since both are in peril of a crippling loss of property (XX.35, XXI.11 f., 15, 25) their position after XVII–XIX is not unreasonable.

The real difficulties are thus posed by IX and XVI.

Now, VIII and IX, as Blass observed (i.378), both appear to have a thematic connection with X, the prosecution of Theomnestos for slander—provided that they are read hastily and superficially. The speaker of VIII is obsessed with what his associates have *said* about him; note κακῶς ἀκήκοεν, κακῶς λέγειν, διαβάλλειν in § 3, ὅτι ἐλέγετε κατ' ἐμοῦ in § 4, κακολογεῖν in § 5, and so on. IX begins τί ποτε διανοηθέντες ... ἐπεχείρησαν διαβάλλειν: διαβολή recurs in § 2, διαβάλλειν in § 3, διαβολή and λοιδορεῖν in § 18, and it is not irrelevant that the fine which the speaker incurred was for his alleged λοιδορία of the generals (§ 6).

A similar community of theme links XVI to XIV. In XIV the crux of the charge against the younger Alkibiades is that he insisted on serving in the cavalry although called up as a hoplite

---

[10] Cf. A. Schweizer, *Die 13. Rede des Lysias* (Borna-Leipzig, 1936), 82 ff.

[11] So in the Demosthenic MS Parisinus 2934 a whole division of symbuleutic speeches, xiii-xvii, is placed at the end, widely separated from the "Philippics" (cf. p. 7).

(§§ 7–11). In XVI the defendant attempts to prove (a) that he did not serve in the cavalry under the Thirty (§§ 3, 6–8), and (b) that although entitled to serve in the cavalry in 395/394 he refused to accept what was regarded as a comparatively safe form of soldiering, at a time when others who had no right to be there were in the cavalry, and insisted on serving as a hoplite (§ 13). The main burden of his self-praise is his military record (§§ 14–17).

It should be observed incidentally that XXII and XXIII are thematically linked by the fact that the accused in XXII are metics (§ 5) and Pankleon in XXIII, formerly believed by the speaker to be a metic (§ 2) is now alleged (§ 12) to be a slave, but asserts that he has the rights of a Plataean.

It now begins to appear that thematic connection between speeches may sometimes have taken precedence over identity of legal genre in determining the position of speeches in the corpus from which our corpusculum was selected. The same principle is conspicuous in the grouping of the private speeches of Demosthenes in Parisinus 2934. Those connected with Demosthenes' own inheritance (xxvii–xxxi) always appear together, though covering several legal genres. The sequence lix–xxxvi–xlv–xlvi is formed by a common connection with Apollodoros, though lix (cf. § 115) was written for him and xxxvi (a παραγραφή) against him; xlv and xlvi, private prosecutions for perjured evidence, arise out of xxxvi. Similarly l–li–liii–xlix–lii appear together, because liii, xlix and lii were written for Apollodoros, l was probably written for him too. and li, like l, is concerned with trierarchic litigation.

Thematic classification, as we have seen, is sometimes the product of very hasty reading. A good parallel is provided by the hypothesis to Pi. *P.* 4, which tells us (Sch. Pi. ii.92.2 [Drachmann]) that the poem was written for Arkesilaos, "son of Polymnestos." At *P.* 4.59 we find the words ὦ μάκαρ υἱὲ Πολυμνάστου: at corresponding points in other poems (as in *P.* 2.18 and *O.* 6.9) Pindar addresses himself directly to the victor in similar terms, and the composer of the hypothesis did not observe that in *P.* 4.59 Pindar is not addressing the victor but apostrophizing the victor's ancestor, Battos I.

Corpus and Corpusculum   11

In the case of Lysias, how early was the corpus organized with divisions on a principle which oscillated between legal genre and thematic affinity?

Oxyrhynchus Papyrus 2537, one sheet of a codex datable to the late second or early third century A.D., presents a list of very brief hypotheses to the speeches of Lysias. These are ordered in divisions according to legal genre, and the number of speeches in each division is stated. I propose to call the speeches which were included in this work when it was intact "Corpus F." At *recto* 6 we have the heading κακηγοριας δ, and this is followed by hypotheses to speeches X, XI, IX and VIII, entitled respectively κα[ταθεο-μνηϲτου α· β·] (the restoration is rendered certain by 7–15), υ[περτ]ουϲτρατιωτου and προ[ϲτουϲϲ]υνουϲιαϲ[ταϲ. We see from this not only how perspicacious Blass was, but also that by the Antonine period:

(*a*) The précis XI had already found its way into Corpus F. The author of the hypotheses is content to note (*recto* 12–15) the arithmetical contradiction between X.4 and XI.2 (cf. p. 166). Presumably XV was also included in Corpus F.

(*b*) The titles as we find them in the corpusculum were already established.

The other divisions discernible in Corpus F are: possibly βιαίων (this suggestion is an inference from one hypothesis [*recto* 2–5], and it is not an improbable neighbour of κακηγορίας); ἐξούλης, five cases (*recto* 29–*verso* 16); παρακαταθήκης, five cases (*verso* 16–32); ξενίας, at least three cases (*verso* 33–41); an unidentifiable genre].ων, seven cases (*verso* 42 ff.). None of these is represented in the corpusculum at all.

It is surprising to find ξενία, which was always the subject of a γραφή and therefore of a δημόσιος λόγος, among genres which were the subject of δίκαι and of ἰδιωτικοὶ λόγοι. Dionysios classifies Deinarchos's prosecutions for ξενία among δημόσιοι λόγοι (i.311.7 f., 19 f.), but there is no room for a new main heading δημόσιοι in verso 33. Yet Dionysios also classifies Deinarchos's prosecution of Proxenos for ὕβρις and defence of Epichares, charged with ὕβρις, under ἰδιωτικοὶ λόγοι (i.318.8–11), after cases of inheritance and immediately before a case of αἰκία, "assault." ὕβρις was the subject of γραφαί, not δίκαι, as we know from (e.g.) Dem. xxi.28. Its relation, however, to αἰκία, βίαια and βλάβη is so obvious, and the distinction often so hard to draw, that the orators themselves occasionally say things which in isolation would imply that ὕβρις falls under δίκαι; note especially fr. 52a and Dem. xxi.25, xxxvii.33. Similarly, Demosthenes in one passage (xxxix.18) speaks as if a prosecution ξενίας is a blow struck in a private vendetta.

We must therefore always be prepared to find that historical realism took precedence over historical or legal pedantry in the ordering of divisions.

Corpus F has VIII–XI of the corpusculum in the order X, XI, IX, VIII. This happens to be alphabetic order, but no doubt by chance, for in other divisions (note especially *recto* 36–44) violation of alphabetic order is observable. Chronological order would have been no more practicable within a division than within a selection (unless the selection were confined to securely datable speeches). In our most important papyrus of Hypereides (*P. Lit. Lond.* 132 = inv. nos. 108 + 115) there were three speeches on εἰσαγγελίαι, in the order: *Prosecution of Demosthenes*, *Defence of Lykophron* and *Defence of Euxenippos*. The order here is not alphabetic: nor is it chronological, for Lykourgos was alive and active at the time of the third case (*Eux.* 12; cf. Blass, iii/2.64) but dead before the prosecution of Demosthenes and others in connection with Harpalos's money. Probably the speech against Demosthenes was put first as the most famous and interesting. It is significant that Dionysios heads his list of the "authentic private speeches" of Deinarchos with the *Prosecution of Proxenos for Damage* (i.317.1 f.), in which Deinarchos himself, as an old man, was the plaintiff; this is the speech which Dionysios treats at some length as primary biographical evidence (i.299.15–303.8) and therefore regards as first in importance. Similarly, the opening poems in Pindar's

Olympian and Pythian victory odes are not the earliest in date but those addressed to the most famous recipients, the Sicilian tyrants. Analogy thus indicates that X may head the division "slander" in Corpus F because it is the most lucid and polished speech in that division. Between early Roman and late medieval times a regress from conscious order to random distribution, through a series of individually untraceable errors, is to be expected.[12]

Was Corpus F identical in content with Corpus G, and was the corpusculum made up by selecting not individual speeches but complete divisions? The division κακηγορία suggests that the answer to both questions is "yes." I can see no positive grounds for distinguishing between F and G, and the only argument against the supposition that the corpusculum is made up of complete divisions is the fact that whereas its first two speeches concern cases of malicious wounding, there existed in antiquity another speech, *Prosecution of Lysitheos*, which (according to the title as cited—without author's name!—in the Patmos scholia on Demosthenes [*Lex. gr. min.* 163]) belonged to the same genre. If this division had come anywhere in the corpusculum from the second to the penultimate position, the theory that the corpusculum is composed of complete divisions would be refuted; as it is, we are left uncertain, since the speech against Lysitheos could have been present as the first item in an ancestor of the corpusculum but lost through mutilation.

The lexicon of Harpokration contains references to more than a hundred speeches of Lysias, and adds εἰ γνήσιος, "if correctly ascribed," to a third of these. I use the term "Corpus E" for the totality of speeches cited by Harpokration under the name of Lysias, whether or not he added a reservation about their ascription in quoting them.

Corpus E resembled Corpus F in using the title ὑπέρ (περὶ

[12] The order of individual speeches is never safe ground for argument, because both rational criticism (cf. p. 20) and error played their separate parts. In Harp. 166.3 the "eleventh Philippic" of Demosthenes is Dem. x, and xi in fact precedes x in the tenth-century MS. Augustanus 485. On the order of poems in ancient and medieval texts of Theokritos cf. Gow's edition, i.lxvi ff.

Harp.)[13] τοῦ στρατιώτου for IX, but differed from it in certain important respects:

(a) Harpokration (98.1) qualifies IX with the tag εἰ γνήσιος, but Corpus F indicates no doubts about the ascription of that or any other speech.

(b) Corpus F includes X and XI as two different speeches against Theomnestos. Harpokration quotes only from X (44.10 al.), and never with the addition of "ᾱ," which we should expect if he had known of two speeches against Theomnestos (cf. his references [160.14, 225.13] to the two speeches of Lykurgos against Lykophron).

(c) Most important of all, Corpus F includes in the division παρακαταθήκης:

]ςτραπ[ε]ζιτικος
τ]ραπεζ . [. .]δικαζεταιχειλ[
]θ . . . [. .]αρακισσοντο[.] . .
]καιπαρεαυτω[γ]ραμμα'τ'[

(verso 24–27)

In Isokrates xvii, the *Trapezitikos*, a litigant sues the banker Pasion for recovery of a sum deposited with him, claiming that Pasion tried to smuggle away a slave named Kittos (§§ 11, 21), who alone knew about the deposit, and also that Pasion falsified a γραμματεῖον (§§ 23 ff.). One cannot be completely satisfied that the speech ascribed to Lysias in Corpus F is identical with Isok. xvii, for the issue between Greek adversaries at law was not always settled by a single lawsuit, and there may have been two different speeches which were only two moves in a protracted battle. Also, Isokrates' client does not say how much money he deposited. But he does at one point (§ 41) claim to have possessed a thousand gold staters, and the compiler of the hypothesis in Corpus F may have identified this sum (unjustifiably) with the deposit, which was in

[13] The confusion between περί and ὑπέρ from the fourth century B.C. onwards is not only so common that changing one to the other hardly ranks as "emendation," but is to a large extent a semantic coalescence, not merely a palaeographical phenomenon.

gold (§44: τὸ χρυσίον τὸ παρ' αὑτῷ κείμενον). It is perhaps pedantic to question the identification of Isok. xvii with the τραπεζιτικός ascribed to Lysias in Corpus F.

Harpokration, however, quotes (89.15 f., 168.17 f., 275.14) from Isok. xvii without any indication that it could be ascribed to anyone else.

According to [Plu.] *Vit. Or.* 836A there were 425 speeches ascribed to Lysias, of which οἱ περὶ Διονύσιον καὶ Καικίλιον regarded 233 as correctly ascribed (γνήσιοι).

Dionysios of Halikarnassos lived and worked at Rome from 30 B.C. until after 8 B.C. (*Ant. Rom.* i.7.2).[14] Caecilius, to whom he refers on one occasion as τῷ φιλτάτῳ Καικιλίῳ (ii.240.14) was his contemporary.[15] Both of them admired Lysias as the model of classical Attic oratory, and both wrote about him (cf. Longin. *Subl.* 32.8); but Caecilius's work is not preserved, and of Dionysios's two essays on Lysias the survivor is primarily concerned with style, not with the chronology and ascription of individual speeches. Whether their two lists of 233 speeches correctly ascribed to Lysias were identical, we do not know: they could on occasion disagree (cf. p. 20)—out of a total of 60 speeches ascribed to Isokrates, 28 were allowed by Caecilius to be genuine, but only 25 by Dionysios ([Plu.] *Vit. Or.* 838D).[16]

I use the term "Corpus D_1" to denote the total of those speeches regarded by Dionysios as correctly ascribed to Lysias, and "Corpus D_2" for those whose previous ascription to Lysias he regarded as wrong. For the sake of completeness I postulate also "Corpus C," those accepted ("C_1") and rejected ("C_2") by Caecilius; but the evidence does not permit me to say any more about Corpus C.

[14] On the nature of Dionysios's critical work cf. M. Untersteiner, *AFC* vii (1959), 72 ff., and Lossau, 68 ff. I find it hard to agree with Lossau's inference (86 ff.), from Didymos, *Dem.* 2.2 f., 11.10 ff., 13.25 ff., that Didymos presupposes a significant degree of pre-Dionysian work on the chronology and ascription of speeches; cf. p. 21.

[15] Their names are linked not only in *Vit. Or.* 836A but also in Quint. iii.1.16, x.3.87; and cf. Ofenloch's edition of Caecilius, p. xiii.

[16] Fr. 110 is evidence for Caecilius's agreement with someone (συνομολογῶν [*sc.* Διονυσίῳ?]) on the genius of Lysias, and frr. 136 f. evidence for someone's (Caecilius's?) disagreement with Dionysios on some problems in Demosthenes.

Corpus D_1 differed from Corpus F in that Dionysios chose the *Trapezitikos* to illustrate how Isokrates' epideictic style influenced his forensic style (i.86.8–11, 90.15–92.4). Obviously he could not have done this if he had taken its ascription to Lysias seriously, and I doubt whether he would have done so if he had even been aware of such an ascription, for the epideictic element in the style of the *Trapezitikos* seems to be connected, in his eyes, with the question whether Isokrates had in fact written any forensic speeches (i.85.8–86.11).[17]

The relation between Corpus D ($= D_1 + D_2$) and Corpus E can only be inferred from the relation between Dionysios and Harpokration in respect of other authors. For example, Dionysios regarded Andokides iii as wrongly ascribed (i.283), and Harpokration qualified his own references to it (111.10, 213.16, 249.10) by adding εἰ γνήσιος. Most of the relevant entries, however, concern Demosthenes and Deinarchos, and the ground on which inference from E to D stands is not quite as firm as one might wish. The minimum differences are:

(a) Dionysios (i.157.4–12, 270.4–7) does not doubt the ascription of the speech *On Halonnesos* (Dem. vii) to Demosthenes, but Harpokration twice (21.7, 109.7; contrast 76.1) qualifies it as εἰ γνήσιος and (146.1–3) names Hegesippos as a possible author—a view adopted firmly by the author of the anonymous hypothesis.

(b) Dionysios (i.20.6–12) refers to Dem. xl as πρὸς Μαντίθεον περὶ τῆς προικός, but Harpokration (like the medieval manuscripts of Demosthenes) calls it πρὸς Βοιωτόν (88.3).

(c) The speech κατὰ Μοσχίωνος, denied to Deinarchos by Dionysios, lacks the reservation εἰ γνήσιος in Harpokration (134.9).

(d) Harpokration knew of more than one speech of Deinarchos relating to Hegelochos, for he cites καθ'

---

[17] I cannot agree with J. Rea, *P. Oxy.* xxxi.24, who interprets Dionysios's sequence of thought otherwise.

Corpus and Corpusculum 17

Ἡγελόχου (sic) συνηγορία ὑπὲρ ἐπικλήρου (193.9), but Dionysios lists only one.

I have described these as minimum differences because there are also certain apparent differences which may admit of reduction:

(*a*) Harpokration cites five speeches of Deinarchos which we do not find in Dionysios under the names which Harpokration gives them. But, of these five, Κροκωνιδῶν διαδικασία (118.6) concerns a priestess and may therefore be the same as the διαδικασία τῆς ἱερείας τῆς Δήμητρος, rejected by Dionysios (i.314.12–17) and cited by Harpokration (100.12) with the reservation εἰ γνήσιος.

(*b*) The manuscript of Dionysios's essay on Deinarchos is mutilated at the end, and we therefore do not have his complete list of private speeches wrongly (in his view) ascribed to Deinarchos. κατὰ Στεφάνου περὶ τοῦ ὀχετοῦ, cited by Harpokration (231.4), may have come in the missing portion.

(*c*) Dionysios ascribes to Deinarchos two speeches περὶ τοῦ ἵππου. Harpokration (299.9) cites πρὸς Ἀντιφάνην περὶ τοῦ ἵππου, and πρὸς Ἀντιφάνην simply (45.15). Of the two titles which appear in Harpokration, but not in Dionysios, κατὰ Θεοδότου (195.10) and πρὸς τοὺς Λυκούργου παῖδας (49.9), one may be the other speech περὶ τοῦ ἵππου.

On the other side, Harpokration (6.14–7.1, 112.7) gives Demosthenes and Deinarchos as alternative authors of the *Prosecution of Theokrines* ("Dem. lviii"); we know that Demosthenes was the author according to the Alexandrian catalogue (cf. p. 23) and Deinarchos the author according to Dionysios (i.311.21–312.1). That Harpokration used Dionysios is demonstrated by his explicit mention of him in questioning the Demosthenic authorship of a speech πρὸς Κριτίαν (113.4–7). Out of the 58 speeches positively ascribed to Deinarchos by Dionysios, apart from the second speech περὶ τοῦ ἵππου and the *Prosecution of Theokrines*, 30 are cited by Harpokration without the reservation εἰ γνήσιος and 28 are not mentioned by him at all. Out of 38 which Dionysios denies to Deinarchos, one (on the claim to the office of priestess of Demeter) has the reservation in Harpokration (100.12), the two against Boiotos-Mantitheos are Demosthenic in Harpokration, as in Dionysios, and 35 are not cited at all.

These data justify a partial and tentative identification of those speeches in the Lysian corpusculum about which Harpokration expresses a reservation ("Corpus E_2") with those which were denied to Lysias in Corpus D. A margin of uncertainty is created by the fact that the reservation εἰ γνήσιος is sometimes added by Harpokration but sometimes omitted in a reference to the same speech. It is also apparent from Harpokration's references to Dem. lviii that he did not necessarily adopt a firm standpoint, but sometimes preferred to mention alternative ascriptions; in 118.5 f. ταῦτα δὲ σαφῶς Ἰσαῖος διδάσκει καὶ Λυσίας ἐν τῷ κατὰ Στρατοκλέους ἐξούλης it is possible (cf. Blass, i.370) that καί should be emended to ἤ, since no other author mentions a speech of Lysias against Stratokles, whereas Harpokration 217.16 has Ἰσαῖος ἐν τῷ κατὰ Στρατοκλέους, 296.5 f. ἐν τῷ κατὰ Στρατοκλέους (v.l. κατ' Ἀριστοκλέους) Ἰσαῖος, εἰ γνήσιος ὁ λόγος ἐστίν and 98.14 and 200.15 Ἰσαῖος ἐν τῷ πρὸς Στρατοκλέα.[18]

The speeches in the Lysian corpusculum relevant to inference from E to D are:

VI, *Prosecution of Andokides* (εἰ γνήσιος in Harp. 17.17, 298.9; reservation omitted in 270.10).

VII, *On the Olive Tree* (ἐπιγράφεται ... Λυσίου in Harp. 272.3; no reservation in 122.3).

IX, *Defence of the Soldier* (Harp. 98.1: εἰ γνήσιος).

X, *Prosecution of Theomnestos* (εἰ γνήσιος in Harp. 44.10, 50.5, 249.1, 251.17; reservation omitted in 127.9, 218.4). The words cited leave no doubt that Harpokration is referring to X, not XI.

XIV, *Prosecution of Alkibiades* (εἰ γνήσιος, Harp. 22.14 f.); the word cited, πρόπαππος, does not occur in XV.

---

[18] Cf. 106.9, 135.1, 174.8, "Menekles or Kallikrates."

XX, *Defence of Polystratos* (Λυσίᾳ [sic] ἐπιγραφόμενος, Harp. 254.11 f.).

XXIV, *Defence of the Cripple* (Harp. 12.4: λόγος τις, ὡς λέγεται, Λυσίου).

XXX, *Prosecution of Nikomachos* (Harp. 122.2); Harpokration has Νικομαχίδου, not Νικομάχου, but the word cited, ἐπιβολή, occurs in XXX.3.

Prosecution of Nikides for ἀργία (Harp. 91.7); this speech was originally in the codex Palatinus between XXV and XXVI.

The only two speeches which occur in the corpusculum and are cited by Harpokration without any reservation are V and XII; the remaining seventeen are not mentioned by him at all.

Since Dionysios was plainly not accepted as sole authority by Harpokration when questions of authenticity arose in connection with Deinarchos and Demosthenes, complete identification of D_1 with E_1 and of D_2 with E_2 cannot be justified, but the analogy of Deinarchos suggests that it is reasonable to postulate a high degree of coincidence.[19]

The fact that a source of Athenaios (408c) apparently regarded Lysias as the author of Andokides iv (cited as Andokides' without reservation by Harp. 112.5 f., 139.4; and the hypothesis to the speech [contrast the hypothesis to And. iii] gives no indication that Dionysios thought otherwise) is not an adequate reason for postulating one more independent Lysian corpus. Andokides iv is a very special case (cf. p. 191) and the problem of its authorship excited as much speculation among ancient scholars as it does today.

By the same process as in argument from E to D, the nature of the *corpus Lysiacum* when Dionysios set to work on it has to be inferred from evidence relating to other authors:

(a) In the case of Deinarchos, the corpus as known to Dionysios was ordered in divisions based primarily on legal

---

[19] The inference of Devries, 15 f., to Dionysios's belief in the correct ascription of certain speeches *non sequitur*.

genre, but with deviations which can be attributed to thematic connections discerned and imposed either by Dionysios himself or by someone before him. Thus Deinarchos's prosecution of Pytheas for ξενία is listed immediately before a prosecution of the same person on a different charge (i.311.7–10), whereas the other case of ξενία included by Dionysios among the public speeches rightly (in his view) ascribed to Deinarchos is the fourth in a block of seven εἰσαγγελίαι and ἐνδείξεις (i.311.16–312.4), and all five of the speeches concerned with Harpalos's money come together at the end of the list (i.312.11–17).

(*b*) Certain titles already established by usage were regarded by Dionysios as inaccurate or inadequate, and he says what title he thinks ought to have been given in each case: Deinarchos's '⟨ἀπολογία⟩ πληγῶν' (i.318.9–11) and 'ὑπὲρ υἱοποιήτου' (i.319.3–6).

(*c*) In some cases, at least, the order of speeches within a division was already established by usage; Dionysios put Dem. i–iii in the order ii–iii–i on historical grounds (i.261.13–20), but according to Sch. Dem. ii Caecilius resisted this, πρῶτον ἀξιῶν τὸν πρῶτον νομιζόμενον.

Dionysios does not always say whom he is correcting when he expresses an opinion of his own on an ascription, a title or a date, but when he does say it appears that he is working directly on that section of the catalogue of Kallimachos which listed the works of the orators.

He named Kallimachos as giving their established titles to Lysias's speech *On Behalf of Pherenikos on the Estate of Androkleidas* (i.98.18–21 = Kallim. fr. 448) and Demosthenes' *On Halonnesos* (i.157.5 f. = Kallim. fr. 443). He also names Kallimachos as wrongly ascribing to Demosthenes the speech against Theokrines (Dem. lviii) which he himself ascribes to Deinarchos (i.311.21–312.1 = Kallim. fr. 444).

We should not readily infer from Dionysios that anyone between Kallimachos and himself had made a significant contribution to the correct ascription of speeches. On two occasions only he mentions the Pergamene school, sharply distinguished by Athenaios (336D), as οἱ τὰς ἐν Περγάμῳ ἀναγραφὰς ποιησάμενοι, from Kallimachos and Aristophanes of Byzantion as representatives of the Alexandrian school.[20] Dionysios mentions Pergamon once (i.317.2–8) to the effect that the speech κατὰ Δημοσθένους παρανόμων, which he denies to Deinarchos, is ascribed ἐν τοῖς Περγαμηνοῖς πίναξι to Kallikrates; "I," says Dionysios, "don't know whether it is his; I've never even read a speech of Kallikrates." In the other reference (i.297.14–16) he says that "neither Kallimachos" (fr. 447) "nor οἱ ἐκ Περγάμου γραμματικοί have written anything about Deinarchos which is at all accurate."[21] Whether the Pergamene scholars in fact made very few changes to the catalogue of Kallimachos so far as it affected the orators, or whether Dionysios chose (perhaps for bad reasons) to play them down, we cannot on present evidence tell.[22] That they made few changes is perhaps indicated by Dionysios's wording when he refers to Demosthenes' speech *On the Symmories* as given that title by οἱ τοὺς ῥητορικοὺς πίνακας συντάξαντες (i.260.16–19), which seems to embrace both Kallimachos (fr. 432) and the Pergamenes. It should be added that Harpokration (113.4–7) in referring to the putative Demosthenic speech *Against Kritias* records the conflicting views on its ascription as that of Kallimachos (fr. 445) and that of Dionysios.

I therefore postulate a "Corpus B" as the total of speeches ascribed to Lysias in the Pergamene catalogue, with the reservation that its individuality is as ill determined as that of "Corpus C." I call Kallimachos's list "Corpus A," and I equate this with the 425 speeches mentioned by [Plu.] *Vit. Or.* 836A.

Since *P. Oxy.* 2537 contains no indications of doubt or dispute

---

[20] How far Aristophanes, in what he wrote πρὸς τοὺς Καλλιμάχου πίνακας (Ath. 408F; cf. 336E), corrected Kallimachos's catalogue, and with reference to what genres of literature, we do not know.

[21] From the context Dionysios does not seem to mean that they had committed themselves to much erroneous detail, but that they had not gone into questions of chronology and ascription at all.

[22] Cf. O. Regenbogen, *RE* xx.1424.

about ascription, it is natural to wonder how far Corpus F was identical with Corpus A. Complete identity seems to be disproved by the inclusion of Isok. xvii and the absence of any suspicion in Dionysios that this speech was ever ascribed to anyone but Isokrates. It is possible, however, that the author of *P. Oxy.* 2537 made a simple error which did not necessarily affect any other part. There existed a τραπεζιτικός ascribed to Lysias, from which Photios (143.22 f. [Reitzenstein]) quotes a word (ἀνομολογήσασθαι) not found in Isok. xvii. If both speeches were commonly designated ὁ τραπεζιτικός, the author of *P.Oxy.* 2537, knowing that a τραπεζιτικός was ascribed to Lysias and possessing the τραπεζιτικός ascribed to Isokrates, may have believed that the ascription of the speech which he possessed was erroneous and summarised it in the belief that he was summarising the τραπεζιτικός of Lysias.

A very substantial agreement between Corpus A and Corpus F is therefore to be entertained; we may even consider them identical, save for (*a*) differences caused by mere error, not by rational criticism,[23] and (*b*) the intrusion of précis; as we have seen (p. 14), XI and XV do not seem to have belonged to Corpus E.

The important consequence of the distinctions which it has proved possible to draw between A ≃ B ≃ F and C ≃ D ≃ E is that criticism of ascription played no part whatsoever in the formation of the corpusculum. When we ask ourselves whether or not Lysias wrote any given speech of those ascribed to him, its presence in, or absence from, the Palatinus has not the slightest relevance.[24]

[23] It is extremely unlikely (*pace* Darkow, 8) that the critical opinions of Paulos of Mysia (Phot., cod. 262, 489ᵃ5–ᵇ2; cf. W. Stegemann, *RE* xviii.2372 f.) had any effect whatever on the selection and transmission of Lysian speeches, seeing that the adverse judgments of earlier scholars had none.

[24] Darkow's statement (95) is the opposite of the truth: "The Lysianic corpus is the result of continued exclusion of supposedly spurious work. . . . Therefore the balance of evidence is in favour of the genuineness of any speech of Lysias preserved."

II

Kallimachos and the Booksellers

WHEN DIONYSIOS and Caecilius fell upon Corpus A and axed nearly half of it, they were not being finicky or pedantic, nor should Dionysios's attitude to Kallimachos be dismissed as exemplifying the conventional and disagreeable way in which Greek writers denigrated their predecessors; he simply inferred, from the conditions of his own time, and from certain hard historical facts which were available to him, the means by which Corpus A had been put together. In brief, Dionysios and Caecilius knew that Kallimachos's inclusion of a speech under a given orator's name was not in itself a guarantee of authenticity, or even strong evidence for authenticity, and that it was up to them to do the job again from the beginning. Posterity, in the main, concurred; Photios (*Bibl.* 491^{b}31) contrasts Kallimachos (fr. 446) with "trustworthy judges" when referring to a speech *Against Chairedemos* which was ascribed to Deinarchos by Kallimachos but does not appear in Dionysios's list of genuine Deinarchean speeches.

Kallimachos did, after all (fr. 444), ascribe to Demosthenes one speech, the *Prosecution of Theokrines*, which contains (Dem. lviii.35 f., 41–44) plainly hostile and contemptuous references to Demosthenes himself. We must be a little wary of the assumption that Kallimachos treated all genres of literature alike—we know that he recorded alternative ascriptions in the case of one philosophical work (fr. 449), and he may have done so in the case of some speeches—but we find among the exiguous references to his critical work one striking example of arbitrary decision and one of grossly careless error.

He believed (fr. 450) that Pindar's *P*. 2 was written to commemorate a victory at the Nemean games. There is nothing in the poem to justify this, and later scholars showed no regard for his opinion; Ammonios and Kallistratos referred it to the Olympic games, Apollonios ὁ εἰδογράφος and some others (whose opinion prevailed) to the Pythian, others (including Dionysios of Phaselis) to the Panathenaic, while others again, including Timaios, did not regard it as any kind of victory ode (Sch. Pi. ii.31.8–16 [Drachmann]).

We learn from the scholion on *Clouds* 552 that Kallimachos, having noted Aristophanes' reference to the *Marikas* of Eupolis, and having found in the διδασκαλίαι that *Clouds* was performed in 423 and *Marikas* in 421, concluded (fr. 454) that the διδασκαλίαι were wrong. Eratosthenes later pointed out that the version of *Clouds* which contains the reference to *Marikas* was revised after 421 and was never performed. The remarkable aspect of this gross error on the part of Kallimachos is that the reference to *Marikas* occurs in precisely that part of the parabasis in which Aristophanes complains of the adverse verdict passed on *Clouds* when it was performed.

Let us not be too hard on Kallimachos. Verifying a point by looking it up in a papyrus roll cannot have been easy, and if we had to work entirely with rolls and without the indices which the labour of the last century and a half was provided we should do worse than Kallimachos—or not take on so vast a labour.[1] For all practical purposes, Kallimachos had to accept the ascriptions with which the books in the Alexandrian library were furnished when they arrived; that he did not so much give titles as record titles is

---

[1] Cf. H. Diels, *Hermes* xxii (1887), 413 f. The critical exactitude of Kallimachos's work seems to me overestimated by H. Herter, *RE* Suppl. v.396 ff., and Lossau, 81 ff.

Kallimachos and the Booksellers 25

suggested by the wording of Sch. Eur. *Androm.* 445: ὁ δὲ Καλλίμαχος (fr. 451) ἐπιγραφῆναί φησι τῇ τραγῳδίᾳ Δημοκράτην. The authority, discernment and integrity of those from whom the books were acquired could vary greatly. Centuries later, Galen had the amusing experience of overhearing an argument at a bookshop about the authenticity of a book which bore his own name (*Scr. min.* [Marquardt] ii.91). The situation was essentially the same in the fourth century B.C., as is revealed by a striking passage in Dionysios's essay on Isokrates (i.85.13–86.8). We learn there that Aphareus asserted that Isokrates (his adoptive father) had never written forensic speeches at all, to which Aristotle (fr. 140) retorted: "Many bundles (δέσμαι) of forensic speeches of Isokrates are in circulation in the bookshops." Dionysios stands aloof from this polemic, and, following the statement of Isokrates' younger contemporary Kephisodotos, ἐν ταῖς πρὸς Ἀριστοτέλην ἀντιγραφαῖς, decides to believe that Isokrates wrote "some speeches for the law courts, but not many." We must stress, and can hardly stress too much, what Dionysios takes for granted: that within a few years of an Attic orator's death there could be serious argument whether he had written many forensic speeches or none. Aristotle's essentially agnostic position, apparent from his reference to the booksellers in connection with Isokrates, is further illustrated by his manner of introducing a citation from a forensic speech against Peitholaos and Lykophron (*Rhet.* 1410ᵃ17–20): ὅ ... τις εἶπε κτλ. Aristotle's *Rhetoric* never mentions Lysias; the defence of Iphikrates, which Dionysios (i.21.9–22.9) found ascribed to Lysias and tentatively reallocated to Iphikrates himself, is cited by Aristotle (*Rhet.* 1411ᵇ1–3) simply as "what Iphikrates said,"[2] and in citing (with a slip of the memory, ἐν Σαλαμῖνι) a passage from the

[2] It must, of course, be remembered that Aristotle says "Sokrates" when he means "the character 'Sokrates' in a Platonic dialogue" (e.g., *Rhet.* 1415ᵃ30 f., where ὁ λέγει Σωκράτης ἐν τῷ ἐπιταφίῳ refers to Pl. *Mnx.* 235D), just as he says (1378ᵇ31) "Achilles says ..." for "Homer represents Achilles as saying ..." It has been argued (cf. Darkow, 9) that this mode of reference to a forensic speech implies that its true authorship is known and universally accepted, but the argument loses its force when we remind ourselves that whereas no one believed that Achilles wrote the *Iliad* or Sokrates *Menexenus* everyone presumed that Iphikrates actually appeared before a jury and was capable of putting his own thoughts into his own words.

Epitaphios which became part of the *corpus Lysiacum* Aristotle says ἐν τῷ ἐπιταφίῳ, without adding an author's name (*Rhet.* 1441ᵃ30–36).³ Aristotle knew at first hand the part played by the booksellers, and we must not be afraid to acknowledge it. People would rather buy and read a speech which bore a famous name than one which bore a little-known name; one might say that in this way the "Canon of the Ten Orators" was essentially established by the quality and reputation of those ten orators. Even the most scrupulous bookseller in the late fourth century would have been little inclined to detach the name of Lysias from any speech which was concerned with events of the early part of the century and could not be ascribed on positive grounds to an orator other than Lysias. We should not imagine that it was only the remoteness in time of these speeches which made false ascription easy. After all, in the list of 38 speeches (and it is a truncated list) which Dionysios regards as wrongly ascribed to Deinarchos, there are 20 which he feels able to reject on chronological grounds alone, without reference to style; and Kallimachos was already a youth when Deinarchos died.⁴ The honesty of booksellers was by no means the only factor relevant to the ascription of speeches in the fourth century, and I shall suggest later (p. 159) that it was not merely impracticable, but actually impossible, for them to attain the standards which we should like them to have attained; but they must wait a little for the clearance of their character.

Thus in attempting to isolate the individual work of Lysias within the body of work ascribed to him we are trying in the first instance to undo what was done in the fourth century; to do what Kallimachos had not the time or equipment to do; to do afresh what Dionysios and Caecilius were the first to attempt on a significant scale. The evidence available to Dionysios was far greater in quantity than that available to us; but we are, after all, two

³ He means by τῷ "the one which contains the words which I am quoting." The difference between this and 1408ᵇ20 τὰ ἐν τῷ Φαίδρῳ is obvious; cf. note 2, above.

⁴ E. Drerup, *Philologus* Suppl. VII (1899), 548 f., argued that false ascription of speeches to Demosthenes before the Alexandrian era was impossible because too many people know the truth. Unfortunately, widespread knowledge of the truth does not suffice to guarantee her victory.

thousand years older, and experience may have taught us something more about the use of evidence.

The origin of the corpusculum and the interrelation of corpora A–G is represented diagrammatically, in Figure I, herewith.

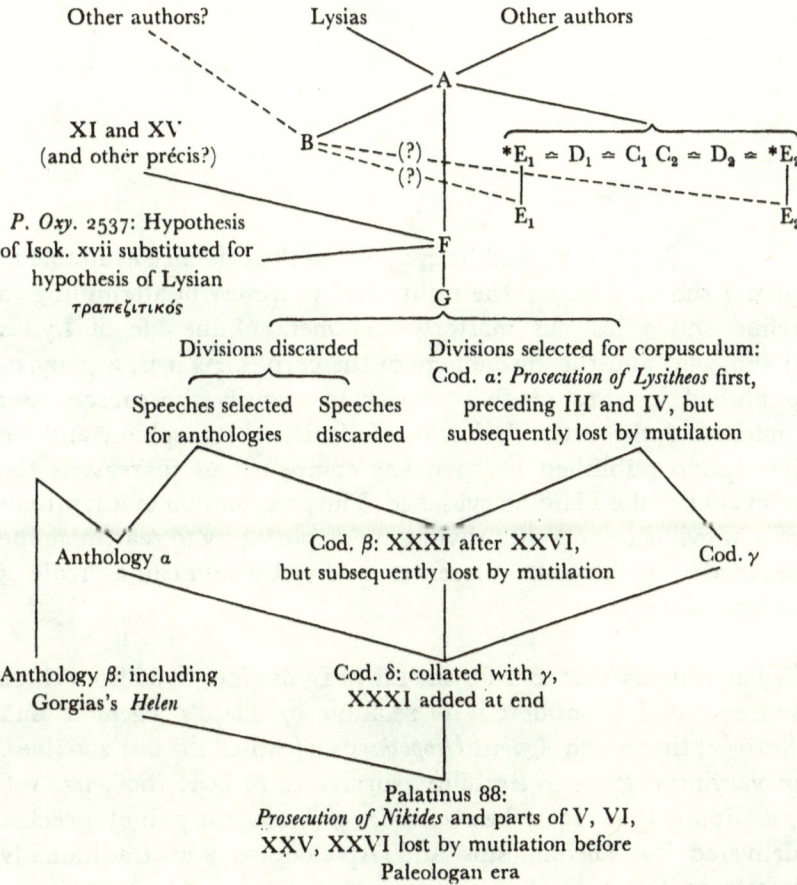

FIGURE I

III

Chronology

IF NOTHING had been added to the evidence available to Blass I should question the utility and propriety of attempting to refine and adjust his masterly treatment of the life of Lysias (i.339–353) and the chronology of the corpus. As it is, a papyrus published in 1919 made it easier to identify the sources and understand the interrelation of Hellenistic biographies, and an inscription published in 1939 has compelled us to reassess the relevance of the Platonic evidence. The presentation of a synthesis of new evidence and old provides the opportunity to rearrange the old evidence with some reference to what I would call a "scale of vulnerability."[1]

The primary evidence for the life of Lysias is derived from three sources: XII, considered in relation to Plato's *Phaedrus* and *Republic*; the speech *Against Hippotherses*, of which the last 200 lines, in varying degrees of legibility, survive in *P. Oxy.* 1606, frr. 1–6 col. iii; and §§ 21–23 of the *Prosecution of Neaira*, the pair of speeches delivered by Theomnestos and Apollodoros and traditionally known as "Dem. lix."

[1] F. Ferckel, *Lysias und Athen* (Würzburg, 1937), took account of fresh evidence, but largely in connection with matters not relevant to our present problem, and his chronological conclusions are too much dominated by "must have . . ." and "cannot have . . ."

The speaker of XII describes himself (§4) as son of Kephalos, "who was persuaded by Perikles to settle in Attica," and as brother of Polemarchos (§§ 12, 16 ff.). Kephalos lived thirty years in Attica, and it is obvious from the narrative that he died before the Thirty Tyrants came to power in 404 (§§4 f.).

At the beginning of the *Republic* Sokrates and Glaukon, on the point of departing from Peiraieus, are persuaded to remain at the house of Kephalos, who has three sons: Polemarchos, Lysias and Euthydemos (328B). Kephalos is "a very old man" (328D). This tells us nothing about Lysias's age, when we recall that the speaker of X (§5 ~ §27) was born when his father was 54 and that Sokrates' children were not all grown up when he was 70 (Pl. *Phdo.* 116B).[2]

In Plato's *Phaedrus* Phaidros has come, when he meets Sokrates, from "Lysias the son of Kephalos" (227A), for whose literary gifts he has extraordinary admiration (228A), and Sokrates takes it for granted that Lysias τῶν λόγων ὑμᾶς . . . ἑστία (227B). At a later stage Sokrates exhorts Phaidros to divert Lysias to philosophy, to which "his (*sc.* Lysias's) brother Polemarchos" is already devoted (257B). This reference accords well with the philosophical enthusiasm displayed by Polemarchos in *Republic* i (331D ff.)—and with the fact that neither Lysias nor Euthydemos is mentioned in the *Republic* after the initial enumeration of the company present.

Sokrates treats Kephalos in the *Republic* as a very rich man (329E–331B), and Kephalos does not carry modesty so far as to disclaim his wealth, though he rates it low by comparison with his grandfather's (330B).

The speaker of XII, whom we may henceforth call "Lysias" without scruple, was also a rich man, and so was his brother Polemarchos. Lysias claims to have had in his house, when it was searched by the representative of the Thirty Tyrants, three talents

---

[2] I am inclined to believe that Kephalos's word νεανίσκοις (v.l. νεανίαις) in 328D refers to his own sons, but the older he is the less the word tells us about their age; and the passage is ambiguous, since he may be referring to Glaukon and Adeimantos (cf. Adam, *ad loc.*).

of silver, in addition to some foreign gold currency (XII.11); and —to judge from comparable cases, notably the estate of Diodotos as described in XXXII.6 f. and that inherited by Demosthenes (Dem. xxvii)—although a rich Greek kept what we would regard as a surprisingly large amount of money "idle," this ready money would be unlikely to represent the major part of his capital. Lysias does not give us a separate figure for the wealth of Polemarchos; he speaks of the workshop close to his own house as if they owned it jointly (§§ 8 ~ 19), and says that at the time of its seizure by the Thirty Tyrants it contained 120 slaves (together with his own and Polemarchos's domestic slaves) and a stock of 700 shields (§ 19). It appears, therefore, that Kephalos, like Demosthenes' father, was a well-to-do manufacturer, whose business his sons inherited.

As we have seen, at the beginning of the *Republic* Kephalos and Polemarchos are represented as living in Peiraieus. Lysias in *Phaedrus* is regarded as not normally living in Athens, for the fact that he is staying with a friend ἐν ἄστει is a matter for remark (227B); nor, on the other hand, does he live abroad, for the word used in Plato of visitors from abroad is ἐπιδημεῖν (e.g., *Ap.* 20A). Lysias was certainly living in Peiraieus in 404, for when he escaped from the clutches of the Thirty he went to the house of a shipowner, Archeneos, and sent him "to the city" to find out what had happened to Polemarchos (XII.16). Whether this means that he happened to know that Polemarchos would be in the city that evening, or that he imagined that Polemarchos had already been arrested and taken off to the city, it certainly does not mean (*pace* Blass, i.347) that Polemarchos must have lived in the city; for the Thirty "divided among themselves the houses" which they were to visit in order to arrest ten metics (XII.7 f.), and when Peison was asked on leaving Lysias's house, where he was going next, he said that he was going to Polemarchos's house (§ 12). It would have been a curious division of labour which assigned to the same man the seizure of one property in Peiraieus and another in Athens on the same evening.

So much for the evidence of XII and Plato on the status of

Lysias and his family. The Platonic evidence poses an interesting chronological problem. The difficulty of assigning a "dramatic date" to the *Republic* is notorious: setting aside the highly controversial question of the festival of Bendis at Peiraieus,[3] we find that Plato's brothers, Glaukon and Adeimantos, are old enough to have distinguished themselves in "the battle at Megara", but Glaukon, at least, was not too old at that time to have had a "lover" who composed elegiacs in his honour (368A). Almost any place but Megara would have been more helpful to those who are hungry for dramatic dates; the definite article in τὴν Μεγαροῖ μάχην does not, of course, imply that the battle was important or famous at the time of writing, but only that the speaker, Sokrates, assumes that his hearers, Glaukon and Adeimantos, know to what occasion he is referring. Even if we confine ourselves to fighting at or near Megara mentioned by extant historians (and, given the contiguity of Attica and the Megarid, this restriction is by no means necessary) our choice is wide; we must certainly include among the alternative possibilities the battle described by Diodoros xiii.65.1 f. (presumably from Ephoros) and dated by him to 409. No conclusion can be drawn as to Sokrates' age at the time of the dialogue from his reference to τοῖς σφόδρα πρεσβύταις as having travelled a road "which we too shall perhaps have to travel" (328D); this is a remark (including the "perhaps") which a man can make at any

[3] This sounds cavalier, in the face of the argument of W. S. Ferguson, *Hesperia* Suppl. VIII (1949), 131 ff., 152, that *SEG* x.64, the decree which established the festival (*Rep.* 327A), must be dated to 429. But Ferguson's thesis depends in the first place (to say nothing of the second stage, the relation between festival and conciliar years in 430/429) on his restoration of 64b.18 (=64a.27) as ... ἐνάτει ἐπὶ δέκα τὸ Θαργηλιῶνο]ς μένὸς τῆι ἐνδεκάτηι [τῆς δεκάτης πρυτανείας..., and it is not credible to me that the date of a festival should be specified in terms of the conciliar calendar (cf. W. K. Pritchett, *BCH* lxxxi [1957], 296 n. 1, and *SEG* xvii.5). We shall know in what year the festival began when we know (if we ever do) when Pasiphon was Secretary of the Council, and even then we shall have to consider which elements in a Platonic dialogue constitute, for Plato, the dramatic date (cf. K. J. Dover, *Phronesis* x [1965], 10 f.). There is no doubt that the festival of Bendis at Peiraieus was celebrated on 19 Thargelion (cf. L. Deubner, *Attische Feste* [Berlin, 1932], 219 f.), but the problems raised by the fictional relation between *Republic* and *Timaeus* (17A) and the identification of the panegyris of Athena mentioned in *Ti.* 21A have no relevance to the question of the year in which the festival began.

time, and even at his trial Sokrates, though βραδὺς καὶ πρεσβύτης (*Ap.* 39B), would hardly have thought of himself as being in the decrepit condition in which he had found Kephalos.

Phaedrus makes a more positive contribution. Phaidros himself is designated as son of Pythokles, of the deme Myrrhinous (244A). It has always been known that a man called Phaidros was among those who fled from Athens in the summer of 415 when denounced by Teukros for taking part in the parodying of the Mysteries (Andokides i.15). It was only when the fragmentary records of the sale of the property of the men condemned for impieties in 415 were greatly augmented by the excavation of the Agora that identification of Plato's Phaidros with Andokides' Phaidros gave a salutary shock to students both of Plato and of Lysias: *SEG* xiii.17.112 (= x.238.63; cf. xiii.13.188 f.) records the sale of the property of Φαίδρο τô Πυθο[κλέος] Μυρρινοσίο. Phaidros, then, left Athens in 415; and it does not seem possible that he can have returned until the "recall of the exiles" consequent on the imposition of Spartan peace terms in 404 (Xen. *HG* ii.2.23; And. i.80). Certainly Alkibiades had been recalled earlier, and so had Adeimantos (*SEG* xiii.17.53, 17.116 ~ Xen. *HG* i.4.21); but they had not been denounced by Teukros—whose evidence, so far as we know, was never rebutted—and it was possible to recall them by a decision to adopt the view that the evidence given in 415 by Agariste and the slave Andromachos (And. i.12 f., 16) was false. The third of the three persons denounced by Agariste, Axiochos (another kinsman of Alkibiades [*SEG* xiii.21.6]) was recalled under the same decision; I take [Pl.] *Ax.* 369A (~ Xen. *HG* i.7.12) to be valid as historical evidence for his presence at Athens in 406, and he may well be the Axiochos who proposed a decree concerning Thracian Neapolis in or shortly after 408 (*IG* i^2.108.39 ~ Thuc. viii.64.3 ff., Xen. *HG* i.4.9).

For the "dramatic date" of Plato's *Phaedrus* we therefore appear so far to have a choice between two alternatives: one a short period, the other a *terminus ante quem*. The short period is the earlier part of the rule of the Thirty Tyrants, when the exiles have returned but Polemarchos has not yet been murdered; and the evidence of Xenophon favours the hypothesis that the murder of Polemarchos and other wealthy metics preceded the rift in the Thirty which led to the death of Theramenes (*HG* ii.3.21). It could no doubt be said that "there is nothing in *Phaedrus* to suggest that the Thirty Tyrants are in power," but fortunately we are spared the necessity of falling back on statements of such a kind, which are innocuous but of limited significance. In 268c Sokrates and Phaidros agree that "if someone approached Sophokles or Euripides and said (εἰ ... τις λέγοι) ... that he could teach tragic composition ... they would laugh at him ... (οὗτοι ἂν ... καταγελῷεν)." Sophokles and Euripides both died before the end of the Peloponnesian War, and one does not speak of the dead in such terms. If, therefore, Plato envisaged a possible historical situation for *Phaedrus*—and students of ancient philosophy will know how heavy a weight is borne by that word "if"—the situation cannot be that of 404, and we are thrown back on the alternative, that it is earlier than the summer of 415. We recall with interest that Lysias is already a distinguished writer, and that Sokrates speaks of him in terms appropriate to someone who lives in Attica, but not Athens. In 278E–279A Phaidros and Sokrates speak of Isokrates in terms which suggest that he is younger than Lysias, or at least—which is not quite the same thing—at an earlier stage of development. All that we know for certain about the age of Isokrates is that he was 82 when he wrote the *Antidosis* (xv.9), 94 when he began the *Panathenaikos* (xii.3) and 97 when he finished it (xii.270). It is customary to accept 436/435 as his date of birth (the figure is given by [Plu.] *Vit. Or.* 836F) and to date the *Antidosis* and *Panathenaikos* accordingly. This, however, is to put the cart before the horse. *Vit. Or.* 837F shows that his age at death and the interval between the *Panathenaikos* and his death were disputed, and it would be safer, inferring his approximate date of birth from the political circumstances which the *Antidosis* and *Panathenaikos* presuppose, to locate it within the limits 438–435. *Phaedrus* therefore may be held to imply a date somewhat earlier than 440 for the birth of Lysias.

For the moment, we must be content to note these data; we shall encounter before long other data with which they are difficult to reconcile.

Harpokration refers twice to a speech of Lysias *Against Hippotherses* (68.208., 159.17). *P. Oxy.* 1606, of the late second or early third century A.D., contains fragments of several speeches, one of which is entitled (fr. 6, col. iii) πρὸς Ἱπποθέρσην ὑπὲρ θεραπαίνης. The legible portion of the speech is actually about Lysias, who is not only named (lines 36, 79, 136, 222) but identified beyond doubt by the statements that he was a metic (154) who lost both his property and his brother under the Thirty Tyrants (7 ff., 80 ff., 155 ff.). Litigation has arisen out of his attempts to recover some part of what the Thirty sold when they had taken it from him; with the details of this litigation I am not now concerned, but rather with certain other statements made about Lysias in the course of the speech.

The restoration "richest of the metics" is inescapable in εω[c]μ[ε]νγαρυ | [μεισηνδα]ιμονειτε | πλου[σιωτατοσ η]ντωνμετοι | [κων (152 ff.), and it appears that the value of the property—the total property, presumably, of Lysias and Polemarchos—sold by the Thirty was 70 talents: ουc]ιαν | δεεβδ[ομηκο]ντατα | λαντων [.....]ντο (29 ff.). These statements fill in the outline already provided by XII and the *Republic*; from the new data in the speech (163 ff.) it appears that after Lysias fled—destitute, one might have imagined from XII—he provided the democrats who were gathering in exile with (*a*) 300 of some commodity or other; (*b*) a sum of money, the total being illegible; (*c*) some other contribution, the description of which occupied six missing lines of papyrus; and (*d*), from a foreign friend, a further two talents. This list of contributions is a useful reminder (though it ought not to surprise anyone) that the realisable assets and sources of credit of a wealthy Greek were not necessarily all located in the city where he lived.

The case against Neaira was brought in the 340's, probably after 343 (cf. Blass, iii/1.536). The second speaker, Apollodoros, after describing the audacious ways in which Neaira has acted as if she were a respectable Athenian married woman, says (§115): "And when you have seen her face (ὄψις), reflect on this only, that she—Neaira!—has done what I have recounted." As the written words stand, the point is in doubt. Apollodoros may mean that Neaira looks a mild, harmless old woman,[4] and he may be urging the jury not to be deceived by appearances. Alternatively, it may be that she is still a woman of striking beauty, and he is trying to reduce the proverbial susceptibility of juries to the charm of women; we may recall the anecdote ([Plu.] *Vit. Or.* 849E) that Hypereides secured the acquittal of Phryne by bringing her into court "topless." Of these two interpretations, two factors favour the second. One is the phraseology, Νέαιρα οὖσα ταῦτα διαπέπρακται, which does not imply "Remember that despite appearances she is still Neaira," but simply emphasises the enormity of the contradiction between Neaira's character and her pretensions; and we may recall the words attributed to Iphikrates in Arist. *Rhet.* 1398ª5 f., "Well, then, if you, who are Aristophon, would not betray the fleet for money, would I, who am Iphikrates, do so?" The second point is the fact that Neaira's defence (as represented by Apollodoros) turns largely on the claim of Stephanos that he keeps her as a hetaira—that he does not pretend, and has never pretended, that she is his wife (§119). Now, if Neaira at the time of the trial looked old and wizened, Apollodoros had a splendid opportunity to use the argument, "We discard hetairai when they grow old; if Stephanos still keeps Neaira, that proves that they mean to pass as man and wife." This argument would have been in keeping with Apollodoros's own generalisation that men keep hetairai solely for pleasure (§122). It would also have been in keeping with the kind of social and psychological generalisation, true or false, which is abundantly exemplified in the orators—for example: VII.35, "Slaves are naturally more hostile to their own masters than to anyone"; Dem. xxiv.124, "Slaves who have been freed feel no gratitude towards their former master, but hate him more than

---

[4] Cf. the technique of Dem. xxxvii. 44, where the slave Antigenes is exhibited and his master says sarcastically, "This is the man who (*sc.* is alleged to have) evicted Pantainetos and got the better of Pantainetos's friends!"

they hate anyone, because he knows that they were slaves"; xxxix.26, "If Mantias was so extravagant as to keep a mistress as well as a wife, how could he have left any substantial property when he died?"; Hyper. i.15, "It is impossible that a man should start to be an adulterer at the age of fifty; either he has always been that sort of man, or the accusation is false."

I would conclude that at the time of the trial Neaira was still a seductive woman. Now, Apollodoros alleges, with witnesses to support his allegation (§§ 33 f.),[5] that she was present as a hetaira at the party given by Chabrias to celebrate his Pythian victory in 374, and that earlier she had been kept by a succession of lovers (§§ 24–32), the first of whom, the Thessalian Simos, came to Athens with her on the occasion of a Great Panathenaia (§ 24) and thus not later than 378. Her previous visit to Athens (according to Apollodoros) was when Lysias "the sophist" (§ 21) brought his own mistress Metaneira to be initiated at Eleusis (§§ 21 f.). At that time Neaira was already earning money as a prostitute, although "rather young ⟨for this⟩ because she had not yet attained the age of puberty" (§ 22: νεωτέρα οὖσα διὰ[6] τὸ μήπω τὴν ἡλικίαν αὐτῇ παρεῖναι). Metaneira is the fourth, Neaira the seventh, of the seven girls listed by Apollodoros (§ 19) as brought up from infancy by Nikarete, who (he says) had a sharp eye for potential hetairai and pretended that the girls whom she acquired were her own daughters (§§ 18 f.).

We do not have to believe Apollodoros's assertion about the behaviour of the nymphet Neaira, nor do we know the difference in age between Metaneira and Neaira. The documentary testimony which names Lysias as "son of Kephalos" may be authentic, in the sense that (unlike many documents incorporated in speeches, notably the clumsy fabrications in Dem. xviii) it was probably included in the stichometric edition from which the markers in Parisinus 2934 are derived. The interval between the

[5] Since witnesses sometimes contradicted each other, some witnesses cannot have told the truth. Thus must be borne in mind throughout my argument from Dem. lix.

[6] διά is odd; but cf. VIII.12 οἱ δ' ἄρα οὐκ ἀντέλεγον ἀλλ' ἀντέπραττον, καὶ διὰ τοῦτο ἀντέπραττον, ἵνα τὸν ἐμὸν λόγον εἰδείη Πολυκλῆς, which seems to mean "... and they carried their hostile activity to the point of ensuring..."

Chronology 37

marker B (at ἐκτήσατο Νικαρέτη in §18) and Γ (at γεγενημένην ὁρᾶν in §30) is 70 lines of speech in Rennie's edition, plus $14\frac{1}{2}$ lines of documents. From Γ to Δ (at the end of §38) there are 72 lines of speech and 11 lines of documents. The markers are then missing until we come to I, which is placed after τῇ γυναικί in the document cited in §87. From I to K we have 74 lines of speech and a two-line document; from K to M, 144 lines, plus a two-line epigram and an eight-line document, totalling $154 = 2 \times 77$.[7] Normally the interval between one stichometric marker and the next corresponds to 77–79 lines as printed in Rennie or Butcher, when there are no documents or when fabricated documents (which are in a majority) have been subtracted. It is therefore virtually certain that at least one of the three documents incorporated between §22 and §30 of the *Prosecution of Neaira* was absent from the stichometric edition.[8] Crude arithmetic points to the absence of the six-and-a-half-line document in §25. That is in fact the only one of the three which adds nothing to what Apollodoros has already said (for the document in §23 gives the demotic of Hipparchos). This argument is far from decisive, since the fictitious documents in Dem. xviii are notoriously furnished with an excess of plausible-sounding detail, but the private speeches are in a different category, and the balance of probability inclines to the presence of the testimony involving Lysias in the stichometric edition of Demosthenes. Even if it be rejected, it is hard to see whom, among men living about 380, a speaker in the 340's could describe as "Lysias the sophist" (cf. p. 155 on λογογράφος and σοφιστής) except our Lysias.

It is no part of Apollodoros's purpose to denigrate Lysias. He is interested in establishing the association of Neaira with Metaneira and their common owner Nikarete, and in relating how Lysias, having a wife and an old mother at home (§22), put Metaneira and Nikarete to stay with Philostratos he is leading up to Philostratos's

[7] Data from F. Burger, *Hermes* xxii (1887), 654.

[8] E. Drerup, *JbClPh* Suppl. xxiv (1898), 343 ff., argues for the authenticity of the documents in Dem. lix as a whole; but I find nothing surprising in the idea that the presence of some genuine documents in the text of a speech should inspire the forgery of some more.

evidence on the presence of Neaira in Athens at that time. If my argument about Neaira's age is sound, we can hardly date Lysias's importation of Metaneira as a mistress much earlier than 380. Generalisation about the onset of senility is perilous; we have no means of assessing the rejuvenating effect of Metaneira; and Lysias's mother may, of course, have been a centenarian. But if the *Prosecution of Neaira* were our only evidence, we should hesitate to date Lysias's birth earlier than 440, and we might well wish to bring it down a little further.

Good biographical evidence on the orators was not always available to Dionysios.[9] All he can say about the chronology of Isaios, for example, is: "He flourished after the Peloponnesian War, as I infer from speeches of his, and lasted until Philip's rise to power" (i.93.5–7), which is no more than we could infer ourselves from the surviving speeches. In the case of Lysias, however, he adds some important data (i.8.2–17) to what we have already gathered:

(a) Kephalos was a Syracusan by birth.
(b) Lysias was born after Kephalos moved to Attica.
(c) Lysias and his two brothers went to Thurioi when it was founded by the Athenians, and Lysias was at that time 15.
(d) After the defeat of the Athenians in Sicily, 300 citizens of Thurioi, including Lysias, were compelled to flee, charged with ἀττικισμός, and Lysias returned to Athens in 412/411.

Dionysios dates the foundation of Thurioi "in the twelfth year before the Peloponnesian War" (i.8.6–8), from which he calculates (i.8.15 f.) that Lysias was 47 in 412/411; and, of course, he implies either 459/458 or 458/457 as Lysias's date of birth, which leads him to postulate that he died at the age of 80 (a purely hypothetical figure) in 379/378 or 378/377 (i.20.23–21.2). This

---

[9] The inadequacy and conflicting nature of biographical data on classical authors has recently been well illustrated by the *Life of Pindar* in *P. Oxy.* 2438.

Chronology 39

would incidentally imply that Kephalos died by 428, and—if we take the *Republic* seriously—that there was a gap of twenty years between Plato and his brothers.

The *Lives of the Ten Orators* do not in general command our respect, and in historical technique they fall far below the standards of Plutarch, in whose *Moralia* they were transmitted to the Middle Ages. Their author compiled information, without adequate synthesis, from two or more sources; thus he says (836A) that Lysias died "at the age of 83, or, as some say, 76, or, as some say, past 80." He is even led to repeat himself; thus he appends to his statement about Lysias's death: "They say that he was born in the archonship of Philokles," though this has already been stated a few lines earlier (835C).

The author follows Dionysios quite closely, but with certain adjustments and amplifications:

> (*a*) Kephalos was already dead when Lysias, at the age of 15, went to Thurioi at its foundation (835D).
> (*b*) Lysias was accompanied to Thurioi by Polemarchos, "for he had two other brothers, Euthydemos and Brachyllos."

The former statement is wholly irreconcilable with the *Republic*, where Kephalos is a very old man at a time when Lysias and Polemarchos are grown men. More important, it is virtually irreconcilable with XII. If Kephalos lived at Athens 30 years (XII.4) but died before the foundation of Thurioi, it is hard to imagine how he was "persuaded by Perikles" (a very young man in the 470's) to abandon Syracuse for Athens—unless he was in danger as a political enemy of the tyrant Hieron, and if that had been so Lysias could have turned it to good account in XII.4.

As for Brachyllos, there is some reason to think that the author of the *Life* has misinterpreted Dem. lix, a speech which he uses and names (836B) in dealing with Lysias's affair with Metaneira; but he uses it carelessly, for he makes this affair precede Lysias's marriage. Now, Dem. lix.22 says that Lysias's wife was his ἀδελφιδῆ, the daughter of Brachyllos. ἀδελφιδῆ often means "brother's daughter," but it also means "sister's daughter," as in III.6 and Is. iii.43, and I presume (with Blass, i.346 n.1) that Brachyllos was not Lysias's brother, but his brother-in-law.

It may be seen from the following confrontation (cf. Grenfell and Hunt *ad loc.*) that the speech *Against Hippotherses* was a source of the anonymous *Life*:

P. Oxy. 1606.163 ff.	Vit. Or. 835F
φευ]γωνωιχετο	ἐπιθεμένων δὲ τῶν ἀπὸ Φυλῆς
[ ]τριακοσι	τῇ καθόδῳ, ἐκεῖ (Westermann: ἐπεὶ codd).
[ ]ειστηκα	χρησιμώτατος ἁπάντων ὤφθη,
[θοδονκαιπ]αρεσχετο	χρήματά τε παρασχὼν
[δ]ραχμας	δραχμὰς δισχιλίας
. . .	
. . .	καὶ ἀσπίδας διακοσίας
. . .	
. . .	πεμφθείς τε σὺν Ἑρμᾶνι
. . .	
. . .	ἐπικούρους ἐμισθώσατο τριακοσίους
. . .	
[ηλει]ονξ[ενον]οντας	δύο τ' ἔπεισε τάλαντα δοῦναι
αυ[τω]ιεπει[cεν]αυτονδυ	Θρασυδαῖον τὸν Ἠλεῖον,
οταλαντιαπ[αρ]ασχειντ[ε	ξένον αὐτῷ γεγονότα
λη[[ι]]	

Blass surmised (i.350) that the ultimate source of the secondary biographical evidence was the work *On His Own Benefactions*, ascribed to Lysias by Harpokration (173.3; 203.12; 300.6). But, in addition to the passage cited above, there are two slight reasons for giving priority to the speech *Against Hippotherses*.

One is that at the beginning of the fourth century Syracusan origin was a liability at Athens, for Syracuse had inflicted a humiliating defeat on the Athenians in 413 and had helped the Peloponnesian fleet in the Aegean in the closing years of the war.

Chronology 41

In XII.4 Lysias avoids saying whence Kephalos came to Peiraieus; but in a defensive speech, and in a case where his adversaries, in the manner of Greek litigants, would naturally have exploited what prejudice they could against his origins, he would have found it politic to rebut this διαβολή, and from his doing so (however he did it) later readers could learn that Kephalos was a Syracusan. Lysias would take the same opportunity to assert that he himself was born in Athens.

If the work *On His Own Benefactions* was early, Lysias would have had the same reason to avoid mention of Syracuse in it as he had in XII. If, on the other hand, it was a later work, and belonged to the time when Athens was cultivating the friendship of Dionysios I (*IG* ii².18, 103)—to whom, on the other hand, the *Olympikos* ascribed to Lysias was implacably hostile (Dion. Hal. i.45.22–48.18)—Lysias had a different motive for silence on his origins: as we have seen, his father must have left Syracuse after it had expelled the Deinomenid tyranny and established a democracy.

Secondly, there existed in the late fourth century a law (and for all we know, it was an old law) which forbade a metic ἐξοικεῖν ἐν τῷ πολέμῳ (Hyper. v.33; cf. iii.29). If part of Hippotherses' διαβολή against Lysias was to the effect that Lysias had gone to Thurioi in time of war, Lysias can have rebutted this by saying that he was only 15 when he went there, and that the οἶκος of Kephalos remained at Peiraieus. We may compare how the speaker of X rebuts an accusation of parricide by saying that he was only 13 when his father was executed by the Thirty (§4). It is less easy to see why Lysias need have mentioned in the work *On His Own Benefactions* how old he was when he went to Thurioi.

For these reasons I am inclined to treat the speech *Against Hippotherses* as the source of those statements in the biographical tradition which we cannot find in XII or in Plato.

If Dionysios is right—if, that is, Lysias left Athens in 443 and did not return until 412/411—Plato's *Phaedrus* has no possible dramatic date, for Phaidros went into exile in 415 and did not return until 404, by which time Sophokles and Euripides were dead. Moreover, if Lysias was born in 459/458 or 458/457, he was approaching 80 when he kept Metaneira as a mistress. Neither of these conclusions suffices to prove Dionysios wrong. I am well aware of the criticisms which can be levelled against my interpretation of Dem. lix, and if Plato was capable of anachronisms as audacious as *Menexenus* it is hard to assert that he cannot have created an impossible situation for *Phaedrus* (cf. p. 33). None the less, the conflict justifies scrutiny of Dionysios's statements.

That Lysias went to Thurioi at 15 seems to me the least vulnerable of these statements. Unlike "35" as the numerical equivalent of one generation, "40" as the ἀκμή of an individual career, "18" as the age of entering manhood, "25–27" for participation in public life (Dion. Hal. i.310.4 f.), "70" as the boundary of old age (i.303.4 f.), or "80" as the age of death (i.20.23–21.1), "15" has no conventional significance for Hellenistic biographers or historians of literature.

But did Lysias go to Thurioi when it was founded? This may well be a pure assumption on the part of Dionysios (cf. Blass, i.340). Suppose instead that he went in 430/429, when Kephalos's powerful friend Perikles was in temporary disgrace and the plague had begun its ravages in Athens (Thuc. ii.59). This hypothesis would put Kephalos's arrival in Attica between 450 and 445, Lysias's birth about 445, and Kephalos's death between 420 and 415; it would make Lysias's mother (say) a little over 80 in 380; and the dramatic date of the *Republic* would fall within the limits 420–415—if it is possible to bring Lysias back from Thurioi by that time, and not when Dionysios dates his return, 412/411.

We need not doubt that Lysias returned on an occasion when it was perilous to be identified at Thurioi with Athenian interests. I wonder whether Dionysios, learning from historical works available to him that there was a major upheaval of this nature at Thurioi in 412, jumped to the conclusion (ctr. Blass, i.346, n. 3: "ohne Zweifel nach Lysias selbst") that this was the only appropriate occasion for the flight of Lysias. What we know of the disturbed history of Thurioi suggests that it was by no means the only such occasion; there seems to have been a strong movement for independence from Athenian influence even before the Peloponnesian War (Diod. xii.35). When the Sicilian Expedition sailed along the Italian coast in 415, "the cities did not allow them to enter the walls or buy commodities, but granted only watering and anchorage, and Taras and Lokroi did not grant even that" (Thuc. vi.44.2). Unless Thucydides is exaggerating (as he sometimes does),[10] Thurioi at that date was unfriendly to Athens; admittedly, Diod. xiii.3.4 gives a different account, to the effect that Thurioi displayed the greatest φιλανθρωπία to the Athenian forces, but certain other data persuade me to take Thucydides' silence more seriously. Alkibiades succeeded in jumping ship at Thurioi on his way back to face his trial at Athens, and could not be found (vi.61.6). In 414 Thurioi rebuffed Gylippos (vi.104.2); but it regarded his little fleet as ineffectual (§3)—as well it might, seeing that Syracuse herself had abandoned hope and was opening negotiations with Nikias (vi.103.3 f., 2.2). When in the summer of 413 Demosthenes and Eurymedon called at Thurioi they found that "the opponents of Athens had lately been cast out" (vii.33.5) —which confirms our impression from vi.44.2 and 61.6 that the friends of Athens were in eclipse in 415 and only began to gain strength in 414. Thucydides maintains complete silence on the attitude of Thurioi during the Athenian activities of 427-424 and Phaiax's diplomatic mission in 422 (v.4.1, 5.1). I suggest for serious consideration the hypothesis that pro-Athenian elements in Thurioi were frequently, perhaps continuously, threatened in the late 420's, and that Lysias returned to Athens during that period. This hypothesis has the advantage that it offers an entirely plausible and self-consistent dramatic date for Plato's *Phaedrus*— say, 418–416, when Phaidros and Sokrates were as we see them in the *Symposium*, Lysias was in his late twenties, and Isokrates about twenty.

[10] E.g., vi.46.3, where Segesta borrows gold and silver plate "from the neighbouring cities, both Phoenician and Greek"; the only Greek city which could possibly be called "neighbouring" was Selinus, with which Segesta was at war.

44 Lysias and the *Corpus Lysiacum*

The earliest datable speech in the corpusculum is XX. The man there defended, Polystratos, was one of the compilers of the citizen list under the oligarchy in 411 (§§ 13 f.). For that he had already been fined (§§ 14, 18); he now faced a fresh charge, of indeterminate nature but belonging (in the speaker's view) to a group of charges currently brought against men involved in the antidemocratic proceedings of 411 (§§ 6 f.). No allusions in the speech positively indicate a date later than 409, and an accumulation of arguments *ex silentio* shows that it was certainly composed before the defeat of Athens.

The latest speech in the corpusculum to which a virtually certain date can be assigned is XXVI, an attack on a man who has drawn by lot the office of eponymous archon (§ 12 ~ '*Aθ.π*.56.6) and is undergoing the required scrutiny (§§ 1 *al.*) by the Council (§ 21). The beginning of the speech was lost when the Palatinus was mutilated, and we owe to the table of contents in the manuscript the knowledge (no doubt based on the opening sentences; cf. XXXI.1) that the man's name is Euandros. This was in fact the name of the eponymous archon of 382/381, and since coincidences in the Attic archon list, though by no means unknown, should not be multiplied beyond necessity, it is reasonable to presume that XXVI was an unsuccessful attack delivered in the summer of 382.

The latest speech in the corpusculum which can be dated without even the margin of doubt which some may wish to attach to XXVI is X, composed "in the twentieth year" from the democratic restoration (§ 4) and thus in 384/383.

The only speeches in the whole corpus other than XX which could possibly be dated on positive grounds earlier than 403/402 are a pair defending a litigant against "Alkibiades," who has been identified by some with the elder Alkibiades (but cf. p. 53). XII belongs to the end of 403, for although the charge made by Lysias personally against Eratosthenes is a charge of murder, the case must have formed part of the εὔθυναι to which any of the surviving Thirty Tyrants could submit himself (cf. p. 8). IV, V, VIII and XXIII are not datable. The remaining speeches of the

Chronology 45

corpusculum are either datable within the limits 403–388 or reveal an upper terminus lying between those limits.[11]

Of the speeches included in Corpus A two were composed in the interests of Iphikrates. On historical grounds Dionysios dates one of these later than 372/371 (i.20.15–21.9) and the other later than 356/355 (i.21.9–19). Since he accepts 459–458 as the date of the orator's birth and assumes that he died at the age of 80—and hence in 379/378 or 378/377 (i.20.23–21.3)—Dionysios is bound to reject the two speeches for Iphikrates as wrongly ascribed. Isokrates, of course, was still writing at the age of 97, as Dionysios well knew (i.56.7); but, after all, that information comes from Isokrates' own pen (xii.270), and clearly Dionysios, in the absence of any information at all on the date of Lysias's death, had to fall back on an assumption. If we think (as I do) that he dated Lysias's birth too early, we have no rational grounds for sharing his assumption about the date of Lysias's death; the assumption could be right, but if it is, it is right by chance. Dionysios alleges, in the case of the second speech for Iphikrates, that his suspicions were first aroused by its lack of what he regards as Lysias's stylistic merits, and that his historical enquiry into its date came second (i.21.9–15). In the case of the earlier speech, Dionysios does not state in so many words that suspicion of its style preceded discovery of its date, but he rather suggests that it did (i.20.15–21.9). It is important to remember, however, that what Dionysios says about the speeches for Iphikrates is only a digression in his essay on the style of Lysias. Since we do not possess the essay which he devoted to the discussion of the true and false ascription of speeches to Lysias (cf. i.22.8 f., 25.3–7), we do not know how many speeches datable after 378/377 but indistinguishable from the genuine work of Lysias by Dionysios's stylistic criteria were rejected by him on chronological grounds alone. Although on occasion (i.306.6–15; cf. i.97.10–101.18) he seems to speak with assurance of the

[11] Darkow, 71, n. 6, considers the possibility that XXII antedates 403, but there was no time before then at which all that is said in §14 would make sense. No one now, I think, believes that Κτησικλέους τοῦ ἄρχοντος in IX.6 is the eponymous archon of 334/3; for ἄρχων = "commander (in the field)" cf. XXVI.21, XXVIII.5.

recognition of Lysias's style, he does not, in the last resort, treat this style as unique and inimitable, for he admits that the speech *On Halonnesos* (Dem. vii) τὸν Λυσιακὸν χαρακτῆρα ἐκμέμακται εἰς ὄνυχα (i.157.9 f.). In that instance he feels safe in his admission, for no one's reconstruction of the chronology of Lysias could possibly encompass the speech *On Halonnesos*. But it is legitimate to wonder whether there may not have been occasions on which Dionysios's chronological decision made him abnormally sensitive to stylistic phenomena which appeared to support it or insensitive to those which did not.

The majority of the speeches known to us only by titles and citations or fragments are undatable. The only one which takes us outside the limits observable in the corpusculum is the speech on the estate of Androkleidas, a Theban who fled to Athens when the Kadmeia was seized by Phoibidas in 382 (Xen. *HG* v.2.31; Plu. *Pel.* 5.3); he died in exile. The speech was ascribed to Lysias by Kallimachos (fr. 448). Since the ascription is accepted by Dionysios (i.98.18–100.12), it presumably contained no obvious allusion to any event which he could date after 378.

IV

Ideology and Political Association

IN XII Lysias speaks, and in the speech *Against Hippotherses* another speaks for him, as a "democrat": that is to say, as an active helper of those men in exile who fought against the oligarchy established after the defeat of Athens, re-entered the city triumphantly in the autumn of 403, and re-established a full democracy which endured without serious challenge until again suppressed by external power three generations later. If we were to divide the population of Athens into three categories, "democrats," "oligarchs" and "quietists," we should deny the authenticity of any speech which defends an "oligarch" or a "quietist." But I hope no one will want to found a conclusion wholly on any such division, for this would be to ignore all but one aspect of Athenian politics.

In the first place, whatever Lysias's own sentiments may have been when the Thirty Tyrants came to power, the Thirty made him their enemy on their own initiative and by the most effective means imaginable: they killed his brother, tried to kill him, and seized his family property. Thereafter he could revenge himself only by taking the same road as those who were in armed opposition to the Thirty.[1]

[1] It is worth remembering, as a possible analogy, that Kleon "declared war" on Aristophanes *before* our earliest extant play of Aristophanes, and it is open to question whether *Babylonians* had ridiculed Kleon in particular.

Those historians who have not forbidden themselves on principle to speculate on hypothetical courses of events may well wonder what the political development of fourth-century Athens would have been if the oligarchy of the Thirty had included no Kritias and more than one Theramenes: if, instead of alienating the middle class by undiscriminating proscriptions (cf. Pl. *Ep.* 7.324C–325A), it had conciliated and flattered them and had made the sailors the scapegoat for Athens' defeat.[2] It might be injudicious to suggest that in those circumstances Athens would have remained an oligarchy for more than twenty years; but, given the facts, it would certainly be naïve to suppose that everyone in the twenty years after 403 who vilified the Thirty, attacked individuals who had been allowed by the Thirty to stay in the city, and sang the praises of the restored democracy must also, in earlier years, have vilified the Four Hundred, voted for every proposal made by Kleophon, and defended the political rights of what Aristophanes rightly called (*Ach.* 162) ὁ θρανίτης λεὼς ὁ σωσίπολις (cf. [Xen.] *Resp. Ath.* 1.2).

In Athenian politics—and when I speak of "Athenians" I include, except when I refer specifically to the holding of magistracies and personal appearance in Assembly or Council, metics whose wealth and personal connections made them people to be reckoned with—we may distinguish three separate and sometimes conflicting moments.

The first is the ideological moment. There certainly existed at Athens, through the lifetime of Lysias, men who could defend democracy as such, on objective grounds (I call a moral or political value "objective" wherever and whenever two or more people discuss rationally its relation to any other value which they have

---

[2] The oligarchic revolution of 411 must have been facilitated not merely by the physical distance separating hoplites in Attica from sailors at Samos, but also by a feeling on the part of each class that the other had been to blame for the disaster in Sicily; and the breach was healed by naval successes in 411/410. We may compare the extent to which the German capture of Crete in 1941 produced among British forces in Egypt contempt of sailors for soldiers and resentment of soldiers against airmen. If the three services had been drawn from different economic classes, the political consequences might have been far reaching.

both or all adopted). There existed also men who defended an oligarchic ideology which was (in the same sense) equally objective, and men who regarded moral evaluation itself as systematic deception. I do not doubt that it was possible to find men in each of these three categories whose political principles and motives were consistent and enduring; but I do doubt whether the ideological moment was the decisive one at any stage, however critical, of Athenian political history.

The second moment is that of economic self-interest. There were, as always, rich men who resented the claims made upon them by the community as a whole, a community from which they felt themselves estranged. There were other rich men (probably the majority) who were animated by the powerful force of φιλοτιμία (cf. XXI.22), and who knew how lavish expenditure could pave the way to high standing, respect, influence and power in the community. The anonymous speaker of XXV, who is greatly addicted to generalisation, makes the point (§8) that "no man is oligarchic or democratic by nature, but everyone is an enthusiast for the establishment of that constitution which is in his own interest." Yet he does not suggest—as is suggested by the so-called Old Oligarch ([Xen.] *Resp. Ath.* 1.4 f.) and later (disingenuously) by Demosthenes (e.g., xxi.208–212)—that rich men are oligarchs and poor men democrats; he means that those who can press a legitimate claim on the gratitude of the people have an interest in the maintenance of democracy, while those who have suffered punishment, loss or dishonour have an interest in oligarchic revolution.

The third moment is the association of individuals. The speaker of IX makes a revealing statement (§13): "I become a friend of Sostratos ... knowing he was a man of importance in the life of the community (περὶ τὴν πόλιν ἄξιον λόγου γεγενημένον). Although I became prominent (γνώριμος) because of his power (δυναστεία) I did not take my revenge on any enemy or confer a favour on any friend." The δυναστεία of Sostratos has not left much of a mark on history, but the speaker's brief reference to it is perfectly in accord with two strands which are conspicuous in

Athenian political life. One of these, familiar to us from Demosthenes, is the inseparability of private feuds from political rivalries fought out in the law courts with a mustering of influential individuals on either side.[3] The other is Thucydides' presentation of political issues in terms of rivalry between eminent individuals competing for προστασία τοῦ δήμου: I draw attention especially to his assessment of the successors of Perikles (ii.65.7–12), his description of Alkibiades' opposition to Nikias in relation to the peace of 421 (v.43.2 f.; cf. vi.89.2) and the Sicilian Expedition (vi.15.2), and his treatment of the breakdown of the oligarchy in 411 as exemplifying the disruptive forces which are inherent in oligarchies (viii.89.3).

These three moments are of different interest to different historians, and which of the three dominates and absorbs the other two is a matter of disagreement, in which each historian's presuppositions about politics play some part. It seems to me that the third moment matters most, and that the evidence supports my view;[4] but the reader must bear in mind the possibility that an unconscious selectivity operates on my observation of relevant data.[5]

The most important characteristic of the third moment is that the alignment of individuals could, and did, change between the emergence of any two political issues, so that although it might be pedantic, and sometimes cumbrous, to dispense with the word "party" in all discussion of Athenian politics, it is important not to assume that the composition of (say) the "North Aegean" party in year n is exactly the same as that of the "North Aegean" party in year $n + 3$ or of the "Peace with Sparta" party in either year. As the speaker of XXV observes (§9), Phrynichos and Peisandros (the latter a lively watchdog of the people in the disturbances occasioned by the sacrileges of 415 [And. i.27, 36, 43]) were instigators

---

[3] Cf. Lavency, 57, 80 ff., 97.

[4] Dion. Hal. i.315.7–15 has an interesting argument from political association.

[5] The "dynastic" interpretation of Athenian democracy is adopted with considerable (but, as sometimes happens, salutary) exaggeration by G. Prestel, *Die antidemokratische Strömung in Athen des fünften Jahrhunderts bis zum Tode des Perikles* (Breslau, 1939).

of the oligarchic revolution in 411. On a level which we might call "sub-political," VIII exhibits, with a degree of allusive detail which baffles our attempts to unravel the story, and in a tone of indignation which touches the sense of humour of readers separated from the event by two millennia, the progress of a nexus towards its dissolution in ἑκὼν ὑμῖν ἐξίσταμαι τῆς φιλίας (§18). Between these two extremes is the relationship between Demosthenes, Apollodoros and Phormion. Apollodoros, the victim of a sustained and venomous attack in Dem. xxxvi on Phormion's behalf, appears almost at once (Dem. xlv) as a close associate of Demosthenes—a change of alignment so rapid and complete, and finding expression in such extravagantly rhetorical terms, that it enabled Aischines in 343 (ii.165) to charge Demosthenes with the most treacherous kind of dishonesty.[6] Even to the modern student of Greek history it wears a grotesque look; but it would perhaps seem less so if he were also a student of modern countries which have many small political parties.

In the light of what has been said above, how are we to reconstruct the history of the political loyalties and attitudes of Lysias? His father, according to XII.4, had been an acquaintance of Perikles. The family was wealthy. These two data in themsleves tell us precisely nothing about his politics between his return from Thurioi and his flight from the Thirty. I would be reluctant even to draw conclusions from his experience at Thurioi; if a statement made on his behalf in the speech *Against Hippotherses* was (as I have suggested) the sole evidence available to Dionysios, it is evidence tainted by advocacy, and we should need to know much more about his nexus of associations at Thurioi before we could decide whether he fled as a member of a defeated democratic faction or—which is not the same thing in the West (though on a rebellious Aegean island it might have been)—as a man whose interests were too closely bound up with those of a father who lived in Attica.

[6] Cf., however, Lionel Pearson, in L. Wallach, (ed.), *The Classical Tradition* (Ithaca, N.Y., 1966), who points out how far the evidence—including the allegation of Aischines—falls short of proof that Demosthenes wrote speeches for Apollodoros.

52 Lysias and the *Corpus Lysiacum*

More interesting questions are raised by the Platonic evidence. The associations between the men whom we encounter in Plato are best displayed not in columnar lists, as if they were distributed among parties in a parliament, but in a diagram bearing a rough resemblance to that of a "chelate" molecule. If we perform this exercise with reference to *Protagoras* 314E–316A, *Republic* 328B and the *Symposium*, we get the result sketched in Figure II.

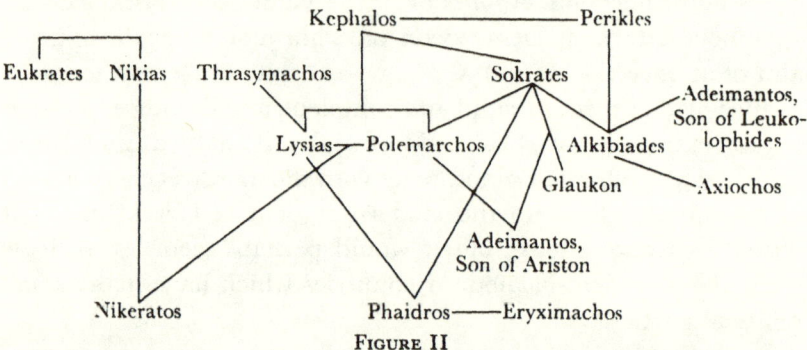

FIGURE II

The bottom right quarter of this diagram includes five people—Adeimantos, Alkibiades, Axiochos, Eryximachos and Phaidros—who were denounced in 415 for profanation of the Mysteries (And. i.13–16, 35); one, Sokrates, who was allowed by the Thirty Tyrants to stay in the city (cf. Pl. *Ap.* 32c, Xen. *Mem.* i.2.31 ff.); and two, Adeimantos and Glaukon, whose family at least was not conspicuous for devotion to the radical "establishment." Lysias is linked to Alkibiades by three different routes: via his own father and Alkibiades' guardian, Perikles; via Phaidros; and via Polemarchos and Sokrates.

The least irrational expectations that could be entertained about the politics of Lysias before the end of the Peloponnesian War would be based on the assumption that he had a place on the periphery of the δυναστεία of Alkibiades. As for his attitude to political principles, we ought to ask ourselves why Plato represents Thrasymachos as present in Kephalos's house at the beginning of the *Republic*. Perhaps Thrasymachos was brought by Lysias's friend Kleitophon (*Rep.* 340A, *Clit.* 406A); but perhaps he was himself a friend of Lysias, with whom he had a common interest in rhetoric and with whose name his is coupled in *Phaedrus* (266c, 269d and 271c; cf. Dion. Hal. i.13.23–14.6). This, however, would be too selective an interpretation of our "molecule" and too rigid a schematisation of political alignment. Nikias's son Nikeratos is, after all, under the same roof as Thrasymachos, Lysias and Polemarchos in the opening scene of the *Republic*. No doubt it would have been difficult to support Nikias and Alkibiades simultaneously, actively and overtly in 421–415, but it would have been no more difficult then than in a civilised society today to be friendly with some friends of both, and certainly impossible to predict, in respect of a man in such a position, what his relations with the two families would be a few years later. As the speaker of XIX reminds us (§53), change of mind is the hallmark of honesty and rationality.

The corpus contains much that is hostile to Alkibiades:

(a) XIV, a prosecution of the younger Alkibiades (on XV cf. pp. 7, 166), with a sustained attack on the elder.

(b) A speech πρὸς Ἀλκιβιάδην περὶ οἰκίας, cited by Harpokration 192.8, 211.9 f. (both times without περὶ οἰκίας, and in the latter passage with εἰ γνήσιος ὁ λόγος) and 237.16 f. This speech I take to be against the younger Alkibiades.

(c) A work (of unspecified nature) in which Lysias spoke of the "self-indulgence" (τρυφή) of the elder Alkibiades, cited by Ath. 534F. This could be the same as b.

(d) A λόγος κατ' αὐτοῦ (sc. Ἀλκιβιάδου) cited by Ath. 574E, which may be identical with c if c does not = b.

(e) A speech cited by Sch. Patm. Dem. (Lex. gr. min. 163) as ὁ πρὸς Ἀλκιβιάδην ὕστερος. It contained the words ἔρρε εἰς ὄλεθρόν τε καὶ Ἄβυδον, "for by now I am tired of abusing you." This may be identical with c and with d, if we assume an error in the title (cf. pp. 4f.), or with b, unless we have any reason (and have we?—Blass, i.368, is hardly adequate) for supposing that the younger Alkibiades could not be told to get out of Athens and go to live at Abydos.

(*f*) The speaker of XXI adduces (§6) as evidence for the condition of his ship when he was trierarch the fact that Alkibiades, as general, chose to sail on it, and adds "I would have given anything not to have him on board with me."

This last passage reminds us of an extremely important factor in Greek oratory. In making his tactical plan for success in a lawsuit, the speech-writer must take into account (among much else) the currents of feeling which are predominant in juries at the time of the suit. The composer of XXI judged it profitable to exploit hostility to Alkibiades. In XIX.52 the atmosphere is different; although the opportunity for expressing outspoken hostility to Alkibiades exists, and the assumption that he profited from his command is made, the scale and duration of his naval dominance of the Aegean is exaggerated. Just as in 405 the question of the day was "What should we do about Alkibiades?" (Ar. *Frogs* 1422 ff.), so in the fourth century his reputation fluctuated and the facts of his career became embellished and distorted (Dem. xxi.143–147 afford a particularly interesting example).[7] On the assumption (which I make without doubt or hesitation) that a litigant does not gratuitously offend a jury by the manner in which he refers to a politician already dead, it appears from the confrontation of XIII.8–12 with XXX.10–12 (note especially §12, "Well, there *are* charges one could make against Kleophon...") that attitudes to Kleophon also fluctuated in the early fourth century.

Doubts of the authenticity of one speech or another have occasionally been based on apparent inconsistencies of a remarkably tenuous kind; for example, it has been held[8] that the chilly words in *Epitaphios* 59–60 about the revival of Persian naval power under Konon's leadership can hardly have been written by the

---

[7] Cf. Bruns, 509 ff.
[8] P. Treves, *RIFC* N.S. XV (1937), 280 f.

same man who displays in XIX warmth towards Konon and zeal in the interests of one of Konon's associates. One might argue similarly that the same man cannot have made the bold assertion in XIV.38 "Alkibiades went so far as to betray the fleet, with Adeimantos, to Lysander" (cf. Xen. *HG* ii.1.32) and yet in *Epitaphios* 58 have touched so delicately on this same topic; "When the fleet was lost in the Hellespont, either through defective command (ἡγεμόνος [-νων Ald.] κακίᾳ[9]) or by the will of the gods..."

One could argue in this way if the corpus were something other than what it is. But he who best λέγει τὰ καίρια best conceals himself. For a solemn epideixis, as for a Pindaric victory ode (or a good after-dinner speech), a sense of occasion is indispensable, and silence or ambivalence may be not only a substitute for the expression of the speaker's disapproval but also a compromise between his own positive approval and either the contrary sentiment of his audience or the range within which the sentiments appropriate to the occasion in question fall. As for forensic speeches, their purpose is to win, not to enlighten. No one in his senses would expect, by collecting and reading the speeches delivered in court by a modern advocate, to obtain an accurate picture of the moral and political attitudes of the advocate himself. In bringing this analogy to bear upon the *corpus Lysiacum* we do not need to beg any questions by regarding Lysias as a professional, paid advocate. We need only remind ourselves of the personal nature of Athenian political associations and of their potential (and sometimes demonstrable) instability; of the overriding compulsion to win a case, especially in a community which so lightly inflicted the death penalty and even more readily pauperized and disenfranchised those who had displeased it; of the readiness, hardly less conspicuous in ancient Athens than today, to sacrifice consistency, even integrity, in the interests of victory;[10]

[9] For κακός = "incompetent," without imputation of treachery or cowardice, cf. Ar. *Th.* 837, Thuc. vi.38.2 ("bad at ...," with an infinitive), Pl. *Phdr.* 248B.

[10] I have never been involved in a legal action, but as a member of the public I have been interested to see and hear advocates practicing crude forms of deception which in academic life would earn them at least ridicule, at worst ostracism, and

and, finally, of the intricate relationship between the persona of the litigant, the nature and weight of the evidence against him, and whatever attitudes to current political issues were predominant in the community at the moment of litigation—a relationship which could be assessed by the man on the spot, but can be assessed only fractionally and tentatively by us.

What I have said may give the impression (which I should greatly regret) of a pre-Socratic παίγνιον, an attempt to prove that rational consideration of political alignment as a criterion of ascription is a waste of time and that mortal men can only wallow in ignorance. My intention, however, was of the opposite kind: to suggest that ascription founded on political criteria depends on an unreal schematisation of ancient political and forensic activity, on the assumption that what we happen to know is all we need to know, and on a natural but disastrous tendency to believe that if a man writes well he is also a man of inflexible integrity and consistency. It is not the spirit of Gorgias or Euthydemos, but a wish to clothe the skeleton of a dead writer with flesh and blood, that encourages me to assert that we have *no* political or ideological grounds for denying the ascription to Lysias of *any* extant or lost speech in the corpus, including VI (possibly delivered [cf. p. 78] by an accuser of Sokrates), XX (the *Defence of Polystratos*), the *Defence of Eryximachos* "who remained in the city," XXV (cf. p. 188), the *Defence of Sokrates* (cf. p. 192), and the *Epitaphios*. More accurate chronological data than we have might well justify modification of this statement. As matters stand, linguistic criteria are less unpromising than political criteria.

---

would certainly be a serious obstacle to their professional advancement. As it is, they have gone on to become Queen's Counsel and, in some cases, judges. Lawyers assert that deliberate misleading of a jury is regarded as professionally disgraceful, and no doubt they believe their own assertion; but a lawyer's notions of what is or is not "misleading" are very different from a scholar's.

V

Genre and Ethos

TECHNICAL CRITERIA of ascription comprise the means by which a plea is presented and the language in which it is presented. The means cannot be wholly separated from the language. It would be impossible, for instance, to plot the occurrence of arguments from probability without regarding where and how the words εἰκός and εἰκότως are used, because well before the end of the fifth century the value and limitations of argument ἐκ τῶν εἰκότων had become the subject not only of theoretical discussion and illustration (e.g., Ant. ii.α.5, β.5, δ.10), but also of comment in the course of forensic argument (e.g., Ant. v.25 f., 64). It is an open question whether the word εἰκός fell on the ears of a jury in the early fourth century with greater weight than expressions such as "it is to be presumed," "in all probability" or "it is only reasonable to suppose" carry with us, or whether it had already become so debased that a man who seriously depended on argument from probability would be careful not to use the word. The absence of εἰκός from XXIX, where the life and estate of Philokles appear to hang upon a weak basis of probability, rather suggests that in such a case more was achieved by eschewing the word than by wielding it.[1] Again, if we enumerated sentences in the corpus in which an infinitive depends on a neuter adjective

---

[1] Cf. A. Schweizer, *Die 13 Rede des Lysias* (Borna, 1936), 84, 100, on the alternatives to explicit argument from probability in XIII.

(e.g., XII.1, οὐκ ἄρξασθαί μοι δοκεῖ ἄπορον εἶναι), we should necessarily include (e.g.) XVI.7, καίτοι πᾶσι ῥᾴδιον τοῦτο γνῶναι, ὅτι ἀναγκαῖον ἦν κτλ. But ῥᾴδιον γνῶναι is not merely a syntactical phenomenon; it is also a forensic weapon. And what about καίτοι? It is a particle of which the semantics are, as we would expect, discussed by Denniston; but the step in reasoning, valid or invalid, which is taken by καίτοι, the charge of indignation or scorn which it carries, its manipulation of the juryman's mind, all belong, as clearly as anything can, within the sphere of forensic technique. I would have little regard for the conclusions of a dissertation on the relation between oratory and the law unless I had reason to think that the writer had checked and pondered on every instance of the word καί in the orators.

A good illustration of the difficulty of deciding which of two labels, "linguistic" and "forensic," should be attached to a phenomenon is afforded by the occurrence of εἰ...ἤ... in the sense "whether...or..." in IV. This occurs four times in IV (and in Ant. v.14 = vi.2 and And. i.7), but nowhere else in the corpus.[2] At first sight, therefore, it represents a linguistic singularity of IV. Consider, however, the context of each of the four occurrences:

§§ 10 f. τοῦτ' ἂν κατεῖπεν, πότερα κοινὴ ἡμῖν ἦν ἢ ἰδία τούτου, καὶ πότερα τὸ ἥμισυ τοῦ ἀργυρίου ἐγὼ συνεβαλόμην ἢ οὗτος ἅπαν ἔδωκε, καὶ εἰ διηλλαγμένοι ἢ ἔτι ἐχθροὶ ἦμεν, ἔτι δ' εἰ μεταπεμφθέντες ἤλθομεν ἢ οὐδενὸς καλέσαντος, καὶ εἰ οὗτος ἦρχε χειρῶν ἀδίκων ἢ ἐγὼ πρότερος τοῦτον ἐπάταξα.

§15. εἰ δὲ μεταπεμφθέντες ἢ μή, καὶ πότερον πρότερος ἐπλήγην ἢ ἐπάταξα, ἐκείνη μᾶλλον ἂν ᾔδει.

In both cases the speaker is exploiting his adversary's refusal to allow the examination under torture of the concubine whom they owned jointly. The substitution of πότερ-α/-ον for εἰ in §§ 10 f. would have given a fivefold accumulation of that word, which any Greek orator would have found aesthetically intolerable (the

---

[2] Fr. 79 is wrongly classified in Holmes's *Index Lysiacus*.

Genre and Ethos 59

nearest parallel would be the direct questions—where εἰ is inadmissible—in VII.38: ποτέροις χρὴ πιστεύειν μᾶλλον ... καὶ πότερον εἰκὸς μᾶλλον τοῦτον ... ψεύδεσθαι ἤ ... ἐμέ ... ἐργάσασθαι, καὶ πότερον οἴεσθ' αὐτόν ... βοηθεῖν ... αἰτιᾶσθαι ... [cf. Ant. v.36]). The variation which was aesthetically inevitable in §§ 10 f. then served as a model for § 15. In this speech the primary phenomenon is the argument "All these questions could have been settled by torturing the concubine"; the occurrence of εἰ ... ἤ ... is secondary.

The first step is to discriminate between speeches which are forensic and speeches which are not—a process which proves to have some bearing on discrimination between forensic speeches.

A distinction between δικανικοὶ λόγοι and ἐπιδεικτικοὶ λόγοι is made by Isokrates (xiii.20, iv.11). Aristotle, dividing what Plato regards as essentially one (*Sph.* 222c δικανικὴν καὶ δημηγορικήν ... τέχνην: cf. *Rep.* 365D), makes a threefold division: συμβουλευτικόν, δικανικόν, ἐπιδεικτικόν (*Rhet.* 1358ᵇ4–13; cf. 1359ᵃ14 f.). Corresponding to these three γένη are three kinds of language (*Rhet.* 1414ᵃ8–19): δημηγορική (cf. 1354ᵇ22–29, 1413ᵇ3–5, 1415ᵇ33 f.), δικανική, ἐπιδεικτική. Dionysios also uses the terms δικανικός and συμβουλευτικός (i.11.13 f.), and ἐπιδεικτικός in antithesis to δικανικός (i.91.9–12), but he subdivides the epideictic genre into the serious πανηγυρικοί (i.9.1, 11.15) which are epideictic *par excellence* (i.26.22–27.1), and what he calls, with reference to Lysias, οὓς μετὰ παιδιᾶς ἔγραψεν (i.11.16 f.)—a category including works in epistolary form, ἐρωτικοί and ἑταιρικοί (i.9.1, 11.15 f.). μετὰ παιδιᾶς reminds us of the words with which Gorgias (39.21) concludes his *Helen*, Ἑλένης μὲν ἐγκώμιον, ἐμὸν δὲ παίγνιον, and justifies us in making a generic distinction between panegyric oratory, designed for solemn occasions, and παίγνια, which are a kind of intellectual titillation.

In the *corpus Lysiacum* we have one panegyric, the *Epitaphios*, preserved in Part I of the Palatinus, and a substantial citation from another, the beginning of the *Olympikos*, cited by Dionysios (i.46.11–48.16).[3]

Argument is different from adornment, and we naturally expect that the language which a man uses when he is trying to convince a jury (often with the litigant's life at stake) or an assembly (sometimes on a vital issue of war and peace) to differ from what he uses when he is expressing acceptable sentiments on a ceremonial occasion to an audience which does not need to be subjected to persuasion but looks for aesthetic and emotional satisfaction.

The terms used by Aristotle (*Rhet.* 1414^{a}18–28) to characterise ἐπιδεικτικὴ λέξις are uninformative. We gain much more from Dionysios's analysis of a passage of Isok. xvii (i.91.15–92.4), in the course of which he remarks (91.3–15) that the sentence (xvii.9)

καὶ πρὸς τούτοις, ὦ ἄνδρες δικασταί,
νομίζων, εἰ μὲν αὐτοῦ μένειν ἐπιχειροίην,
ἐκδοθήσεσθαί με ὑπὸ τῆς πόλεως Σατύρῳ,
εἰ δ' ἄλλοσέ ποι τραποίμην,
οὐδὲν αὐτῷ μελήσειν τῶν ἐμῶν λόγων,
εἰ δ' εἰσπλευσοίμην εἰς τὸν Πόντον,
ἀποθανεῖσθαί με μετὰ τοῦ πατρός

is not only more elaborate in structure than one expects in a forensic speech but also "borrows from epideictic parallelisms" (cf. Isok. xii.2) "and assonances"; that is to say, the parallelism of the three conditional clauses and the assonance ἐπιχειροίην . . . τραποίμην . . . εἰσπλευσοίμην are epideictic features.

This observation can be tested with reference to the surviving

[3] J. Klowski, *Zur Echtheitsfrage des lysianischen Epitaphios* (Diss. Hamburg, 1959), 51 ff., argues that the *Epitaphios* should be compared with the funeral orations ascribed to other orators, not with the *Olympikos*, for the latter, as he reminds us (p. 52) was designed to persuade the audience to adopt a certain political view and course of action (Dion. Hal. i.45.22—46.10, Diod. Sic. xiv.109.3). The reminder is opportune, but Klowski's conclusion that we should classify the *Olympikos* as symbuleutic does not follow. We should expect the language used by Lysias in a panegyric at Olympia to conform to that of panegyrics in general, even though he was using it towards an unusual end; and Dion. Hal. i.48.19–21, having taken the *Olympikos* as typical, clearly distinguishes from it (on stylistic grounds) the symbuleutic speeches of the *corpus Lysiacum*.

portion of the *Olympikos* and the equivalent portions of the *Epitaphios* (§§ 1–7), XII, XIII and XIX (each §§ 1–9).[4]

(1) Simple parallelism
   (a) With terminal assonance of at least one complete syllable

*Ol.*2:   τοὺς τυράννους ἔπαυσε
         καὶ τοὺς ὑβρίζοντας ἐκώλυσεν

Ibid.: τὰ μὲν ὀψομένους
       τὰ δ' ἀκουσομένους

Epit. 4: ᾕρουν μὲν   τοὺς φεύγοντας
        ἀπέλειπον δὲ τοὺς διώκοντας

Epit. 6: τῆσδε μὲν τῆς πόλεως διὰ τὴν   ἀρετὴν
              ἀθάνατον ⟨τὴν⟩ μνήμην ἐποίησαν
       τὴν δ' ἑαυτῶν πατρίδα διὰ τὴν ἐνθάδε συμφορὰν
             ἀνώνυμον   κατέστησαν

XII.1: ἢ τὸν κατήγορον ἀπειπεῖν
      ἢ τὸν   χρόνον ἐπιλιπεῖν

XII.7: ἀποκτιννύναι γὰρ ἀνθρώπους περὶ οὐδενὸς ἡγοῦντο
      λαμβάνειν δὲ χρήματα περὶ πολλοῦ
                               ἐποιοῦντο

   (b) With partial terminal assonance

*Ol.*3:   ἀνδρὸς δ'   ἀγαθοῦ
        καὶ πολίτου πολλοῦ ἀξίου

*Ol.*4:   τῶν μὲν παύσασθαι
        τὰ δὲ κωλῦσαι

*Ol.*6:   περὶ μὲν τῶν παρεληλυθότων   αἰσχύνεσθαι
        περὶ δὲ τῶν μελλόντων ἔσεσθαι δεδιέναι

---

[4] I exclude passages of the form $A_1B_1C + A_2B_2$ (sc. C)—e.g., XII.1 μήτ' ἄν... δύνασθαι—except as in section 2, below; I also exclude sentences in which one of the parallel members contains a subordinate or participial clause to which nothing in the other member corresponds—e.g., *Epit.* 7 ἐκείνους μέν ... ἀσεβεῖσθαι—and the form $A_1B_1C_{1,2}+A_2B_2$ (or variants on this) unless it is an ingredient in a larger unit which also contains $A_3B_3+A_4B_4$.

Ol.7: καὶ διὰ τὴν ἔμφυτον ἀρετὴν
καὶ διὰ τὴν περὶ τὸν πόλεμον ἐπιστήμην

Epit. 4: ταῖς ψυχαῖς διαφέρειν
ἢ ταῖς ἰδέαις ἐλλείπειν

(c) Without terminal assonance

Epit. 2: καὶ τοῖς ποιεῖν δυναμένοις
καὶ τοῖς εἰπεῖν βουληθεῖσιν

Epit. 5: ἔργῳ μὲν τοὺς περὶ αὐτὰς καταδεδουλωμέναι
λόγῳ δὲ περὶ τῆσδε τῆς χώρας ἀκούουσαι κλέος
μέγα

ibid.: πολλῆς δόξης
καὶ μεγάλης ἐλπίδος

Epit. 6: τήν τε σφετέραν αὐτῶν δυστυχίαν
καὶ τὴν τῶν ἡμετέρων προγόνων ἀρετήν

XII.4: μήτ' εἰς τοὺς ἄλλους ἐξαμαρτάνειν
μήθ' ὑπὸ τῶν ἄλλων ἀδικεῖσθαι

XII.5: τῶν ἀδίκων καθαρὰν ποιῆσαι τὴν
πόλιν
καὶ τοὺς λοιποὺς πολίτας ἐπ' ἀρετὴν καί
δικαιοσύνην τραπέσθαι

XII.6: τὴν μὲν πόλιν πένεσθαι
τὴν δ' ἀρχὴν δεῖσθαι χρημάτων

XIII.5: αἱ νῆες αἱ ὑμέτεραι διεφθάρησαν
καὶ τὰ πράγματα ⟨τὰ⟩ ἐν τῇ πόλει ἀσθενέστερα
ἐγεγένητο

(2) With insertion of postpositive or concomitant[5]

Epit. 2: ὁ μὲν λόγος μοι περὶ τούτων
ὁ δ' ἀγὼν οὐ πρὸς τὰ τούτων ἔργα
ἀλλὰ πρὸς τοὺς πρότερον ἐπ'
αὐτοῖς εἰρηκότας

[5] For the definition of these terms see Dover, 12 f., 40 ff.

Genre and Ethos 63

Epit. 4:   διὰ τὴν εὐψυχίαν μᾶλλον ἄνδρες
         ἢ διὰ τὴν φύσιν   γυναῖκες

XII.1:   τοιαῦτα αὐτοῖς τὸ μέγεθος
       καὶ τοσαῦτα   τὸ   πλῆθος

XII.7:   οὐ χρημάτων ἕνεκα   ταῦτα πέπρακται
       ἀλλὰ συμφέροντα τῇ πόλει   γεγένηται

(3) Simple chiasmus

XII.6:   τιμωρεῖσθαι μὲν δοκεῖν
       τῷ δ' ἔργῳ   χρηματίζεσθαι

(4) Parallelism of greater complexity

*Ol.*2:   ἀγῶνα   μὲν   σωμάτων ἐποίησε
      φιλοτιμίαν ⟨δὲ⟩ πλούτου
      γνώμης   δ'   ἐπίδειξιν

*Ol.*5:   ἡ μὲν ἀρχὴ   τῶν κρατούντων τῆς
                                           θαλάττης
      τῶν δὲ χρημάτων   βασιλεὺς   ταμίας
      τὰ δὲ τῶν Ἑλλήνων σώματα τῶν δαπανᾶσθαι
                                        δυναμένων

Epit. 2:   πολλὰ τοῖς προτέροις περὶ αὐτῶν εἰρῆσθαι
       πολλὰ δὲ καὶ ἐκείνοις   παραλελεῖφθαι
       ἱκανὰ δὲ καὶ τοῖς ἐπιγιγνομένοις   ἐξεῖναι εἰπεῖν

Epit. 3:   ὑμνοῦντας   μὲν ἐν ταῖς   ᾠδαῖς
       λέγοντας   δ' ἐν ταῖς τῶν ἀγαθῶν μνήμαις
       τιμῶντας   δ' ἐν τοῖς καιροῖς τοῖς τοιούτοις
       παιδεύοντας   δ' ἐν τοῖς τῶν τεθνεώτων ἔργοις
                                              τοὺς ζῶντας

Epit. 4:   μόναι μὲν ὡπλισμέναι σιδήρῳ τῶν περὶ αὐτὰς
       πρῶται δὲ   τῶν πάντων
              ἐφ' ἵππους ἀναβᾶσαι

XIX.9: ἐστερημένοι μὲν κηδεστῶν
ἐστερημένοι δὲ τῆς προικὸς
παιδάρια δὲ τρία ἠναγκασμένοι τρέφειν.

(5) Antithesis between participial clause and main clause[6]

*Ol.*6: τῆς ἀλλοτρίας ἐπιθυμοῦντας: τῆς σφετέρας αὐτῶν στερεῖσθαι

Epit. 2: οἱ τὰ αὑτῶν πενθοῦντες κακὰ: τὰς τούτων ἀρετὰς ὑμνοῦσιν

Epit. 6: ἐκ τῶν ἡμαρτημένων μαθούσαις: περὶ τῶν λοιπῶν ἄμεινον βουλεύσασθαι

Ibid.: τῆς ἀλλοτρίας ἀδίκως ἐπιθυμήσασαι: τὴν ἑαυτῶν δικαίως ἀπώλεσαν.

These samples are consonant with Dionysios's characterisation of epideictic style, and they suggest (a fact to which it will be necessary to return shortly) that the epideictic element in XII is substantially larger than might be expected in a forensic speech.

Epideictic differ from forensic speeches also in respect of vocabulary. The *Olympikos* contains the following words which are "non-forensic" in that they are not attested in the forensic speeches of the corpus, Andokides i–ii, Isokrates xvi–xxi, or Isaios:[7]

ἀήττητος (§)
ἀθάνατος (§7): *Epit.* 6
ἀναμένειν (§8): *Epit.* 23
ἀντέχεσθαι (§6): *Phormis.* 4
ἀπόρθητος (§7)
ἀστασίαστος (§7): *Epit.* 55
ἀτείχιστος (§7)
ἔμφυτος (§7)
ἡγεμών (§7): *Epit.* 47

[6] Cf. Hollingsworth, 43 f.
[7] I ask the reader to take the definition of "non-forensic" very strictly. I am not suggesting that (e.g.) ἀήττητος would necessarily strike an Athenian jury as pretentious or poetic; I simply state that it does not occur in the body of speeches which I have listed.

Genre and Ethos 65

καίνειν (§7), if καινομένην (Hude) is an acceptable emendation of καιομένην.[8]
μικρολογεῖσθαι (§3)
στέργειν (§4)
σύλλογος (§2): And. iii.38
συναγείρειν (§1)
ὑφηγεῖσθαι (§3): in Is. iv.22 ὑφηγοῦνται is Schömann's emendation (ἡγοῦνται δεῖν Dobree) of ἡγοῦνται.

This is a formidable list (15 words), from so short a specimen. The corresponding portion of the *Epitaphios* (§§1–7) yields (in addition to ἀθάνατος, already listed):

ἀναίρεσις (§7)
ἀνέλπιστος (§4): And. iv.24
ἔθνος (§5)
ἐπιγίγνεσθαι (§2): *Phormis.* 1
εὐψυχία (§4)
κλέος (§5)
μάχιμος (§5)
μνήμη (§3)
πρόσταξις (§1)
ὑμνεῖν (§§2, 3)
ᾠδή (§3): Isok. x.64

These total 12.

The corresponding yield from XII.1–9 is only two words:

ἀθυμία (§3)
ἀφθονία (§2): *Epit.* 2

The total of non-forensic words in the *Epitaphios* is 70. Those not already listed are:

ἄγασθαι (§40)
ἀγήρατος (§79)
αἰδεῖσθαι (§12)
ἀναμένειν (§23): *Olymp.* 8

---

[8] If καιομένην is right, substitute καίειν for καίνειν; it too is non-forensic (*Epit.* 37).

ἀντίπαλος (§38)
ἀνιτιτάττειν (§40): middle in And. i.107
ἀπαραίτητος (§78)
ἀστασίαστος (§55): Olymp. 7
ἀφειδεῖν (§25)
ἄφιξις (§26)
βαρβαρικός (§38)
βούλευμα (§§40, 64): And. iii.29
δεξιοῦσθαι (§37)
διαβιβάζειν (§28)
διορύττειν (§29)
δουλοῦσθαι (§21)
ἐγκαθιστάναι (§59)
ἐμβαίνειν (§§30 al.)
ἐξυβρίζειν (§9)
ἐπιπλεῖν (§32)
ἐρημοῦν (§37): And. iii.21
ἐρίζειν (§42)
εὐκλεής (§23)
εὐκτός (§69)
ζευγνύναι (§29)
ἡγεμών (§§47 al.): Olymp. 7
θεᾶσθαι (§35): And. iv.13
θηρίον (§19): Isok. xi.32
θνητός (§§77 al.): Isok. x.47
ἱκετεία (§39): Isok. x.31
καταστρέφεσθαι (§21): Isok. xi.11
κείρεσθαι (§60)
λήγειν (§74)
μακαρίζειν (§81)
ναυαγίον (§38)
παιάν (§38)
πανδημεί (§49): And. iii.18, Isok. x.27
παρακελευσμός (§38)
πάροδος (§§30, 32)
πεζομαχεῖν (§47)

Genre and Ethos 67

ποθεινός (§73)
πόθος (§39)
πορθεῖν (§37): Isok. x.26
προαπολλύναι (§24)
σοφία (§80): Isok. x.1
στέλλειν (§21)
στενός (§28)
στενότης (§30)
συμμειγνύναι (§38)
συναθροίζειν (§34)
τειχίζειν (§44): And. iii.5 al., Isok. xi.12
τελευτή (§§47, 66): And. iv.24
τοκεύς (§75)
ὑπεκτίθεσθαι (middle, §34): pass. Isok. xix.18
φίλιος (§38)
φιλόνικος (§16)
φιλοψυχεῖν (§25)

The total list in XII amounts to 41. In addition to ἀθυμία and ἀφθονία, we have:

ἀμφίθυρος (§12)
ἀπληστία (§19)
ἄταφος (§21)
ἀφέλκειν (§96), if Reiske's ἀφέλκοντες is a correct emendation of ἀφελόντες.
γυναικεῖος (§19)
δαρεικός (§11)
διαψήφισις (§34)
ἑλικτήρ (§19)
ἐξυπηρετεῖν (§23)
ἐξώλεια (§10)
ἐπαρᾶσθαι (§10)
ἐπιθυμητής (§90): And. iv.6
ἐπιλήσμων (§87): *Phormis.* 2
ἔφορος (§§43, 46): not the Spartan magistracy.
ζήτησις (§30)

68 Lysias and the *Corpus Lysiacum*

θορυβεῖν (§73): And. iv.7
κιβωτός (§10)
κλεισίον (§18)
κόσμος (§19): = "jewellery"
κυζικηνός (§11)
μιαίνειν (§99)
οἰκοδομεῖν (§63)
ὅμηρος (§68)
οὖς (§19)
παράγγελμα (§17)
παράσπονδος (§74)
πλανᾶσθαι (§97): Isok. xiii.15
πρόβουλος (§65)
προσκεφάλαιον (§18)
προσκτᾶσθαι (§39)
σκυλεύειν (§40)
συναγωγεύς (§43)
συναπολλύναι (§88)
συνδιαβάλλειν (§93): Isok. xiii.11
συνωμότης (§43): And. iv.4
συνωφελεῖν (§93)
ὑπηρέτης (§10)
ὑπεροψία (§93)
χαλκός (§19)

It should be noted that the *Epitaphios* is 85 per cent the length of XII and that six of the "non-forensic" words in XII denote material objects.

If we define hiatus as a juxtaposition of final and initial vowels which in Aristophanic comedy is neither accepted nor resolved by elision, prodelision or synizesis,[9] and if we further restrict it to

[9] Any definition of hiatus necessarily contains an arbitrary element. Herodas, for instance, admits far more synizesis than Aristophanes; and while it would obviously be unreasonable to treat as hiatus the juxtaposition of a vowel at the end of a sentence and a vowel at the beginning of the next sentence, there is much room for disagreement on the boundaries of clauses within sentences (cf. p. 131).

Genre and Ethos

pairs of words which are not separated by the boundary of a clause, a parenthesis or a vocative expression, we find that the only two examples in the *Olympikos* are πολλοῦ ἀξίου (§3) and χρόνῳ ἀλλοτρίως (§1); but in the latter there is a pause imposed by an antithetical "colon,"[10] thus:

ἐν μὲν γὰρ τῷ τέως χρόνῳ : ἀλλοτρίως ... διέκειντο·
ἐπειδὴ δ' ἐκεῖνος κτλ.

In *Epit.* 1–7 the only indubitable example is τὰ αὑτῶν (§§2, 7); καὶ ἡττηθέντων in §7 might admit of synizesis, and colon-division is indicated in:

§2: οὔτε γὰρ γῆς ἄπειροι : οὔτε θαλάττης οὐδεμιᾶς
§7: Ἀθηναῖοι : ἡγησάμενοι : ἐκείνους μὲν κτλ.

In XII.1–9, on the other hand, we find δοκεῖ ἄπορον (§1), μέντοι ὡς (§2), ἢ ὑπέρ (§2), ἠνάγκασμαι ὑπό (§3), συκοφάνται ὄντες (§5), πολιτείᾳ ἀχθόμενοι (§6) and ἀργυρίου ἕτοιμος (§9).

Given the limitations of the evidence, we can hardly hope to discover by technical criteria whether XII, the *Epitaphios* and the *Olympikos* are the work of one, two or three writers. Since our only other specimen of the genre before Isokrates' *Panegyric* is the brief citation of the *Epitaphios* of Gorgias, we simply do not have enough of the genre at the right period.[11]

A similar obstacle presents itself in respect of the famous putative παίγνιον of Lysias, the *Erotikos* incorporated in Plato, *Phdr.* 230D–234C. Is it Lysias, or is it Plato exercising his considerable gifts as a parodist? It is easy enough to show that in vocabulary, both positively and negatively, the *Erotikos* resembles XII and

---

[10] Cf. Ed. Fraenkel, *NGG* 1933, 319 ff.

[11] Cf. Darkow, 24. The incidence of hiatus, however, is relevant to the old argument about the chronological relation of the *Epitaphios* and Isok. iv. Hiatus is certainly not avoided in the *Epitaphios* as carefully as in speeches of the later fourth century; cf. J. Walz, *Philologus* Suppl. xxix/4 (1936), 37.

70 Lysias and the *Corpus Lysiacum*

differs from the reply which Plato puts into the mouth of Sokrates (*Phdr.* 237B7–238C4, 238D8–241D1):[12]

	Erotikos	XII	Sokrates' reply
⎧ ἀξιοῦν	230C7	20, 26, 37, 68, 82, 89, 93	—
⎩ ἄξιος	231B1, B7, C1, 233B4, E1, 234A1, C1	20, 37, 63, 64, 68, 82, 82, 85, 86, 86, 86, 87	239D3
αὖ	—	—	237D4, D6, 238B2, C1, 239C4
δή *solitarium* as connective	—	81? (cj. Scheibe: δέ cod.)	237D5, 238E2, 239A1, A7, C5, E2, 241A2, B3
καὶ μὲν δή	231A7, 232B5, E3, 233A4, D8	30, 35, 49, 89	—
καίτοι	231C7	31, 47, 48, 57, 63, 88, 89	—
παρέχεσθαι	—	(33, 42, 46, 76: all with "witnesses" as the object)	238A5, B2, 239E2, 240C3
περὶ πολλοῦ (etc.) ποιεῖσθαι	231C1, C5, 232C1, 233D1	7	—
ὥστε = "therefore"	231B5, D4, D8, 232A8, D7, E5, 233B5	3, 22, 33, 33, 34, 37, 50, 58, 67, 70, 76, 91, 92, 93	—

We possess no other παίγνιον ascribed to Lysias; therefore we have no means of judging for ourselves whether or not he used in παίγνια language which resembled his forensic language as exemplified in XII. If the *Erotikos* is genuine,[13] he certainly did; if it is a parody, he probably did; but the only evidence which could incline us toward the verdict that it really is a parody would be the discovery of several other παίγνια ascribed to Lysias and the

[12] Cf. G. E. Dimock Jr., *AJP* lxxiii (1952), 381 ff.

[13] The passage of Dionysios (ii.224.13–15) which might have shown us whether he ascribed the *Erotikos* to Lysias is unfortunately mutilated: ἀλλὰ καὶ ⟨ ... ⟩ κρατίστου τῶν τότε ῥητόρων ἕτερον αὑτός (*sc.*, Plato) ἐν τῷ Φαίδρῳ συνετάξατο λόγον ἐρωτικὸν εἰς τὴν ⟨αὑτήν add. Herwerden⟩ ὑπόθεσιν. Dionysios's opinion would have been of interest, since other παίγνια ascribed to Lysias were available to him.

observations that (*a*) they are consistently unlike XII in significant respects and (*b*) the *Erotikos* has features in common with Sokrates' reply and other Platonic speeches but not with them.

The manner in which an Attic orator organised and presented a case was determined by five factors: what had actually happened; his own judgment, skill and technical predilections; the personality of the litigant: the known or presumed intentions of his adversary; and the current attitude of juries.

The problem created by the attitude of the jury has been discussed already (p. 54; and cf. Alkidamas 15.22 f. on the importance of attunement to a jury's mood). That the facts of a case impose certain conditions on its presentation is so obvious that it should not be necessary to say so; but the necessity is revealed by reading much of what has been written about the orators. Some commentators have displayed a childish credulity—for example, in accepting Demosthenes' portrayal of Meidias as just and accurate[14]—and historians, particularly those of an anti-Jacobin persuasion, have sometimes gone so far in the other direction that they read the *corpus Lysiacum* with the feeling that they are witnessing the sacrifice of magnanimous innocents to wild beasts in the amphitheatre.[15] We have to remind ourselves that out of all the cases represented in Palatinus 88 there are only three (VI, XXVI and XXVIII) of which we know the outcome, and only one (VI) where we even know what was said on the other side. The statement of [Plu.] *Vit. Or.* 836A, "It is said that Lysias was defeated only twice," is unacceptable, because no one but Lysias's ghost was ever in a position to know whether it was true or not (cf. p. 160); it is also

[14] For instance, L. W. King's edition of Dem. xxi, p. xiii. Even A. P. Dorjahn, *TAPA* lxvi (1935), 288, seems not only to believe the allegation of XXIX.12, that Ergokles' friends claimed to have bribed 2,100 jurors, but also to believe the claim itself. K. Schön, *Die Scheinargumente bei Lysias* (Paderborn, 1918), 1 ff., has an interesting survey of modern attitudes to the reliability of Lysian speeches as historical evidence. For an analysis of the means by which opponents sought to discredit one another see W. Voegelin, *Die Diabole bei Lysias* (Basel, 1943).

[15] For instance, R. von Pöhlmann, *Geschichte der sozialen Frage und des Sozialismus in der antiken Welt* (3d ed.; Munich, 1925), i.261 ff.

irrelevant to consideration of the extant speeches, because we do not know how many of these are the work of Lysias. Dionysios, who rated Lysias's plausibility very high (i.17.21–18), had more sense than to guess how often this plausibility achieved its object. It sometimes happens, especially in reading Isaios and the private speeches of Demosthenes, that we think we have detected a weak point in the speaker's case, or at least we can formulate questions which we should like to put to the witnesses if the case were being heard before us in modern conditions and we were on the judge's bench. Usually, however, we have to admit, if we are honest, that we do not know whether we are reading ὁ κρείττων λόγος or ὁ ἥττων λογος. When I was much younger, XXIX (*Prosecution of Philokles*) used to give me gooseflesh; but now I am prepared to consider the possibility that the speaker's inference from the dearth of accusers is correct (§1) and that the peculations of Philokles and the relations between Ergokles and Philokles (§3) were a matter of common knowledge (§14).[16] A man with legal experience and intelligence knows that if he is to win his case he must follow whatever path the facts leave open to him. Add to this that the presentation must be suited to the personality of the litigant—which was known to the writer, but is not known to us— and I hope it will be clear why I do not use types of forensic argument as a criterion of authorship.[17]

On the question of foreknowledge of an adversary's argument more will be said later (p. 167); it is inextricably bound up with the question of the relation between what we now read and what was actually said in court.

Certain elements which are sometimes regarded as characteristic of Lysias are in fact older. Since the extant speeches of Antiphon concern homicide and Andokides is a defence on a charge of sacrilege, speeches in the *corpus Lysiacum* are our earliest extant

---

[16] Cf. P. Cloché, *REA* xxi (1919), 191.

[17] Detailed study of the construction and organisation of Greek arguments, as urged by J. J. Bateman, *Gnomon* xxxviii (1966), 803, is highly desirable, but I would not be too sanguine about its bearing on the problem of ascription.

specimens of "administrative" cases—δοκιμασίαι, εἰσαγγελίαι, εὔθυναι, confiscations, prosecutions of generals. Confusion of "earliest" and "earliest extant" is the most powerful and pervasive source of error in the characterisation of historical change, and in the study of Lysias such confusion is easily avoidable by reference to Aristophanes' *Knights*, where the conventions of political prosecution are caricatured fully, even tediously.[18] Observe, for example, how, when Kleon threatens the Sausageman, "I declare that you are descended from those who were cursed of Athena" (445 f.), the Sausageman retorts that Kleon's grandfather was one of the bodyguard of the daughter of Hippias (447–449), and compare XIV, where the younger Alkibiades is attacked through the sacrilegious behaviour of his father (§§ 41 f.) and the politics of his great-grandparents (§§ 39 f.; cf. And. ii.26, Isok. xvi.25). At the end of the play, the Sausageman warns Demos not to be deceived when a prosecutor says, "If you don't bring in a verdict of guilty, you've lost your daily bread" (1358–1360). This is an argument described as familiar in XXVII.1: εἰ μὴ καταψηφιεῖσθε ὧν αὐτοὶ κελεύουσιν, ἐπιλείψει ὑμῖν ἡ μισθοφορά. It is presupposed by the defendant in XIX.11, "It is difficult for me, in making my plea, to contend with the opinion which some people hold about the estate of Nikophemos and with the shortage of money from which our city is at present suffering." Compare XXX.22, "When the Council has enough money at its disposal, it does no wrong, but when there is a shortage it is compelled to accept denunciations and confiscate citizens' property and listen to speakers who make the most discreditable proposals." In XIX.61 the speaker turns the matter to his own advantage; he tells the jury that it will profit more by leaving the defendants in possession of their capital (and thus able to perform liturgies) than by confiscating this capital, and the last words of the speech (§ 64) are: "If you do this, you will give a verdict which is both just and in your own interest." Compare XXI.12: "If, then, you do as I bid you, you will both

---

[18] A. Burckhardt, *Spuren der athenischen Volksrede in der alten Komödie* (Basel, 1924), contains an exceptionally interesting survey of comic representations of symbuleutic and forensic oratory. Cf. also Navarre, 171 f.

give a just verdict and choose what profits you. You see how small is our country's revenue, and how this is embezzled by those who administer it" (cf. *Knights* 1217–1233). "You ought, therefore, to consider that the securest national revenue is the capacity of those who are willing to undertake liturgies." It appears from Aristophanes that this issue was familiar to juries when Athens was an imperial power enjoying the tribute of the Aegean, and did not first come into prominence when her finances were administered in the hand-to-mouth manner of the fourth century.

But if there are many constants, there is at least one variable. One of the most striking features of the speeches which Thucydides cast, with little regard for the individuality of the speaker, into his own idiom, is the frequency of argument based on psychological generalisation—not generalisation about Athenians or Spartans or even Greeks as a whole, but about human beings and human communities as such.[19]

This kind of generalisation is applied in Gorgias's *Palamedes* (44); note especially §3: "For good men must always take the greatest care not to make mistakes, and this applies to what is not remediable even more than to what is; for remedy is possible if men look ahead, but if they change their minds afterwards, there is no cure. The judgment of a man by his fellows belongs to this category; and that is now (ὅπερ ... νῦν; cf. Thuc. ii.60.4, vi.11.5) your situation." Compare §§ 1, 4, 6, 15–17, 20, 25. It is also prominent in the *Tetralogies*, as in ii.α.1, on the difficulty of detecting crimes committed by men of high ability, or iv.δ.2, a denial that outrage is as natural a function of youth, or self-restraint of maturity, as seeing and hearing are of the eyes and ears. These works are theoretical, but psychological generalisation is to be found also in the real forensic speeches of Antiphon:

> i.28 f. "For a man who conspires to kill his neighbour (τοῖς πέλας [cf. Thuc. i.141.1, vi.12.1]) does not do so in the presence of witnesses, but in secret ... and the victim

---

[19] Cf. C. Meister, *Die Gnomik im Geschichtswerk des Thukydides* (Winterthur, 1955), 14 f., 63 ff.

Genre and Ethos

knows nothing until ... but then ... he enjoins on his family to take vengeance. That is what my father enjoined on me ..." (ἃ κἀμοὶ κτλ. [cf. Thuc. ii.61.3].)

v.71–73 "... Thus it is good to subject events to the test of time ... Therefore do not come to acknowledge this (*sc.* what actually happened) when it is too late ... Since (ὡς) there can be no worse counsellors (*sc.* than anger and hostile allegation). For there is nothing that a man can judge rightly when he is angry; for the organ of deliberation, the human judgment, is corrupted. Believe me (τοι) the passage of the days has great power ... And I assure you that I ... For it is right that ... And it is better that your power ... For in delay ... but in immediate anger ..." (Cf. v.5 f., 11, 57, 70, πολλὰ δ' ἐστὶ τὰ συμβαλλόμενα τοῖς βουλομένοις τῶν ἀλλοτρίων ἐφίεσθαι; 86, μεθ' οὗ ... τῶν πραγμάτων [cf. 71 f.]; 91, ἐν μὲν γάρ ... ἐξημαρτηκότας [cf. Gorgias 44.34], 92, ἔπειτα δέ ... ἐξεργάζοιτο; 93, οὗ πλέονος ... τῶν ἀσεβημάτων.)

vi.1 "Nothing is more desirable for a human being than that his life should never be in danger ... But if danger is unavoidable ... that his conscience should be clear ..." (Cf. vi.5, ἔστι μὲν γάρ ... ἀποστεροίη; 18 f., αἰτιάσασθαι μὲν οὖν ... ἐξελέγχοιτο.)

Andokides ii, composed in 407,[20] generalises about the human condition in §§5 f. (ἐμοὶ δέ ... πρᾶξαι), giving credit to "the man who first said ...," and briefly, in a conditional protasis, in §24 (not so much propounding an opinion as suggesting that an assumption is shared by his audience). The generalisation in §18 is political rather than psychological.

To the student of Greek literature an author's silences are often no less significant than his utterances, and argument based on human nature, which we see muted in Andokides ii, seems to have been out of fashion in forensic oratory for a generation after the

---

[20] Cf. Albini's edition, p. 11.

death of Antiphon. Andokides, defending himself in 399, never lets go the rope that ties his argument to the actual situation of himself and the jury, even where a high level of abstraction might have been apposite (i.1, 6 f., 9, 24, 144 f.) and an earlier writer would probably not have resisted the temptation. In the *corpus Lysiacum* the only true psychological generalisation, as distinct from legal and political generalisations, is in III (§§ 4, 39, 44), a speech which is unusual in being concerned with a tempestuous love-affair; XXV.8 (on which see p. 188) is on the borderland of psychological and political generalisation.

Dionysios lists among the excellences of Lysias ἠθοποιΐα, "creation of character" (i.15.7–16.16, 22.21 f.). If he had meant by this that Lysias adapted the speech to the litigant, he would have been making a very rash statement; for when he wrote, the litigants had been dead for more than three centuries, and he could not know—any more than we can—whether their speeches were well or ill adapted to their characters. He would also have been in peril of circular argument, if he had denied the ascription of a speech to Lysias on the grounds that it seemed to him unsuited to the character of an individual about whose character he knew nothing.

In fact, Dionysios did not mean anything of the sort. He says that Lysias is always straightforward and unpretentious (i.10.4–12.10, 15.21–23. 22.17 f.), concise (13.11–22, 22.19 f.), lucid (12.11–13.10, 22.18), vivid (14.17–15.6, 22.20) and attractive (17.19–18.6, 23.3). If he also believed that Lysias suited the speech to the litigant, it would follow for him that Lysias did not compose speeches suited to people who were by nature pretentious, verbose, muddle-headed or repulsive, and these defects mark a fairly high proportion of any community. Dionysios further remarks, in a different connection (i.305.6–11), that one of the distinctive features of Lysias is his consistency of style, in private and public lawsuits alike (αὐτὸς αὑτῷ ὁμολογούμενος). This proposition alone suffices to show that by ἠθοποιΐα Dionysios cannot mean adaptation of the speech to the actual character of the litigant. What he does mean is that Lysias creates for the litigant a temporary character of the kind which most appeals to a jury. "He sets before us

Genre and Ethos 77

(ὑποτίθεται) his speakers as men with honest, decent, reasonable intentions, in such a way that their speeches seem illustrations (εἰκόνες) of their characters" (i.15.14–16). The result is a uniquely persuasive appeal (16.1–3, 17.12–18, 23.3, 28.16–18). Dionysos knows perfectly well that we, as readers, cannot decide whether the speaker is telling the truth; it is precisely our inability which testifies to the writer's competence (30.2–16).[21]

Now, at the same time as he generalises about Lysias's language as a whole and speaks of his consistency Dionysios also says that Lysias τὴν λέξιν ἀποδίδωσι τοῖς ἤθεσιν οἰκείαν (15.16 f.). But since he goes on to say that characters are most effectively revealed by "clear, correct, ordinary language" (15.16–19), he obviously does not mean that Lysias gives to each distinct character the language appropriate to that character. What he does mean is that when a good character has been constructed for a litigant—Lysias, in his view, always did so; that is the point of the plural τοῖς ἤθεσιν—the effect is lost if a speech redolent of rhetorical artifice is superimposed (cf. Arist. *Rhet.* 1408ᵇ21–26). "What is pretentious and recherché and contrived is ἀνηθοποίητον. Lysias composes ἀφελῶς πάνυ καὶ ἁπλῶς ... His style gives the impression of being ἀποίητος ... καὶ ἀτεχνίτευτος." (15.19–16.4.) Similar words are used in Dionysios's criticism of Isok. xvii as admitting epideictic features in a forensic context: he recasts a sentence of Isokrates in a form which, he says, would have been ἀποίητόν τε καὶ ἀφελές (90.17–91.3).

I have dwelt at some length on Dionysios's view of ἠθοποιΐα in Lysias not simply because it has been misinterpreted[22] but because, paradoxically, he could quite rationally have made four points which he fails to make and we have to make for him.

[21] Devries says (p. 22): "By these and similar means an effect was produced upon the jurymen that was well-nigh irresistible." But how can we know the extent (or grounds) of the jury's resistance in any individual case?

[22] Notably by Devries, in unequal combat against Francken, 1 ff. It is a pity that Devries offers (p. 14 f.) a partial summary of Dion. Hal. i. 15 ff. instead of a translation which would bring out the sequence of thought properly. For a just appreciation of Dionysios's meaning cf. Bruns, 432 f.; W. Motschmann, *Die Charaktere bei Lysias* (Munich, 1905); F. Zucker, *SDA* 1953; S. Usher, *Eranos* lxiii (1965), 99 ff.

(1) The first is a point made long before, by Aristotle (*Rhet.* 1408ª27–32), that a rustic and an educated man do not talk alike or argue alike.

(2) Obviously a litigant must make a favourable impression of honesty and sincerity, and must do everything that will have a persuasive effect; but within those limits, we expect a competent speech-writer to adapt the language to the status and character of the litigant, and if Lysias (or any other speech-writer) did not do so it would be a matter for considerable surprise.

(3) When we read the surviving speeches of the corpus, we get an impression of distinctive personalities. Not everyone agrees in the assessment of these personalities; personally, I find the speaker of XXV the most distinctive,[23] but he has not seemed so to others (e.g., Blass, i.515 f.) who have studied ἦθος in the orators.[24]

(4) There are two speeches which do permit us to say something about the relation between language and character.

VI, the *Prosecution of Andokides*, was composed for delivery (in 399) either by Meletos or by Epichares (And. i.94 f.). It cannot have been delivered by the first prosecutor, Kephisios (And, i.92 f.), because the speaker names Kephisios and appears embarrassed at being associated with him (§42).[25]

XII, the *Prosecution of Eratosthenes*, was delivered by Lysias himself.

Now, in the same year as VI a certain Meletos was one of the prosecutors of Sokrates; Plato treats him (*Ap.* 23E) as "representing the poets" and (26CD, 27C; cf. *Euthyphro* 2C) as a champion of traditional religious ideas. If the two Meletoi were the same man, and if VI was delivered by Meletos, we should expect it not only to exploit the lowest level of religious sentiment but also to have an

---

[23] Despite the fact that I also believe XXV more likely to be a hypothetical speech than to have been written with a real speaker in mind, cf. p. 188.

[24] Cf. Devries, 28; but Bruns (450 f.) treats XXV as an example of the writer's ability to build on the foundation laid by the speaker's personality.

[25] Bruns, 521 ff., regards VI as a fiction (cf. p. 190, below) composed by an unidentifiable enemy of Andokides. The speech is now mutilated; the lost portion may have contained the curious allegations known to us from Tzetzes, *Chil.* vi.367 ff. (printed in MacDowell, 172).

Genre and Ethos   79

abnormally high poetic colouring,[26] and at the same time to be deficient in the sentence structures characteristic of the orator.[27] Aristophanes apparently (fr. 114) referred to a Meletos as the lover of a Kallias, and Andokides (i.112, 115 ff.) treats Kallias the son of Hipponikos as an instigator of the machinations against himself. As for XII, we should not expect Lysias, as a well-known rhetorician, to pose as a helpless and artless innocent; this pose could not carry conviction, and he might well have felt that it would damage his reputation as a craftsman. Moreover, with sentiment running against the former Thirty, he could afford to be himself. Accordingly, we expect XII to exhibit rhetorical sentence structure,[28] to admit poetic colouring only sparingly, and to bring off some audacious oratorical *coups* which Lysias might have hesitated to risk when writing for another man's tongue.

Identification of the two Meletoi might seem to be precluded by Plato's reference (*Euthyphro* 2B) to Meletos as quite a young man in 399; fr. 114 of Aristophanes is from *Farmers*, which is shown by Plu. *Nic.* 8.2, citing fr. 100, to have referred to Nikias's behaviour over Pylos in 425, and the manner of the reference suggests (though it does not force us to believe) that the Pylos affair was recent. But according to the wording of the charge against Sokrates, as given by Diog. Laert. ii.40, the father of Meletos was also named Meletos, and Aristophanes can have been referring to the father's association with Kallias.[29] That Lysias should compose a speech for a man who was not only an enemy of Sokrates but also open to the allegation (And. i.94) of involvement in the arrest of Leon of Salamis under the Thirty Tyrants imposes something of a

[26] Cf. Darkow, 34.
[27] Cf. Hollingsworth, 46, and—on sentence structure as an aspect of ethos—G. Wolgast, *Zweigliedrigkeit im Satzbau des Lysias und Isokrates* (Diss. Kiel, 1962), 28 f.
[28] Cf. S. Usher, *Eranos* lxiii (1965), 114, and A. González Laso, *EC* i (1952), 366 ff.
[29] Cf. P. Mazon, *REA* xliv (1942), 177 ff. (who, however, goes badly astray in saying [181], in connection with the erotic relationship between Meletos and Kallias in Ar. fr. 114, that περαίνειν in its sexual sense belongs to the language of comedy rather than to that of scholia). I do not understand the grounds of MacDowell's statement (209) that Sokrates (*sc.*, in Pl. *Euthphr.* 2B) "appears not to have known any Meletos of Pitthos before 399."

strain even on the interpretation of Athenian politics advocated on p. 50, but we must be careful not to beg the question by assuming Lysias's authorship of the *Defence of Sokrates* ascribed to him (p. 192) or the validity of Andokides' allegation against Meletos (ὡς ὑμεῖς ἅπαντες ἴστε, as observed by the speaker of Dem. xl.53, is the worst of credentials for any allegation).

The fact that VI adopts and exploits the most primitive religious fears, prejudices and beliefs (§§ 17, 19 f., 27, 31 f., 33, 54) and the further fact that it shows a very much larger number of non-forensic words than the corresponding portion (§§ 1–52 [εὔνοιαν]) of XII seem to me stronger arguments for the identity of the two Meletoi than any argument which has been adduced to the contrary.[30]

As we have seen (p. 67), the number of non-forensic words in XII.1–52 is 24. VI contains no less than 77. If we deduct words which denote material objects (e.g., ἄγαλμα [§ 15]), actions or states which, at least in prose, are only used with material reference (e.g., ἐσθίειν and ὄζειν [§ 2]), constitutional and administrative terms (e.g., βασιλεύειν [§ 28], ἱέρεια [§ 51]), and—which makes a great difference to VI, because of its subject—ritual terms (e.g., ἁγνεύειν [§ 51]), there still remain:

> ἀβίωτος (§ 31)
> ἄθεος (§ 32)
> ἀθῷος (§ 4)
> αἴκισμα (§ 26)
> ἄλγιστος (§ 1): Isok. x.34

[30] Blass, i.567 f., takes the possibility seriously. MacDowell's arguments (*loc. cit.*) against identification seem to me open to criticism. "Sokrates' colleague in 404" (And. i.94 ~ Pl. *Ap.* 32c) "could not have been unknown to him in 399" (Pl. *Euthphr.* 2B). But (*a*) this presupposes that Andokides' allegation is literally true (on ὡς ὑμεῖς ἅπαντες ἴστε as a testimonial, see above), and thus that Meletos was actually one of the five men sent to Salamis to arrest Leon; (*b*) as I read Pl. *Ap.* 32c, it does not follow that Sokrates exchanged a word with his four "colleagues"—and he may not even have seen all of them; and (*c*) *Euthphr.* 2B implies (maliciously?) that Meletos was not a well-known man and that Sokrates himself did not know much about him, but it does not imply that Sokrates did not know him at all. The commonplace sneer in Ar. fr. 438 that Meletos was of Thracian origin is no more to be taken seriously than Aischines' sneer at Demosthenes as a Scythian.

Genre and Ethos 81

ἀλᾶσθαι (§30): ctr. πλανᾶσθαι XII.97
ἀνταποδιδόναι (§49)
ἀντικατηγορεῖν (§42)
ἀπαθής (§48): Epit. 27
ἀποδημία (§6)
ἀσέβημα (§§13, 16, 31)
ἀστός (§17): Epit. 66
ἀσχολία (§34)
αὐτόματος (§25): Epit. 79
δαιμόνιος (§32)
δήπουθεν (§36)
διοχλεῖν (§6)
δόγμα (§43): And. iv.6
ἐναργής (§3): Isok. x.61
ἔνθεν (§28)
ἐξείργειν (§16)
ἐπιβαίνειν (§15)
ἐπινοεῖν (§31)
ἐπιτάττειν (§13): Epit. 51; And. iii.11
ἑσπέρα (§51)
εὐχή (§§4, 33)
θεωρεῖν (§5): the reference is to festivals[31]
καταθάπτειν (§47)
κατάπληξ (§50)
κατελεεῖν (§3)
κολακεύειν (§6): And. iv.16
κομπάζειν (§§18, 48)
λήθη (§27)
λιμός (§1)
μαντεία (§33): Isok. x.27
μετοικία (§49)
ναυκληρεῖν (§49)
ξενοῦν (§48)
παρατιθέναι (§2)
περιτρέπειν (§13)

[31] This should perhaps be deducted as a technical term.

πολιτικός (§33): And. iv.1; Isok. x.9
πολλαχόθεν (§20)
πονεῖν (§4): *Erot.* 232A
πρᾳότης (§34): Isok. x.37
προσεύχεσθαι (§51)
πρόσχημα (§33)
προσψηφίζεσθαι (§24)
προτιμᾶν (§50): Isok. x.16, 60
σάλος (§49): metaphorical
τόπος (§28): Isok. x.4, 38
τροφεῖα (§49): *Epit.* 70; metaphorical
ὑπάγειν (§19)

On the other hand, rhetorical parallelism and assonance are much rarer in VI than in XII.1–52, as examination on the lines suggested on p. 61 will quickly show. And to step for a moment outside the limits of XII.1–52, contrast the thunderclap with which XII ends (§100)—παύσομαι κατηγορῶν. ἀκηκόατε. ἑοράκατε. πεπόνθατε. ἔχετε. δικάζετε—with the ending of VI, where an approach to a similar effect is given a blunter edge by a γνώμη (§55): φανερῶς ἔχετ' αὐτὸν ἀσεβοῦντα. εἴδετε, ἠκούσατε τὰ τούτου ἁμαρτήματα. ἀντιβολήσει καὶ ἱκετεύσει ὑμᾶς · μὴ ἐλεεῖτε. οὐ γὰρ οἱ δικαίως ἀποθνῄσκοντες ἀλλ' οἱ ἀδίκως ἄξιοί εἰσιν ἐλεεῖσθαι.

Now: either VI was composed by someone other than Lysias, or it was composed by Lysias with careful regard for the known personality and style of the person who was going to deliver it. If we accept the former alternative on the strength of the political evidence, well and good; it can reasonably be presented as the minimum sacrifice necessary for the achievement of historical coherence. If, however, we accept it solely on the strength of the technical criteria so far considered, we imply either that Lysias was not capable of altering his language to suit the litigant, or that although capable, he was not willing to do so. The former implication leads directly to the conclusion, and the latter gives some plausibility to the conclusion, that no extant speech except XII can be ascribed to Lysias if its language differs significantly from that of XII.

Genre and Ethos 83

But to suppose that Lysias was incapable is absurd; there are scholars today who could do it, and such hard facts as we have about Lysias justify the belief that he was as sensitive to language and the technical aspects of persuasion as any man of his time. If, on the other hand, we suppose that he was not willing to use different techniques for different litigants, on what evidence do we base such a supposition?[32]

If, as seems to be the case, linguistic phenomena conform to the status, profession and personality of the litigant in the only two speeches which permit us to have an opinion on this relationship, it is rational to allow for conformity in all other speeches. This means that considerable linguistic difference is equally compatible with identity and with difference of authorship.

It is, however, demonstrable that conformity of language to litigant falls within certain boundaries, and that in the Lysian period a certain distance between forensic language anad colloquial language was maintained, no matter how simple and plain-spoken the persona of the litigant might be. This is most obvious if we compare passages of continuous forensic narrative with comic narrative.[33] I choose the following for comparison.

> Aristophanes: the Sausageman's narrative, *Knights* 624–852; Strepsiades' autobiographical soliloquy, *Clouds* 43–73, and his description of his quarrel with his son, 1353–1376; Karion's narrative, *Wealth* 653–747. Omitting interruptions and answers to questions, these passages afford 91 examples of simple connection, equivalent to "and," "then," "but" or asyndeton.
>
> Andokides i.34–45, 48–53, 60–66, omitting quoted direct speech—80 examples.

---

[32] The writer's problem was to achieve a satisfactory adjustment (cf. p. 54) between (*a*) his own technique, (*b*) the litigant's personality, and (*c*) the personality most acceptable to the jury. Cf. Bruns, 434.

[33] Cf. Ed. Fraenkel, *Beobachtungen zu Aristophanes* (Rome, 1962), 126 f., on connectives in comic narrative.

84   Lysias and the *Corpus Lysiacum*

Lysias I.11–26, III.5–14, XII.6–18 and XXXII.4–18, omitting quoted direct speech—148 examples.

Isokrates xvii.3–23, xviii.5–12 and xix.5–12, 18–20—99 examples.

The outstanding difference between comic and forensic narrative is that ἔπειτα, ἔπειτα δέ, κἄπειτα, εἶτα and κᾆτα occur 23 times in Aristophanes, namely:

Knights 678:   ἐγὼ δέ ... ἐπριάμην ... ὅσ' ἦν ἐν τἀγορᾷ.
             ἔπειτα ταῖς ἀφύαις ἐδίδουν ἡδύσματα.

Cf. *Clouds* 46; *Wealth* 657, 659, 676, 681, 695, 710, 718, 729.

Clouds 1364:   κἀγώ ... ἠνεσχόμην τὸ πρῶτον.
             ἔπειτα δ' ἐκέλευσ' αὐτὸν κτλ.

   1376:   κἄπειτ' ἔφλα με
Knights 647:   τῶν δ' εὐθέως τὰ πρόσωπα διεγαλήνισεν
             εἶτ' ἐστεφάνουν μ' εὐαγγέλια.

Cf. 675; *Clouds* 66, 1375; *Wealth* 720, 732.

640:   κἀγὼ προσέκυσα. κᾆτα τῷ πρωκτῷ θενών ...
      ἀνέκραγον.

Cf. 665; *Clouds* 1365, 1374; *Wealth* 689.

These same words function as connectives through Aristophanes in shorter narrative statements—for example:

Clouds 149–151: κηρὸν διατήξας, εἶτα τὴν ψύλλαν λαβὼν
             ἐνέβαψεν εἰς τὸν κηρὸν αὐτῆς τὼ πόδε,
             κᾆτα ψυχείσῃ περιέφυσαν Περσικαί.

They appear also in Menander, as in:

Epitr. 310 f.:   ἐπλανήθη γὰρ μεθ' ἡμῶν οὐσ' ἐκεῖ,
             εἶτ' ἐξαπίνης κλάουσα προστέχει μόνον.

Cf. 330; *Dysk.* 119, 529, 537, 617, 627; *Sik.* (Kassel) 244 f.; *Heros* 28–30; fr. 195.

In forensic oratory these words are the rarest of all simple connectives. They are common in enumerations (e.g., And.

i.43.132), and common also as "logical" connectives, co-ordinated with πρῶτον μέν and meaning "secondly"; this logical use can intrude into narrative ("secondly," "but afterwards," etc.) and there are two examples of such intrusion in the Lysian period:

And. i.144: πρῶτον μέν . . . εἰς ἀπορίαν κατέστην, ἔπειτα δὲ καινὸν βίον ἠργασάμην (cf. Ant. vi.11: καὶ πρῶτον μὲν διδασκαλεῖον . . . κατεσκεύασα . . . , ἔπειτα τὸν χορὸν συνέλεξα κτλ., and, from a symbuleutic speech, And. iii.5).

Isok. xvii.7: πρῶτον μὲν αὐτὸς ἀφανίσας ὑφ' ἡμῶν αὐτὸν ᾐτιᾶτ' ἠφανίσθαι, ἔπειτα δὲ συλληφθέντα ὡς ἐλεύθερον ὄντα διεκώλυσεν βασανίζεσθαι, μετὰ δὲ ταῦτα κτλ.

Looking outside the narrative passages chosen, we find only two examples of simple narrative ἔπειτα and εἶτα:

And. i.17: Σπεύσιππος δέ . . . παραδίδωσιν . . . κἄπειτα ὁ πατὴρ ἀναστὰς κτλ.
And. i.112: . . . καὶ ἔδειξεν αὐτοῖς. κᾆθ' ὁ κῆρυξ ἐκήρυττε (cf. And. iii.22 [symbuleutic], εἶτα δέ: Is. xi.18).

There are two reasons for believing that these usages were colloquial, and neither a convention of comic verse nor a convenient opening for iambic trimeters: (1) They are avoided by Euripides: the two great narrative speeches in *Bacchae* (677–768, 1043–1152) do not contain a single example, in 93 simple connections (65 out of the 93 are in fact δέ). (2) Lys. I.14, where the speaker is reporting what his wife said when he asked her why the outer door had creaked in the night: ἔφασκε τὸν λύχνον ἀποσβεσθῆναι τὸν παρὰ τῷ παιδίῳ, εἶτα ("and so") ἐκ τῶν γειτόνων ἐνάψασθαι.

It should be noted that simple καί, which we might have expected to be characteristically colloquial, accounts for only 20 out of 91 comic passages, 17 out of Andokides' 80, 41 out of 142 Lysian and 17 out of 99 Isokratean. Seven out of the Lysian examples occur in XII (§§6, 8, 10 *bis*, 12 *bis*, 18).[34]

A striking difference between comic and forensic usage appears

---

[34] Cf. S. Trenkner, *Le Style KAI dans le récit attique oral* (Assen, 1960), 8, 12 f.

in the use of connective δέ when a sentence begins with a participial or subordinate clause, as in:

And. i.38: ἔφη γάρ ... ἀναστὰς δὲ πρῴ ... βαδίζειν.
Cf. §§38 bis, 39, 40 bis, 41, 43, 44, 45, 51, 62, 63, 65.

Lys. I.18: ἐλθὼν δ' οἴκαδε ἐκέλευον ἀκολουθεῖν μοι τὴν θεράπαιναν.
Cf. §§18, 22, 24; XII.8, 12 (ἐξιοῦσι δ' ἐμοὶ καὶ Πείσωνι κτλ.), 14, 16 bis; XXXII.11, 12.

Isok. xvii.4: πυνθανόμενος δὲ καὶ περὶ τῆσδε τῆς πόλεως ... ἐπεθύμησ' ἀποδημῆσαι.
Cf. §§11, 15, 18, 23; xviii.5, 7, 7, 7, 12 bis; xix.5 (ξένος δὲ γενόμενος), 6, 6 (πλάνης δὲ γενόμενος), 7.

Lys. I.11: προϊόντος δὲ τοῦ χρόνου, ὦ ἄνδρες, ἧκον μὲν ἀπροσδοκήτως ἐξ ἀγροῦ.
Cf. §14, XXXII.4, 7.

Isok. xvii.4: συστήσαντος δέ μοι Πυθοδώρου ... ἐχρώμην τῇ τούτου τραπέζῃ.
Cf. §§16; xviii.5, 6, 11; xix.18.

And. i.34: ἐπειδὴ δ' οὗτοι ἀπεγράφησαν κτλ.
Cf. §§36, 37 (ὡς), 38 (ἐπεί), 48.

Lys. I.12: ἐπειδὴ δ' ἐγὼ ὠργιζόμην κτλ.
Cf. §§14, 19, 21, 23; III.5, 8, 10; XII.10,11 (ἐπεί); XXXII.8, 12.

Isok. xvii.8: ἐπειδὴ δέ ... διεπραξάμην κτλ.
Cf. §§9, 19 (εἰ), 12, 12 (ἵνα); xviii.10 (ἵνα), xix.7, 10, 18 (ὅτε).

Against these 76 forensic examples we can set only Ar. *Pl.* 660 (ἐπεὶ δέ ... καθωσιώθη κτλ.) and 668 (ὡς δέ ... ἀποσβέσας ... παρήγγειλεν κτλ.). In this respect, even the plainest-seeming forensic narrative is close to historiography and far distant from the lively narrative of comedy.

It is well known that when several works of the same author are firmly dated on external grounds it is sometimes (not always) possible to detect consistent tendencies to linguistic or metrical change. The best-known example is Euripides' steadily increasing readiness, in the last twenty years of his career, to resolve long syllables in iambic trimeters. When only one work is dated, it has normally, and quite reasonably, been accepted that other works of the same author can be arranged in chronological sequence in accordance with their similarity to the dated work, provided always that the selection of criteria is not determined by any chronological theory already conceived and that if different criteria give conflicting answers there is no dishonest discrimination. A well-known example of dating by reference to one work is the Platonic chronology which is based on the datum that *Laws* is Plato's last work and on the degree of resemblance which any given Platonic work bears to *Laws* in respect of the frequency of hiatus and the relative frequencies of different types of clausular rhythm.

With three forensic speeches in the *corpus Lysiacum* (X, XII and XXX) securely dated with a few months' margin of error, a fourth (XXVI) almost certainly datable to within a month and several others approximately datable, and the whole period covered (from XX to XXVI) being at least 25 years one might have hoped that a canon of ascription based on the chronology of linguistic change would be practicable; but it proves not to be so,[35] and the fault must be laid at the door of the adaptation of language to litigant.

Even without this complication, there are two other factors which embarrass the use of linguistic criteria either for dating, when authorship is known, or for ascription, when it is not.

(1) Most of us are aware that we have linguistic habits which are temporary, not in the sense that they are one stage in a continuous process but in the sense that we later revert to an earlier habit. It is well known that a Greek dramatist is inclined to use the same word several times in one play and either never or rarely in his other plays; and we should expect the same to be true of an orator. This consideration applies not only to individual words but also to combinations of words and to sentence structure. For

---

[35] Cf. Büchler, 65.

example—to look only at the narratives which were discussed (p. 83) in connection with forensic language—the Aristophanic passages include nine sentences beginning with κἀγώ. In two of these κἀγώ is enlarged to κἄγωγε and is immediately followed by a temporal clause. Both examples occur in *Knights*:

> 632: κἄγωγ', ὅτε δὴ 'γνων ἐνδεχομένην τοὺς λόγους . . . 'ἄγε δή . . .', ἦν δ' ἐγώ, κτλ.
> 658: κἄγωγ', ὅτε δὴ 'γνων τοῖς βολίτοις ἡττημένος, διακοσίαισι βουσὶν ὑπερηκόντισα.

Knights shows two other examples of κἄγωγε followed by a subordinate clause:

> 434: κἄγωγ', ἐάν τι παραχαλᾷ, τὴν ἀντλίαν φυλάξω.
> 769: κἄγωγ' ὦ Δῆμ', εἰ μή σε φιλῶ καὶ μὴ στέργω, κατατμηθεὶς ἑψοίμην ἐν περικομματίοις.

The only approximation to this is *Clouds* 530: κἀγώ, παρθένος γὰρ ἔτ' ἦ . . ., ἐξέθηκα. When elsewhere (*Peace* 1120, *Eccl.* 354, 937) in Aristophanes κἀγώ or κἄγωγε is followed by a subordinate clause it does not mean "and I . . ." but "I too," the verb being understood from the previous speaker's sentence.

We have here a good example of a sentence form *temporarily* favoured by a dramatist. It is not, surprising therefore, if we find two similar sentences both occurring in the narrative of one speech, but not in the others,[36] as in:

> XII.8: καὶ ἐμὲ μὲν ξένους ἑστιῶντα κατέλαβον· οὓς ἐξελάσαντες κτλ.
> XII.13: καταλαμβάνομεν δ' αὐτόθι Θέογνιν ἑτέρους φυλάττοντα· ᾧ παραδόντες ἐμὲ κτλ.

Even more striking is the concentration of the article wth the infinitive in XXXI:

> §2: τῷ δύνασθαι καὶ εἰωθέναι λέγειν ἐν ὑμῖν ἐπαρθεὶς
> §5: πρὸς τῷ εἶναι πολίτας
> §5: διὰ τὸ ἀναγκαῖον σφίσιν αὐτοῖς ἡγεῖσθαι εἶναι

---

[36] Cf. Büchler, 39 f., on the language of I, and Devries, 25, on the *figura etymologica* in VII. 38–41.

§6: διὰ τὸ μὴ τὴν πόλιν ἀλλὰ τὴν οὐσίαν πατρίδα ἑαυτοῖς ἡγεῖσθαι
§11: διὰ τὸ ἡγεῖσθαι ἄκοντας αὐτοὺς ἁμαρτάνειν
§21: διὰ τὸ προσήκειν αὐτῇ
§22: διὰ τὸ εὐνοίᾳ μᾶλλον ἢ ἐλέγχῳ τὰ γιγνόμενα δοκιμάζειν
§26: οὐ περὶ τοῦ βουλεύειν ἀλλὰ τοῦ δουλεύειν
§27: τὸ μὴ παραγενέσθαι ἐν ἐκείνῳ τῷ καιρῷ
§32: οὐ μόνον περὶ τοῦ βουλεύειν ἀλλὰ καὶ περὶ τῆς ἐλευθερίας.

This construction occurs only twice in XII (§§13, 52), and only seven times, distributed over six speeches, in the rest of the corpusculum.[37]

Other speeches show positive features absent from the majority; VIII, for example, shows a remarkable fondness for runs of short syllables,[38] and XVI an abnormal avoidance of hiatus.[39]

(2) There is a limit to what we can explain. Demetrios, *Eloc.* 255 f., appears to regard the word order πάντ' ἔγραψεν ἄν (instead of πάντ' ἂν ἔγραψεν) and παρεγένετο οὐχί (instead of οὐ παρεγένετο) as "harsh" (κακόφωνον) but as possibly contributing, like asyndeton (§269) and hiatus (§299), to the effect of what he calls δεινότης—a quality which strikes the hearer like a physical blow (§274) and keeps him awake.[40]

We cannot entertain any expectation *a priori* of the frequency with which an author will choose to deliver such a blow, and it only rarely happens that we can offer a persuasive explanation of his choice of one occasion rather than another. Much linguistic abnormality must, so far as we are concerned, be relegated to the category of caprice.

XII contains one ἄν which fits Demetrios's first example very well. Normally in XII ἄν follows the negative word in a negative sentence (e.g., §84, δίκην παρ' αὐτῶν οὐκ ἂν δύναισθε λαβεῖν; cf.

[37] Cf. Büchler, 31.
[38] Cf. F. Vogel, *Hermes* lviii (1923), 97.
[39] Cf. S. Usher, *Eranos* lxiii (1965), 109; and cf. Wyse's commentary on Isaios, pp. 178 f., on the difference between Isaian speeches in respect of hiatus, a difference which is not explicable chronologically.
[40] δεινότης does not mean the same in Demetrios as in other critics; cf. L. Voit, *Δεινότης—ein antiker Stilbegriff* (Leipzig, 1934), especially 38 ff.

§§ 1, 46, 47, 82, 85, 98) or the interrogative word, where there is one (§§ 34, 82). In positive statements it normally follows the leading mobile word of its clause (§§ 22, 29, 31, 50, 54, 63, 78, 83, 84, 92, 98). Postponement occurs when the clause is divisible into cola:

§ 22: ἐγὼ δ᾽ : ἐβουλόμην ἂν αὐτοὺς τἀληθῆ λέγειν
§ 47: καὶ τοὺς διδασκάλους τῶν σφετέρων ἁμαρτημάτων : σφόδρ᾽ ἂν ἐκόλαζον, καὶ τοὺς ὅρκους ... οὐκ ἂν κτλ.
§ 88: καίτοι οὗτοι μὲν : σωθέντες : πάλιν ἂν δύναιντο τὴν πόλιν ἀπολέσαι· ἐκεῖνοι δέ, : οὓς οὗτοι ἀπώλεσαν, : τελευτήσαντες τὸν βίον κτλ.
§ 93: καὶ τοὺς ἰδίους οἴκους : οὗτοι μὲν ἄν : ... ἐκτήσαντο, ὑμεῖς δὲ κτλ.
§ 98: οἱ δὲ παῖδες ὑμῶν, : ὅσοι μὲν ἐνθάδε ἦσαν, : ὑπὸ τούτων ἂν ὑβρίζοντο, οἱ δ᾽ ἐπὶ ξένης : μικρῶν ἂν ἕνεκα συμβολαίων ἐδούλευον.

The sole exception in XII is § 37: οἳ οὐδ᾽ ὑπὲρ ἑνὸς ἑκάστου τῶν πεπραγμένων δὶς ἀποθανόντες δίκην δοῦναι δύναιντ᾽ ἄν.

Demetrios's second example has a parallel in VI.27: ἀφικόμενος δ᾽ ἐδέθη καὶ ἠκίσθη. ἀπώλετο δὲ οὐχί, ἀλλ᾽ ἐλύθη.

We have already seen reasons for linguistic abnormality in VI, whoever wrote it; we might even have guessed that out of the 32 examples of negative + verb in the speech one would be inverted. But we could not have guessed from examination of ἄν in the rest of XII that Lysias would prefer δίκην δοῦναι δύναιντ᾽ ἄν to δίκην ἂν δοῦναι δύναιντο in § 37, nor can we say why he did.

I referred earlier (p. 69) to the possibility that the *Erotikos* is a parody composed by Plato, and this has, of course, always been taken into account. It carries an important implication, sometimes overlooked, perhaps because it is taken for granted: that what can be parodied for the hearer's amusement can equally be imitated in an attempt to achieve the same success as the original. We all recognise the speech of Agathon in Plato's *Symposium* (194E4–197E8) as a parody of Gorgias, and do not need the notification of this fact which Sokrates gives us humorously in 198C1–5. We

Genre and Ethos 91

recognise it, however, not through any similarity of its vocabulary to the exiguous remains of Gorgias—no similarity is apparent—but from two features.

(1) We see—indeed, the speaker ensures that we see—the framework upon and around which the speech is built. The bold self-reference of the opening words (194E4 f.) ἐγὼ δὲ δὴ βούλομαι πρῶτον μὲν εἰπεῖν ὡς χρή μ' εἰπεῖν, ἔπειτα εἰπεῖν reminds us of εἰπεῖν δυναίμην ἃ βούλομαι, βουλοίμην δ' ἃ δεῖ (Gorgias 42; cf. 39.2, 5, 8; 44.4, 9–11, 22, 27 f.). Agathon generalises succinctly about the right way to deal with his subject (195A1–3; cf. Gorgias 39.1, and contrast the didactic verbiage of Isokrates on the same topic, x.1–15). His organisation of his points (195A3–6, 8; 196B5, D6) stands out as boldly as if he were ticking them off on his fingers (cf. Gorgias 39.6, 9, 13–15; 44.5, 13, 19, 24, 33). He summarises each point before going to the next (195C6 f.; 196A1 f., B4 f., D4–6; 197C1–3; cf. Gorgias 39.7). At the end he refers baldly to his achievement of his intention (197E6–8; cf. Gorgias 39.21). These features of rhetorical disposition are present also in other speeches in *Symposium* (180D6–8, D1–3, E3 f.; 181A4–6, E2–4; 185C2 f., E6–186A2; 188D9–E4; 189C2 f.; 193D6–E2), but there is no other speech in which they are so concentrated and obtrusive.

(2) The remarkable peroration (197D1–E3) consists of a string of parallel cola grouped in pairs, a high degree of assonance binding the members of each pair together. This can only be compared with the passage from Gorgias's *Epitaphios* (12) preserved in Syrianus (p. 90.12 ff. [Rabe]) via Dionysios (i.127.8–128.15); for approximations compare Gorgias 39.4, 6, 19, and 44.17, 25, 32, 35.

We say that Plato is parodying Gorgias; but strictly speaking, he is parodying Agathon's emulation of Gorgias. Agathon, as Plato portrays him, is not trying to amuse his friends but to excite their admiration for his own artistic accomplishment. Now, this has some bearing on the problem of ascription in forensic oratory. Every artist of distinction has imitators, and every successful practitioner in a technical sphere represents an ideal which lesser men try to attain. The work of Sir John Beazley on Attic vases has taught us how distinctions can be drawn between (say) Douris and imitators of Douris. Is it anything less than certain that there were men in Athens in Lysias's time who tried to compose speeches like those of Lysias—or of Thrasymachos, Theramenes or Archinos?[41] Unfortunately, while there are infinite ways of drawing a stroke and relating strokes to each other, one instance of a written word is not distinguishable in isolation from any other instance of the same word, and its relation to its context and argument is not always easily perceived, still less described intelligibly. No one has an ear for Greek prose which commands the same respect as Beazley's eye for painting.[42]

We know that vocabulary is imitable, and anyone who has translated into Demosthenic prose as a linguistic exercise knows that avoidance of hiatus and rhythmical preferences are imitable. We see from Aristophanes' satires on linguistic fashion (*Knights* 1377–1380 [-ικός] and *Clouds* 317 f. [-σις]) that types of word formation can be parodied; and whatever can be parodied can also be imitated seriously. We have seen from Agathon's speech that disposition and sentence structure can be imitated, and if we had any further doubts we could dispel them by looking at modern parodies of Henry James or William Faulkner. If I have been reading Gibbon, I catch myself writing such sentences as "It is easier to ridicule the pretensions, than to emulate the perspicacity, of the sophists." I would not allow such a sentence to survive revision, because its structure is entirely alien to my normal practice, and I would not want my readers to believe that I had persuaded myself that I could write like Gibbon. But if I were an Athenian with ambitions as a composer of speeches, if I were consulted by an inarticulate friend in legal trouble, and if I knew that Lysias had proved himself an outstandingly successful composer of forensic speeches—in those circumstances I would be very much less inhibited in conscious imitation.[43]

To the complications introduced by difference of genre,

---

[41] Cf. Francken, 20.

[42] And I would not suggest in any case that we could draw Beazley's distinctions between "manner," "imitation," "following," "school," etc.

[43] Cf. Büchler, 39, on the general lack of sustained individuality of language in different speeches; the cases examined on p. 89, above, are extremes.

adaptation of argument to circumstances, adaptation of language to ethos, forensic convention, linguistic change and inexplicable caprice I have now added, as a further complication, the concept of a "school" or "manner" of Lysias. It may be felt that I have shown the problem of ascription on technical grounds to be insoluble. But we have not in fact reached the point at which there is no more to be said, provided that we are not too demanding in our quest for a person, and are prepared, when Λυσίας ὁ σοφιστής eludes us, to be content[44] with τὸ Λυσιακόν.

[44] As Wilamowitz was; cf. *Hermes* lviii (1923), 68 f.

VI

Crude Stylometry

DIONYSIOS DISCUSSES at length (i.17.19–20.15) what he calls the "charm" (χάρις) of Lysias. He proclaims that when all other evidence for or against the authorship of a speech ascribed to Lysias is inadequate he has recourse to this criterion for the "final verdict" (i.19.14–18), and he implies that in some cases suspicions originally aroused by the absence of "charm" were subsequently verified on more objective grounds (i.20.7–15). It is easy to decry this approach to the history of literature, particularly as Dionysios recognises (i.18.12 f.) the difficulty of communicating to us just what he means by charm (instead of "he proclaims" I originally wrote "he confesses," and only changed my wording when I realised that I was misrepresenting Dionysios). Yet it would be foolish to refuse even to consider the opinion of an experienced and sensitive critic. Dionysios's judgment is not open to criticism simply on the grounds of "subjectivity"; nor would it be open to criticism even if we knew that he and Caecilius formed equally strong but entirely opposed opinions on the same speech. Irreconcilable "subjective" judgments passed by critics who are equal in experience and, to the best of our belief, in sensitivity, do not "cancel out" like $+x$ and $-x$, and to suppose that they do is a categorical error. Both judgments are items of evidence, and their co-existence simply makes the evaluation of the sum of evidence more difficult.[1] We have to scrutinise the sequence of reactions which has caused each of the two critics to form the opinion which he holds, and the result of this scrutiny may sometimes be discreditable to the intelligence of either or both. But it is not always discreditable, nor is scrutiny always practicable. Perception of similarity and classification of characteristics sometimes work, in the sense that they are supported by subsequent investigation, even when the sorting process is one which we cannot even formulate to our own satisfaction, let alone communicate it to others.

The real weakness of Dionysios's "final verdict" is circular argument. If we have ten works known to be by a certain author, and we are asked to pass judgment on an eleventh, then, however erroneous or ill founded our judgment may be, it will not be a *peritrope*. But Dionysios was faced with 425 speeches, of which only a small number were datable, and only one was a forensic speech composed for delivery by Lysias himself; Dionysios found more than 200 speeches in this corpus which seemed to him "attractive" and he made the tacit assumption that no one among Lysias's contemporaries could write just as attractively and that Lysias could not write unattractively. These assumptions have only to be stated for their insecurity to be apparent. Even if they were more secure, they would be of limited utility, for out of the 30 speeches contained in the Palatinus there is not one on which Dionysios's opinion is known for certain, and it is only by identifying his ascriptions with those of Harpokration that we can infer his probable opinion on one third of them (cf. p. 16).

This does not mean that we must not even attempt to form an opinion of our own. We do not know as much Greek as Dionysios, but we know some.

---

[1] We tend to ignore the existence of evidence which is hard to communicate in quantified form, but it is there. For example: P was accused by Q of perpetrating a scholarly fraud. Neither Q nor I knew P personally; but R knew him well, and I knew R. Whether R's assertion that P was incapable of fraud would have carried any weight in a court of law, I do not know; but I would have been imposing an extremely artificial restriction on my own freedom to judge the issue if I had pretended that I was ignorant of R's assertion or that I was devoid of opinions on R's judgment of character.

In personal relationships we are all aware of a phenomenon which we call "uncharacteristic behaviour." A man does something which he has never done before or something which we regard as a *kind of thing* he has never done before. We cannot translate our observation into mathematical terms, partly because the boundaries of a "kind" of behaviour are hazy, partly because although we can be certain beyond question that the occasions on which he could have acted in this way, but did not, are numerous, we cannot count them. From observation of uncharacteristic behaviour we may infer the onset of neurosis or the existence of hitherto unsuspected pressures, and we can learn to draw increasingly correct inferences.

Now, to read a text thoroughly is to form a partial acquaintance with its author. The observation that an expression or structural phenomenon in his work is uncharacteristic has neither more nor less validity than a comparable observation of uncharacteristic behaviour in someone we know.[2] A famous example is the circumlocution for "women" in Aischylos, *Seven Against Thebes*, 872 f., "All those who encircle their clothes with a girdle." This is not, in my view, unique in Aischylos, and therefore does not make a decisive contribution to the question of authenticity posed by other aspects of the last scene of the *Seven*, for I regard it as akin to the circumlocution for "fish" in *Persians* 577 f., "The voiceless children of her who is undefiled." In any author there must logically be an expression which is the *most* enigmatic (or most tautologous, etc.) in that author's work. Delete it as spurious, and the second "most . . ." automatically moves up to first place; if we delete that too, we are logically committed to going on until there is nothing left.

A more important illustration is provided by [Dem.] vii.45, "Assuming that you go around with your brains between your

[2] Textual criticism, above the level of linguistic trivialities, often depends on the editor's readiness to say, "I know this author, and what the manuscripts have here is not consistent with the way his mind works." To the opponent who demands proof the editor can only say, "Live with the author, as I have done, for the next ten years or so, and then come back and tell me what you think."

temples and not trodden underfoot in your heels." I have a certain affection for this passage, because it struck me with great force, as showing a kind of coarseness which I thought uncharacteristic of Demosthenes, before I read the hypothesis to the speech and discovered that the author of the hypothesis not only treated precisely that passage as "no small testimony" that the speech was not Demosthenic (§2) but also possessed historical grounds for believing that it was delivered by Hegesippos (cf. pp. 4f.). I was further encouraged by the discovery that although Dionysios did not, apparently, entertain any doubt about the Demosthenic authorship of the speech, he describes it as almost wholly lacking the majesty and power which he regards as the hallmark of Demosthenes (i.157.4–12).

Unfortunately, discrimination between the characteristic and the uncharacteristic, always deserving of consideration in poetry, historiography, philosophy and any series of symbuleutic speeches which we have *prima facie* grounds for thinking were composed and delivered by the same person, is of very limited value when speeches are composed for delivery by different people. It is one thing to recognise that Sokrates in *Theages* has a personality quite unlike that of Sokrates in the other Platonic dialogues and to infer that the writer who created this personality was not the writer of those other dialogues; it is quite another thing to say that because Demosthenes did not intend himself to deliver the speech *On Halonnesos* he did not write it either. Confronted, as we are in the *corpus Lysiacum*, by a series of speeches each composed for a different litigant and—as we are bound to assume, in default of evidence to the contrary—accommodated, within reason, to the litigant's personality, we gain little or nothing by the detection of uncharacteristic passages. Indeed, in the extant forensic speeches the least characteristic passage is the peroration of XII, and the reason for its peculiarity is perhaps that when Lysias was writing for himself he knew that he could achieve a daring effect which he could not trust others to achieve. In the epideictic field suspicion on grounds of this kind can be attached only to the fictitious speech of Nikias (fr. 71) before his Syracusan captors, a speech which

Theophrastos, cited by Dion. Hal. i.23.16–24.16, accepted without comment as Lysias's. The few words quoted from it include ἀμάχητον καὶ ἀναυμάχητον ὄλεθρον and ἀνακαλοῦντές τε συγγένειαν, εὐμένειαν. The word play of the former phrase and the two-term asyndeton of the latter are alien to the *Epitaphios* and the *Olympikos*. We can say with assurance that the author of the *Epitaphios* had several dozen opportunities to use each of these devices. Obviously we cannot attach a more precise number to opportunities which a man does not take; but if a statistician rejects as invalid or meaningless the argument from language that the *Speech of Nikias* was not written by the author of the *Epitaphios* he is uncovering a limitation in the application of statistics to language.[3] It is, of course, open to us to say that the *Speech of Nikias* was a comparatively early experiment by Lysias in the genre, but the strong condemnation by Dionysios (i.24.20–25.3) must suggest (cf. Blass, i.448)—except to those who believe that because his method incurred the danger of circularity it was always necessarily circular—that he knew of no other speech in the *corpus Lysiacum* in which opportunities for childish word-play and two-term asyndeton were taken.

The statistical treatment of linguistic phenomena in bulk is at the present time pursued vigorously and rewardingly, in many different branches of literary history; and while not all phenomena can be quantified with exactitude, many can. In describing this treatment as "crude" stylometry and distinguishing it from "refined" stylometry (chap. vii) I use the adjectives not in blame and praise, but with reference to the scale of the quantities involved.

[3] When alternative forms, *a* and *b*, occur in the same author's work, it makes sense to consider the ratio $a:b$, but when only *a* occurs we cannot know whether *b* belongs to the author's individual language at all. If it does not, the probability that he will use *a* in all cases where he can say what he means by using either *a* or *b* is 1; if it does, and the conditions under which he would use *b* are not known, the probability of his using *a* falls short of 1 by an unknown amount. Comparable difficulties beset the use of lexical studies to establish authorship; cf. C. Udny Yule, *The Statistical Study of Literary Vocabulary* (Cambridge, 1944), 44, 69, on the unknowable size of that portion of an author's total vocabulary which he happens not to have used in his extant works.

Crude Stylometry

One possible misunderstanding must be cleared up at the outset. A table stating the frequency with which a writer uses given words or constructions is not like his electroencephalogram, a photograph of his fingerprints, or a description of how he opens doors or lights cigarettes; it is more like a list of his reactions to all the pictures in a large art gallery. I know very well that I have hardly ever uttered a sequence of words in public or committed it to a printer in the form which it had when I first framed it by talking to myself or writing on rough paper. Certainly I cannot use "and," "but," "as," an abstract noun, a participle, a relative or any punctuation mark without deliberate consideration and the exercise of a succession of aesthetic preferences, an exercise in which initial preferences are constantly discarded. I take it for granted that Lysias and people like him were more sensitive to the aesthetic aspects of communication than I am, not least because, whereas a scholar is primarily concerned with lucidity of exposition, an orator is primarily concerned with persuasion, to which calculated obscurity may sometimes contribute more than lucidity (depending on the facts of the case) and calculated roughness more than elegance (depending on the character created for the litigant). Therefore, although the preferences of an orator are ultimately determined by factors which neither he nor we can explain, it is unwise to assume that his choice on any given occasion is ever made unconsciously. In comparing two authors we must make the initial assumption that we are comparing their conscious and deliberate preferences, not their reflexes.[4] This initial assumption holds better for some authors than for others. Its validity decreases in inverse ratio to the time which a writer has at his disposal and to his own sensitivity; people who are tone deaf do not write music, nor do the colour-blind paint, but aesthetic indifference to language seems to impose no such restraint upon volume of utterance. The validity of the assumption is also dependent on the practicability of exercising choice. For example,

---

[4] We do not usually regard Polybios as much of a stylist, but even he apologises (xxxix.12.10 f.) for the fact that the scale and nature of his work make it hard for him on occasion to avoid describing similar situations in the same words.

when we find, by taking samples from two writers, A and B, in the same genre, that they differ consistently in respect of word length or sentence length, it might be unrealistic to suppose that each of them has paid conscious attention to the shape and size of every sentence, and it would certainly be unrealistic to imagine them as counting the letters in their words and discovering the mean length arithmetically. There are likely to be many occasions on which they exercise deliberate preferences for long or short sentences or words, and alter what they first wrote; but these occasions can be the surface manifestation of an unconscious current. In general, if statistical comparison of A and B reveals differences which have escaped the notice even of a scholar or connoisseur who in reading them has focussed his attention on their language, we are justified in believing that if B were trying to write like A, his imitation would not penetrate below a certain level, and his underlying individuality would be revealed by quantification. The same consideration would apply in reverse if A or B were trying to write in different styles. There is, of course, no guarantee that A and B will be found to differ in respect of the first criterion chosen, but experience suggests that if tests are made with a succession of criteria patience is eventually rewarded, and time spent on the initial choice of criteria is not wasted. No one who cares about a problem of ascription can afford to neglect stylometric tests of this kind; to perform them is boring, but exposition of the results of a month's boredom need not bore the reader for more than a few minutes, and the tester himself is sustained by the possibility of neat or even spectacular results. It is worth seeing whether the application of crude stylometry to the *corpus Lysiacum* can help us to isolate the individual Lysias.

Many tedious jobs which used to be done with paper and pencil, at much expense of human eyesight, are now done by computer. None of the tests described below has been done by computer (except one, which gave negative results), and I have to make excuses for pencil and paper, just as I would have to make excuses for cutting the lawn with scissors if a motor-mower were standing idle. There are some stylometric tasks of such a kind that the argument for mechanisation is simple and irrefutable: they cannot be done in any other way.[5] If, for example, I wanted to discover a writer's sensitivity to assonance by recording how often the same sequence of two, three, four or five phonemes is repeated within *n* following phonemes up to a given limit, I would not ask a human being to attempt to make this record. But although the computer is a godsend for many tasks, above all for the compilation of word indices and concordances, there are positive arguments for not mechanising tests which involve straightforward counting and calculation of percentages. One is the time required for the translation of print into perforated tape and for the construction of a programme: the calculation can sometimes be done more quickly with pencil and paper. Since the *corpus Lysiacum* has already been put onto tape, this argument does not apply to our present problem; but another, and more important, argument does apply. I believe that the one thing which is indispensable for the effective study of Greek literature is intimate familiarity with Greek texts—familiarity of such a kind that the student cannot open any text at random and read more than ten lines without being reminded of a second passage, in some other text, which is relevant, and therefore illuminating, in form or content. It is this kind of recollection which makes it possible to interpret literature without confinement to the paths trodden by previous commentators. It does not always come (and certainly it never comes to me) as a result of deliberate efforts at memorisation; it comes rather from the constant rereading of texts for different purposes, with different questions in mind. To recall the analogy of the scissors and the mower, I would certainly cut grass with scissors if I were interested in the ecology of a grass lawn and not solely in the aesthetic satisfaction of contemplating a neat green patch. If, therefore, I have performed stylometric tests in the hard old way, that is because I have counted the incidental gain. Only when the cost outweighs the gain and long labour adds little to one's own store is it time to transfer this

[5] Cf. Jacob Leed (ed.), *The Computer and Literary Style* (Kent, Ohio, 1966), especially the essay of L. T. Milic (72 ff., 79 ff.) on the possibilities for the study of syntactical structures and word classes.

labour to a computer and to stock an electronic memory instead of one's own.

I have deliberately restricted my use of the technical terminology of statistics, and this restriction too calls for an excuse; as a rule, the appearance of a conglomerate of imprecise words where one precise word would do is as much a blemish in philology and the history of literature as it would be in the physical sciences. My excuse is that I am posing questions of such a kind that answers offered in terms of "chi squared" and "standard error" cannot claim greater validity or utility than answers offered in terms of similarity and rank. If I said of five works, A–E, that in a given respect C is at the top, E at the bottom, and B and D closer to each other than either of them is to any of the other three, you might reasonably expect me to translate "top," "bottom" and "closer" into arithmetical terms, but the bearing of my statement would not be increased by elaboration above the level of simple arithmetic.[6] Here again principle is at stake. Uncomprehending hostility is not the only possible relation between "the two cultures"; it is sometimes offset by a servility which implies no less a

---

[6] An interesting illustration is afforded by D. R. Cox and L. Brandwood, *Journ. Royal Stat. Soc.*, Ser. B, xxi (1959), 195 ff. The authors examine the ordering of seven Platonic works—*Critias, Laws, Philebus, Politicus, Republic, Sophist* and *Timaeus*—by applying statistical technique to the percentage distribution of clausular rhythms in those works. The argument is as unintelligible to a classicist as a page of Greek would be to someone who has not learned the language. If, however, we ignore all of it, including "Π_0," "Π_1" and the "$\hat{s}_i$" column in table 1, look only at the rest of table 1 (where the percentage distributions are listed), remember that the distinction between short and long is no more likely to have been felt before a pause in prose than at the end of a verse in poetry, and rank the six works other than *Laws* in accordance with their likeness to *Laws*, we arrive at the order: *Rep., Ti., Crit., Sph., Plt., Phlb., Laws*. The authors' conclusion (p. 199) is, in fact: "The final ordering is *Rep., Tim., Soph., Crit., Pol., Phil., Laws*: there is reasonably strong evidence that *Tim.* is correctly placed before *Soph.*, but the position of *Crit.* could be anywhere between somewhat before *Tim.* to before *Pol.*." I should be sorry to seem ungrateful to Cox and Brandwood for their valuable presentation of data in table 1, but their article raises a question of urgency at a time when collaboration between philologists and statisticians is active: do conclusions reached by statistical techniques always and necessarily add anything to what is already perceptible to those who can operate with simple arithmetic, and may not circumstances arise in which statistical language proves to be an elaborate way of saying what can be said more briefly and simply?

failure to comprehend the nature of literary and historical studies. As I occasionally observe in linguists signs that they do not expect their subject to be taken seriously unless they adopt the terminology of physical science or mimic it by inventing a superfluous jargon, I avoid any more adoption or mimicry than is necessary.

The most important contributions made by the statistician to the stylometric issues which concern us in the *corpus Lysiacum* are essentially admonitory. He offers the benefit of logical demonstration when our common sense and experience do not suffice to deter us from treating a very small sample as if it were very large,[7] and he tells us something of which common sense gives us hardly a hint: how often a random sample can rationally be expected to diverge from the mean of all the random samples chosen from the same population, and by what function of the mean. This is important in so far (and only in so far) as the works tested constitute one population in respect of what is being measured; if, for example, I realise in composing one lecture that I have unconsciously become over-addicted to "but" and that I want to reduce its incidence, that lecture does not belong to the same population as my previous lectures in respect of "but." It is not hard to tell when an author is never linguistically self-conscious; but when he is generally or sometimes so, we cannot know *a priori* the extent, duration or direction of his self-consciousness, and this means that we cannot be sure that we are sampling from the same population. A special complication is that most writers who care at all how they express themselves are more or less sensitive to the attractions of variation in vocabulary or structure, but the incidence of this sensitivity too is unpredictable. It can be discovered, so long as we know on independent grounds that all our samples are taken from the work of one author; but it is precisely when we do not know this that we are most inclined to trust statistics to give us an answer, and the danger of circular argument becomes considerable.

[7] Büchler's use (p. 45) of the term "statistical" is not justified by the data which he has presented (41 ff.).

What criteria shall we choose? There are eight main sources of suggestion.

Simple observation through familiarity with Greek texts.

For those of us whose education has included much translation from English into Greek, recollection of the occasions on which we have hesitated between alternatives.

For those of us who have edited texts, recollection of the occasions on which we have found it impossible to make a rational choice between the variants presented by manuscripts of equal status.

Occasions on which an author appears to have used alternative ways of saying exactly the same thing, and we can neither express the difference in translation nor offer any convincing reason why he should not have made the opposite choice in each case.[8]

Alternatives specified by ancient critics, either in hypothetical examples or in the discussion of particular texts. The brief remarks of Demetrius *Eloc.* 256 on word order are an important example. Dionysios's detailed discussion (i.10.15–92.1) of Isok. xvii.6, 9, 11 and (i.97.10–107.18) his comparison of Isaios's prooemia with those of Lysias are exceptionally valuable for the alternative wordings which, he suggests, would have been less epideictic and more appropriate to forensic oratory (cf. Demetr. *Eloc.* 41).

Variations in recurrent formulae, which abound in documentary inscriptions and in certain forensic contexts.

Changes made when (as often happened in fourth-century oratory [cf. Dion. Hal. i.29.6–10]) an author borrowed a passage from another; the use of And. iii.3–9 by Aischines ii.172–176 is the most striking example.

Changes made when an author re-used a passage which he had originally composed for another occasion. The most extensive example of this practice is Demosthenes'

---

[8] Cf. Büchler, 32 ff., on variation between simple and compound verb (without apparent semantic distinction) within the same speech.

refurbishing of parts of the speech against Androtion (xxii.47–66, 69–73) for use against Androtion's associate Timokrates (xxiv.160–173, 176–181). The systematic adaptation of the passages to their new context distinguishes them clearly from post-Demosthenic interpolations such as the insertion of xxiv.174 and 182 after xxii.66 and 73.

From these sources the following criteria suggest themselves.

(1) The frequency of the definite article, which is the commonest word in Greek. Those who have tried to translate from English into the language of Plato know best how often one can be undecided whether to use it or not, and how many surprises Plato can spring on us if we have acquired too firm a faith in what we learned from grammar-books at school. No one has yet explained satisfactorily, and perhaps no one ever will, the principles underlying the presence or absence of the article with proper names. Add to this the contrasts ἃ γεγένηται/τὰ γεγενημένα (etc.) and ἡ τοῦ στρατηγοῦ οἰκία/ἡ οἰκία ἡ τοῦ στρατηγοῦ, and it is obvious that the potential difference between authors in the frequency of the article is very great. It is equally obvious, however, that where so many contrasting pairs exist, it would be possible for two authors to make opposite choices consistently in each pair and yet emerge with the same overall frequency of the article.

(2) The frequency of occurrence of the next commonest words, καί and δέ. Since it is easy to distinguish simple connective καί from adverbial and "prospective" καί and from particle complexes such as καίτοι and καὶ μὲν δή, it would seem sensible to make the distinction at the outset, and only the simple connective will be considered here for statistical purposes.[9]

(3) The ratio of participles to finite verbs and infinitives.[10] Dionysios, for example, suggests (i.90.21–91.3) that Isok. xvii.6, ἡγούμην δέ, εἰ μὲν προείμην τὰ χρήματα, κινδυνεύσειν, could have been expressed more simply and less artificially as ἡγούμην δὲ

[9] The statistics of (undifferentiated) καί in the *corpus Lysiacum* are presented by A. Q. Morton and J. McLeman, *Paul, the Man and the Myth* (London, 1966), 73 ff. and tables 21–23.

[10] Cf. Büchler, 49 f., on participles in forensic narrative.

παραδοὺς τὰ χρήματα κινδυνεύσειν. One of the most striking differences between the *Tetralogies* ascribed to Antiphon and his three speeches of normal forensic genre is the far higher ratio of participles to other verbal forms in the former.[11]

(4) The ratio of the aorist to the imperfective and perfective aspects. The possibilities of this criterion are suggested by Isok. xxi.5 μάλιστα συκοφαντεῖν οἱ λέγειν μὲν δεινοί, ἔχοντες δὲ μηδέν, τοὺς ἀδυνάτους μὲν εἰπεῖν, ἱκανοὺς δὲ χρήματα τελεῖν. Νικίας τοίνυν Εὐθύνου πλείω μὲν ἔχει, ἧττον δὲ δύναται λέγειν. Thucydides (vi.23.1) makes Nikias say, towards the end of his cautionary speech: ὅτι ἐλάχιστα τῇ τύχῃ παραδοὺς ἐμαυτὸν βούλομαι ἐκπλεῖν. In the following chapter (24.1), he speaks of Nikias as νομίζων ... μάλιστ᾽ ⟨ἂν⟩ οὕτως ἀσφαλῶς ἐκπλεῦσαι. Similarly in vii.34.7 f. he describes how both Corinthians and Athenians regarded themselves as victorious in naval battle fought near Patras; the Corinthians εὐθὺς τρόπαιον ἔστησαν ὡς νικῶντες and the Athenians ἔστησαν τρόπαιον καὶ αὐτοὶ ἐν τῇ Ἀχαΐᾳ ὡς νικήσαντες. It would be inaccurate to say that the aorist and imperfective aspects in these and similar examples are synonymous, for they express different ways of looking at events; but in so far as the author can look at an event either way, and express himself accordingly, they are as good as synonymous. This is even more obvious from Demosthenes' refurbishment in xxiv.216 of a sentiment which he had expressed in xx.154: "If everyone were to abstain from evil-doing, through fear of the penalties imposed by the law ..." In xx he says τὰς ἐν τοῖς νόμοις ζημίας φοβούμενοι, in xxiv τὰς βλάβας καὶ τὰς ζημίας τὰς ἐπὶ τούτοις κειμένας φοβηθέντες. Compare also xxii.53 ὃν οὐδ᾽ ὑπὲρ αὑτοῦ δίκην λαμβάνειν ἐᾷ τὰ πεπραγμένα καὶ βεβιωμένα with xxiv.165 ὃν οὐδ᾽ ὑπὲρ αὑτοῦ δίκην ἐᾷ λαβεῖν τὰ πεπραγμένα καὶ βεβιωμένα. Either the aorist or the imperfective aspect can be used in the formula with which witnesses are summoned (e.g., XIX.23 κάλει μοι Εὔνομον ~ XXI.10 κάλεσον δέ μοι καὶ Ναυσίμαχον), even within the same speech (e.g., Is. iii.53 ἀναγίγνωσκε αὐτοῖς ... ἀνάγνωθι δὴ καὶ τοὺς νόμους). φέρε, φερέτω and ἔνεγκε, ἐνεγκάτω are used indiscriminately in comic dialogue. The same phenomenon appears in the finite indicative

[11] Cf. K. J. Dover, *CQ* xliv (1950), 57.

tenses (e.g., in the Demosthenic adaptation, xxii.69 ἐπεσκεύασεν ~ xxiv.176 ἐπεσκευάκασιν, xxii.72 ἀντεπιγέγραφεν ~ xxiv.180 ἀντεπέγραψεν), but these tenses should be excluded for stylometric purposes unless the samples are extremely large, since the picture could easily be distorted by the preponderance of generalisation in the present tense in some samples and of simple narrative in others.

(5) Dem. xxii.53 λαμβάνειν ἐᾷ ~ xxiv.165 ἐᾷ λαβεῖν and Th. vii.34.7 τρόπαιον ἔστησαν ~ 34.8 ἔστησαν τρόπαιον, quoted above, illustrate change of word order in the re-use of a passage or phrase. Here too variation in formulae is striking; for instance, *IG.* ii^2.1283.9 f. (263/2) ὅπως ἂν οὖν φαίνωνται καὶ οἱ ὀργεῶνες ~ 1324.10 f. (s. II a.C.in.) ὅπως ἂν οὖν καὶ οἱ ὀργεῶνες φαίνωνται.[12] I have argued elsewhere that the determinants of word order in classical Greek prose are logical and lexical, not syntactical, and that the difference in certain works between observed and random order of subject, verb and object is epiphenomenal.[13] When logical and lexical determinants are not operative, we might expect that order will be "arbitrary," that is, determined by causes which are not accessible to us and may be merely habitual to an individual. Unfortunately for our present purposes, order is affected by genre and ethos, since the arrangement of syntactically identical ingredients in parallel members in the same order, in a different order, or in alternation between the same and different orders, is a function of conscious art.[14] There are, in my view, certain aspects of word order which have a claim on our attention as criteria of ascription; but they fall within the province of refined stylometry, not the crude stylometry with which I am now concerned, and I therefore defer them for the moment (p. 127).

(6) Sentence length has been extensively used as a criterion,[15] and its value is obvious when the samples are chosen from modern

---

[12] Cf. Dover, *Greek Word Order*, 1 f., 53, 58, and A. S. Henry, *CQ* N.S. xvi (1966), 296 f.
[13] Cf. Dover, *op. cit.* (n. 12), 65.
[14] Cf., *ibid.*, 68.
[15] Cf. W. C. Wake, *Journ. Royal Stat. Soc.*, Ser. A, cxx (1957), 331 ff.

108   Lysias and the *Corpus Lysiacum*

authors who use the same system of punctuation and may be presumed to have read the proofs of what they have published. In the case of a Greek author, "sentence" can be defined as "a sequence of words terminated by a full stop, colon or question mark in the text edited by A.B.C. and published by X.Y.Z. in the year *n*." This definition assumes editorial consistency, which is in general a reasonable assumption, but it is not beyond criticism. I have the soundest of reasons for asserting that an editor can be inconsistent: I myself vacillate between comma and colon at many places in the composition or edition of a passage of Greek; I may reverse within a day a choice which when taken seemed final and free from objection; and by comparing my final edition of an Aristophanic scene with a provisional edition which I made five years earlier I found that I had tended towards a higher proportion of colons and stops—that is, towards a shorter mean sentence length, on the definition of "sentence" offered above. I must not, of course, assume that other editors are necessarily so infirm of principle; but it strikes me that (for example) Burnet's punctuation of the last part of Agathon's speech in Plato's *Symposium* (197D1–E5) is not consistent with his treatment of a comparable passage in Diotima's myth of the birth of Eros (203D6–E5), and it could rationally be suggested that the observable difference in mean sentence length between samples from the *Anabasis* and samples from the *Hellenica* might be a datum relevant not to the life of Xenophon but to the life of E. C. Marchant.[16] It is theoretically possible that identity of mean sentence length between two works edited by the same person may be the product of different authorship and change in editor's practice. *A fortiori* I am unwilling to compare in respect of sentence length Greek authors edited by different people. Systematic repunctuation of all samples in accordance with the principles detectable in some Hellenistic

---

[16] The consistent difference in sentence length between *Hellenica* (including i–ii) and *Anabasis* was demonstrated, with a good distribution of samples, by N. D. Thomson, *A Computer Investigation of Stylometry, with Particular Reference to the Works of Xenophon* (Diss. St. Andrews, 1965). I do not in fact believe that Marchant's principles changed, or that Thomson's results are affected by such a factor, but I would expect anyone considering the results to raise the possibility.

copies of classical authors (e.g., *P. Lit. Lond.* 132, of Hypereides [see Kenyon's facsimile and C. H. Roberts, *Greek Literary Hands*, pl. 100*b*]) is hardly possible; there is too often room for doubt whether the space between two letters is a punctuating space or not, the shortness of the lines makes punctuation by spaces an inefficient system in any case, and differences between ancient and modern punctuation of the same passage are numerous enough to rob us of confidence in any attempt to apply ancient principles.[17] Moreover, the available fragments in which the application of ancient principles is apparent are later, sometimes by half a millennium or more, than the composition of the texts themselves; the earlier the material, the harder it becomes to understand such principles as are applied.[18]

It might be practicable, if enough people competent in Greek were interested, to re-punctuate a set of samples in accordance with rigorously defined syntactical and rhetorical principles on which they were all agreed, and after full discussion of doubtful cases. This exercise would be fruitful for the comparison of samples taken from works of closely similar character and purpose. The fact that since Bekker editors of the same prose text have substantially agreed on its punctuation is not of great importance, for some editors, instead of beginning their task with an unpunctuated transcript of a medieval manuscript and constantly reciting it aloud—acting it, in fact—until they have arrived at a system of punctuation which satisfies them, commonly begin with a cut-up copy of a previous edition; and this does not encourage reappraisal of punctuation.

There is one novel statistical procedure, based on sentence length, which is certainly (to my mind) of value in many types of literature. This is the "cumulative sum" ("cusum") technique,[19] in which we record the difference in length between the first

---

[17] *P. Oxy.*, plate vii (no. 2538), is interesting as not having space punctuation where we should expect to find it: col. iv, 5, 12, 17.

[18] *P. Hibeh* 14 (s. III a.C.) has some good examples of space punctuation.

[19] Cf. A. Q. Morton, *The Integrity of the Pauline Epistles* (Manchester Statistical Society, 1965), with acknowledgment to W. C. Wake.

sentence and the mean length of all sentences in the sample, and so on to the sum of the first n sentences and n times the mean. The resulting column or graph of positive and negative numbers displays the pattern of the sample in respect of convergence on, and divergence from, its own mean sentence length. I have carried out this exercise on the *Erotikos* incorporated in the *Phaedrus*, Sokrates' reply to it (*Phdr.* 237B7–238C4, 238D8–241D1), Agathon's speech in the *Symposium* and Gorgias's *Helen*. I was able to punctuate all four samples at one session, settling doubtful sentences in any one sample by comparing them with similar sentences in the other samples. The result showed that Sokrates' speech and Agathon's speech are more alike in pattern than are Sokrates' speech and the *Erotikos* or Agathon's and the *Helen*. This may be regarded as slightly favouring the hypothesis that the *Erotikos* is not a parody composed by Plato; but in the absence of any other extant παίγνιον ascribed to Lysias one cannot put the matter more strongly. I have examined cusum charts for the forensic speeches based on Hude's punctuation, but I am not willing to derive any arguments from such patterns as are discernible. Considering that forensic speeches vary greatly in respect of the ratio and position of narrative ingredients, it was perhaps overoptimistic to expect enlightenment from the cusum procedure for this particular genre.

No one can determine *a priori* the size of samples needed for stylometric tests. We have to discover experimentally the minimum size which reveals consistent differences between works which are known on independent grounds to be by different authors.

The two longest of the extant forensic speeches ascribed to Lysias are XII and XIII. In the Budé edition XII has 610 lines and XIII has 596. If we subtract from XII the passage of question and answer in §25 we reduce it to 604 lines, and this makes the two speeches virtually equal. The halfway point in XII falls at ὑπὲρ ἑαυτῶν γιγνομένας in §51, and the halfway point in XIII at σωθῆναι in §52. This division gives us four samples, each of approximately 300 lines. Each half of each speech contains about 600 verbs, of which 250–300 are not indicatives.

Now, Demosthenes xviii and xix and Aischines ii and iii are each very much longer. Since Dem. xviii and Aischines iii are opposing speeches in the same case, we may treat them as exactly contemporary, and the same applies to Dem. xix and Aischines ii. If we take the first and the last 300 Budé lines, the first and last 600 verbs and the first and last 300 non-indicative verbs of each of these speeches, we can see what variation in respect of a given criterion is possible within one speech, and by adding together two samples from one speech to make a single sample we can see also what variation is possible between two speeches of the same author when the sample is as large as the largest available from the corpusculum.

Equipollent variants in a text of which there are only two primary medieval manuscripts (e.g., Antiphon, and Andokides iii–iv)[20] remind us that some errors must remain for ever unsuspected by editors in a text, such as our corpusculum, which depends on one medieval manuscript. The relation between the medieval texts and fragmentary ancient texts of a classical prose author suggests, however, that in respect of crude stylometric tests the margin of error is small. Whatever modern editor's text I have used, I have not hesitated on occasion to disagree with it and to delete a word which the editor has added or liberate from square brackets what he has condemned. Sometimes, no doubt, he was right and I am wrong.

Allowance must also be made for my own errors in counting. By repeating the same count at intervals I have convicted myself of some carelessness, but at the same time satisfied myself that I have not been so careless as to affect the issue.

I do not think that the total margin of error arising from textual corruption, mistaken editorial judgment and careless counting exceeds two percent, and no one's opinion on a question of ascription will (I hope) be affected by a difference of that order in a stylometric text.

[20] E.g., Ant. iv.β.1, where γέγονεν and ἐγένετο are variants.

112   Lysias and the *Corpus Lysiacum*

1. Frequency of ὁ

	300-line samples	600-line samples
389	Ais. iii (A)	
335		(av.) Ais. iii (A+B)
330	Ais. ii (B)	
324		(av.) Ais. ii (A+B)
317	Ais. ii (A)	
312	Dem. xviii (B)	
301	Dem. xix (A)	
299		(av.) Dem. xviii (A+B)
297	XIII (A)	
285	Dem. xviii (A)	
280	Ais. iii (B)	(av.) Dem. xix (A+B)
260		(av.) XIII (A+B)
258	Dem. xix (B), XII (B)	
253		(av.) XII (A+B)
248	XII (A)	
223	XIII (B)	

2. Frequency of simple connective καί

	300-line samples	600-line samples
142	Dem. xviii (B)	
141	Dem. xix (A)	
137	Ais. ii (A)	
135		(av.) Ais. ii (A+B)
132	Ais. ii (B)	
131		(av.) Dem. xviii (A+B)
124		(av.) Dem. xix (A+B)
119	Dem. xviii (A)	
109	Ais. iii (A)	
107	Dem. xix (B)	
101	XII (B)	
100		(av.) Ais. iii (A+B)
94	XIII (A)	
92		(av.) XIII (A+B)
91	Ais. iii (B)	
89	XIII (B)	
85		(av.) XII (A+B)
69	XII (A)	

3. Frequency of δέ

	300-line samples	600-line samples
87	XII (A)	
83		(av.) XII (A+B)
80	Ais. ii (A)	

Crude Stylometry   113

79	XII (B)	
78		(av.) Ais. ii (A+B)
75	Ais. ii (B)	
69	XIII (B)	(av.) XIII (A+B)
68	XIII (A)	
64	Ais. iii (A)	
62	Dem. xix (B)	
61		(av.) Ais. iii (A+B)
60	Dem. xviii (A)	
57	Ais. iii (B)	(av.) Dem. xix (A+B)
54		(av.) Dem. xviii (A+B)
52	Dem. xix (A)	
43	Dem. xviii (B)	

4. Participles as percentage of all verbal forms

	(c.) 600-verb samples	(c.) 1,200-verb samples
36	Ais. ii (B)	
33	Dem. xviii (B), XII (B)	(av.) Ais ii (A+B)
31	Ais. ii (A), Ais. iii (B)	(av.) Dem. xviii (A+B)
30		(av.) Ais. iii (A+B), XII (A+B)
29	Dem. xix (A), Ais. iii (A)	
28	Dem. xviii (A), XII (A)	
26		(av.) Dem. xix (A+B)
23	XIII (A)	
22	Dem. xix (B)	(av.) XIII (A+B)
21	XIII (B)	

5. Aorists as percentage of all non-indicative aorist, imperfective and perfective verbal forms

	(c.) 300-verb samples	(c.) 600-verb samples
44	XIII (B)	
43		(av.) XIII (A+B)
42	Ais. ii (A), Ais. ii (B), XIII (A)	(av.) Ais. ii (A+B)
41	Dem. xix (B)	
36	Dem. xviii (A)	(av.) Dem. xix (A+B)
35	XII (B)	(av.) XII (A+B)
34	Ais. iii (B), XII (A)	
31		(av.) Dem. xviii (A+B)
30	Dem. xix (A)	(av.) Ais. iii (A+B)
26	Ais. iii (A)	
25	Dem. xviii (B)	

Lysias and the *Corpus Lysiacum*

We see from these tables:

In all five tables two samples from the same speech can differ by more than either of them differs from a sample belonging to another speech. In particular, in tables 1, 3 and 5 the two speeches of Aischines differ by more than either of them differs from the nearest speech of Demosthenes, and in table 4 the two speeches of Demosthenes differ by more than either of them differs from the nearest speech of Aischines.

In table 2, XII and XIII are neighbours, but the difference between them is greater than the difference between Dem. xviii and Aischines ii.

Only in table 1 do the six speeches arrange themselves in the order Aischines iii, Aischines ii, Dem. xviii, Dem. xix, XIII, XII. But here there is much greater disparity between the two halves of XIII than between XIII (A) and any of the 300-line samples from Demosthenes and Aischines except Aischines iii (A), and even if this were not so it would be difficult to argue for anything more than a difference between the first and third quarters of the fourth century. The predominant (not necessarily universal) linguistic characteristics of a period or stage of culture constitute a real phenomenon which must not be by-passed through eagerness to establish individual authorship (cf. p. 93).

Since there are only two other speeches in the corpusculum which exceed half the length of XII or XIII—VI, which is just over 50 percent their length, and XIX, which is just over 60 percent—I have not judged it profitable to apply crude stylometric tests to any of them.

VII

Refined Stylometry

Vocabulary

The purpose of examining the vocabulary of the corpus is to discover the likeness and unlikeness of each speech to XII in respect of (*a*) the number of non-forensic words (as defined on p. 64) which it contains in proportion to its length, and (*b*) the particular types of non-forensic word which are concentrated in it. We are bound to take our bearings from XII, because it is the only landmark we have, and if we lose sight of it we go round in circles.

For comparison with XII, I deduct from every speech (including XII) words which denote material objects (natural or manufactured), properties of material objects or activities and functions which relate solely to such objects. I also deduct words which may reasonably be regarded as technical terms in so far as they refer to administrative, ceremonial, legal, commercial and military functions or family relationships. Since there is room for disagreement about the classification of some words, I list under each speech all the words which I have deducted for purposes of comparison. Each reader is likely to transfer a few words from one category to another, and must modify my figures accordingly. Some words are included which are closely related to "deductible" words but are so formed that the speaker had the opportunity to

116   Lysias and the *Corpus Lysiacum*

avoid their use without modification of his meaning,—for instance, διαδίκασμα (XVII.10).

The non-forensic words in the *Epitaphios, Olympikos* and VI have already been cited (pp. 64, 80). In arriving at a total of 24 non-forensic words in XII (p. 67), the following have been deducted: ἀμφίθυρος (§12), δαρεικός (§19), ἑλικτήρ (§19), ἐξώλεια (§10), ἐπαρᾶσθαι (§10), ἔφορος (§43), κιβωτός (§10), κλεισίον (§18), κόσμος (§19 = "jewellery"), κυζικηνός (§11), οἰκοδομεῖν (§63), ὅμηρος (§68), οὖς (§19), παράσπονδος (§74), πρόβουλος (§65: with reference to the special magistracy instituted in 413/412), προσκεφάλαιον (§18), χαλκός (§19).

I: εἴσοδος	(§20)	
μοιχεία	(§36)	And. iv. 10, Isok. xi. 38
οἰκονόμος	(§7)	
παροινία	(§45)	
πολυπραγμοσύνη	(§16)	Isok. xiii.20
πρεσβῦτις	(§15)	
διπλοῦς	(§9)	
μεστός	(§17)	*Epit.* 37
φειδωλός	(§7)	
χείριστος	(§2)	*Epit.* 77
διακονεῖν	(§16)	
δυσκολαίνειν	(§11)	
ἐμπίπτειν	(§18)	Isok. x.52
ἐπεγείρειν	(§23)	
ἐπιτηρεῖν	(§8)	
καταισχύνειν	(§49)	
μετιέναι	(§37)	
πειρᾶν	(§12)	
περιάγειν	(§25)	
περιστρέφειν	(§27)	
συνεθίζειν	(§10)	
ὑποπέμπειν	(§15)	
ἐπίτηδες	(§11)	
κάτω	(§9)	*Epit.* 7

Refined Stylometry 117

Total, 24. Deducted: ἀνδρωνῖτις (§9), αὔλειος (§17), γυμνός (§24), δάμαρ (§30), δᾷς (§24), δύεσθαι (§22), ἐνάπτεσθαι (§14), ἐνεδρεύεσθαι (§49), ἐφέλκεσθαι (§13: of locking a door), θηλάζειν (§9), κλῖμαξ (§9), λούειν (§9), λύχνος (§14), μέταυλος (§17), μυλών (§18), σιδήριον (§42), σίδηρος (§27), τιτθός (§10), ὑπερῷον (§22), ψιμυθιοῦν (§14), ψοφεῖν (§14).

III: θρασύτης   (§45)
     μέθη   (§18)
     παιδιά   (§43: παιδιῶν Laur. 57.4, παιδικῶν Pal.)

     ἄκοσμος   (§45: ἀκοσμότατος Emperius; κοσμιώτα-
                    τος [Pal.] is nonsense)

     ἀπαράσκευος   (§33)
     ἄφιλος   (§18)   Epit. 73
     περιβόητος   (§30)
     ἀπομάχεσθαι   (§25)
     βάλλειν   (§8)
     ἐκκαλεῖν   (§8)
     ἐκπηδᾶν   (§12)
     ἐνίστασθαι   (§8)
     ἐπιδιώκειν   (§35: in Is. fr. 157 = "prosecute for a
                    second time" [Poll. viii.67])

     κράζειν   (§15)
     παροινεῖν   (§19)
     συνεισπίπτειν (§15)
     συνεξαμαρτάνειν (§12)

Total, 17. Deducted: ἀριστᾶν (§11), γναφεύς (§16), ἕλκος (§41), μέτωπον (§8), πανστρατιᾷ (§45), τέγος (§11).

IV: βαρυδαιμονία   (§9)
    λύσις   (§13)
    δυσέρως   (§8)
    εὔκολος   (§9)
    ὀξύχειρ   (§8)
    πάροινος   (§8)
    ἀποκινδυνεύειν (§7)

Lysias and the *Corpus Lysiacum*

παροξύνειν (§8)
περιφέρειν (§9)
συναλλάττειν (§2)

Total, 10. Deducted: ἀπολαγχάνειν (§3), αὐλητρίς (§7), ἐγχειρίδιον (§6), πύξ (§6), ὑπώπιον (§9).

V: None

VII: ἄερκτος (§28)
ἀλόγιστος (§12)
ἄπρακτος (§6)
ἐπαίτιος (§39)
κάτοπτος (§28)
μέτοχος (§7)
πολυτελής (§31)
σῶος (§17)

ἀπελέγχειν (§2)
ἀπομισθοῦν (§9)
ἀποτολμᾶν (§28)
ἐκμισθοῦν (§4)
ἐκτέμνειν (§19)
ἐξήκειν (§11)
ἐξορύττειν (§26)
ἐπεργάζεσθαι (§24)
περιοικεῖν (§28)

ἀμφοτέρωθεν (§28)
κυκλόθεν (§28)

Total, 19. Deducted: ἄμπελος (§14), βοηλάτης (§19), γνώμων (§25), δασύς (§7), δένδρον (§28), ἐπιμελητής (§29), μορία (§7), πρέμνον (§19), πυρκαϊά (§24), σηκός (§5).

VIII: ὁμιλία (§6)
σόφισμα (§8)
ἀπόθετος (§17)
ἐλευθέριος (§16)

ἀντιπράττειν (§11)
ἐπεγκαλεῖν (§1)

Refined Stylometry 119

  κακολογεῖν (§5)
  ξυνθεωρεῖν (§5)
  ὁμιλεῖν (§8)
  ὑπερευδοκιμεῖν (§7)

Total, 10.

IX: δικαίωσις (§8)

  ἀστράτευτος (§15)
  παράλογος (§10)
  συνήθης (§18)

  ἐννοεῖν (§7)
  ἐπικρύπτεσθαι (§18)
  κατολιγωρεῖν (§16)
  μεταπείθειν (§7) Isok. xi.34
  παραμελεῖν (§1)
  πλημμελεῖν (§10)
  σχολάζειν (§14)
  ὑποτοπεῖσθαι (§4)

Total, 12. Deducted: ἀρχεῖον (§9), διωμοσία (§11), λεύκωμα (§6), προπέρυσιν (§4), συνέδριον (§10).

X: μαλακία (§11)
  ῥαθυμία (§11)

  ἀνελεύθερος (§2)
  ἔννους (§20)
  ἐξαίρετος (§3) And. iii.7
  σιδηροῦς (§20: metaphorical)
  σύμφυτος (§28)
  φιλόδικος (§2)

  ἐπαναγιγνώσκειν (§18)
  κατασκεδαννύναι (§23: κατασκέδασται Brulart; κατεσκεύασται Pal.)
  μελετᾶν (§9) Isok. xi.15

Total, 11. Deducted: ἀνδραποδιστής (§10), ἐκδύεσθαι (§9), ζυγόν (§18), μητραλοίας (§8), πατραλοίας (§8), and words cited from archaic laws.

XIII: ἀγώνισμα (§77)
κατασκαφή (§8)
κραυγή (§71) *Epit.* 38

ἀκλεής (§45)
ἀνόμοιος (§58) Isok. xiii.13
μιαρός (§77)
σύσκηνος (§79)

ὁποιοστισοῦν (§11)
τοιουτοσί (§61)

ἀμφιεννύναι (§40)
ἀνιέναι (§93)
ἀποσφάττειν (§78)
διαιρεῖν (§9) Isok. xi.15
ἐλαττοῦν (§9)
ἐπαρκεῖν (§93)
καταμηνύειν (§49)
κατατάττειν (§79)
παραδέχεσθαι (§86)
παρορμίζειν (§25)
προσαπογράφειν (§56)
συναπιέναι (§52)
συσσιτεῖν (§79)
ὑποφαίνεσθαι (§19)

ἐντευθενί (§67)

Total, 24. Deducted: ἀποτυμπανίζειν (§78), βάθρον (§37), δήμιος (§56), θέατρον (§32), κακοῦργος (§78), κόραξ (§81), λιμήν (§34), μάχαιρα (§87), παραφρυκτωρεύεσθαι (§67), πύλη (§81), ταξιαρχεῖν (§7).

XIV: ἀναφανής (§11)
ἄνηβος (§25)
ἀρεστός (§15)
δειλός (§44)
ἐπιφανής (§12) Isok. xi.28
ἀκοσμεῖν (§12)
ἀναλογίζεσθαι (§47)

Refined Stylometry 121

  ἀτακτεῖν (§18)
  εἰσηγεῖσθαι (§35)
  κατακυβεύειν (§27)
  καταποντίζειν (§27)
  ὀπίσω (§5)
  πλεονάκις (§30)

Total, 13. Deducted: ἀέτωμα (§25), ἐξοστρακίζειν (§39), νῆσος (§30), στρατοπεδεύεσθαι (§7).

 XVI: ἀκολασία (§11)
  ἀναδύεσθαι (§15: metaphorical)
  ἀναπράττειν (§6)
  ἀποχωρίζειν (§6)
  ἐνθνῇσκειν (§15)

Total, 5. Deducted: ἀκληρωτί (§16), κύβοι (§11), σανίδιον (§6), φρουρά (§8), φύλαρχος (§7).

 XVII: ἀκρίβεια (§6)
  διαδίκασμα (§10)
  εὔγνωστος (§4)
  περιττός (§7)
  ἐκδικάζειν (§5) Middle in Is. fr. 77 (BS)
  ὁρίζεσθαι (§6) Active in Is. fr. 27
  ἑτέρωθεν (§4)

Total, 7. Deducted: ἀποκηρύττειν (§7), ἀστικός (§3), διαδικασία (§1).

 XVIII: εὐδαιμονία (§23) Isok. xi.14, xiii.4
  πρόσφατος (§19)

Total, 2. Deducted: ξένια (§12).

 XIX: βοήθεια (§21)
  σύλληψις (§7)
  ἀρχαιόπλουτος (§49)
  πολλαπλάσιος (§44)
  σύμμικτος (§27)
  σῶς (§36)

ἀφαρπάζειν (§31)
καταχορηγεῖν (§42: Reiske; καὶ ἐχο-Pal.)
καταχρῆσθαι (§22: = "misuse" in Is. vi.56)
προαναλίσκειν (§57)
προσδανείζειν (§26)
προσδεῖσθαι (§21)
προσλογίζεσθαι (§44)
συνεκδιδόναι (§59)
χρᾶν (§22: = "lend")
ἐφεξῆς (§52)

Total, 16. Deducted: ἀγγεῖον (§31), ἀπόστολος (§21), ἔκπλους (§55), ἤπειρος (§25), θύρωμα (§31), πελταστής (§43), πρέσβεις (§21), χωρίδιον (§28).

XX: παιδεία (§11)
συλλογή (§26) Apparently in a different sense (Harp.) in Is. fr. 103 (BS)
φόβος (§8) *Epit.* 39; Isok. x.25, xi.25
ἄπολις (§35)
ὠφέλιμος (§23) *Phormis.* 4; Isok. x.24
ἀνασῴζειν (§24)
ἐκκλέπτειν (§7)
καταπροδιδόναι (§6)
νεωτερίζειν (§16)
συστρατεύεσθαι (§29)

Total, 10. Deducted: καταδρομή (§28), καταλογεύς (§13), ὅρκιον (§26), ποιμαίνειν (§11).

XXI: ἀνάθεσις (§2)
δωροδοκία (§21) And. iv.30
ἐπίπονος (§19) *Epit.* 16; Isok x.11
ἁμιλλᾶσθαι (§5) And. iv.27
διαδύεσθαι (§12: metaphorical)
περιάπτειν (§24)

Total, 6. Deducted: ἀγένειος (§4), κυβερνήτης (§10), κυκλικός (§2), κωμῳδοί (§4), πλήρωμα (§10), ὑπηρεσία (§10).

XXII: κακόνοια (§16)
ἀνεκτός (§20)
τίμιος (§8)
ὁποσοστισοῦν (§15)
ἀναρπάζειν (§15)

Total, 5. Deducted: ἀγορανόμος (§16), σιτοπώλης (§1), σιτοφύλαξ (§16), συνωνεῖσθαι (§5), φορμός (§5).

XXIII: βιαιότης (§11) And. iv.10
διαμνημονεύειν (§16)

Total, 2. Deducted: ἀντιγραφή (§10), δημοτεύειν (§2), τυρός (§6), χλωρός (§6).

XXIV: ῥώμη (§5) *Epit.* 80
ὑβριστής (§15) And. iv.14
ἄγριος (§7: metaphorical)
δείλαιος (§43)
ἐλεήμων (§7)
πολυπράγμων (§24)
φιλαπεχθήμων (§24)
ἀντιδιδόναι (§9)
ἀπέχειν (§20) Isok. xi.32, xiii.2
κωμῳδεῖν (§18: metaphorical)
προβαίνειν (§16)
ἀμοῦ (§20: cj. Bekker, ἄλλου Pal.)

Total, 12. Deducted: ἀστράβη (§11), βακτηρία (§12), γλάμων (§25), ἱππική (§10), μυροπωλεῖον (§20), ὀχεῖν (§12), σκυτοτομεῖον (§20).

XXV: σύμβουλος (§27)
δημοκρατικός (§8)
ἐπιλύεσθαι (§33)
καταγγέλλειν (§30)
κατανοεῖν (§34)
ὁσάκις (§9)

Total, 6.

XXVI: δοκιμαστής   (§16)
ἡσυχιότης   (§5)
μισοδημία   (§21)
ὀρφανία   (§12)

διακλέπτειν   (§3)
ἐπισύρειν   (§3)
καθήκειν   (§12)
λωβᾶσθαι   (§9)
προσενθυμεῖσθαι   (§13)

Total, 9. Deducted: αἰχμάλωτος (§24), ἅρμα (§10), αὔριον (§6), ἱππαρχεῖν (§20).

XXVII: κολαστής   (§3)
μισθοφορά   (§1)
ἐνδεῖν   (§2)
καταδωροδοκεῖν   (§3)

Total, 4.

XXVIII: κόλαξ   (§4)   Isok. x.57

ὁμογνώμων   (§17)
ἀντιλαμβάνειν   (§15)
ἐμπιμπλάναι   (§6)

Total, 4. Deducted: πρόξενος (§1), πρώην (§9).

XXIX: None.

Deducted: καταχειροτονεῖν (§2), μεσεγγυᾶν (§6).

XXX: διοίκησις   (§22)
εὐτέλεια   (§21)

καταπειρᾶν   (§34)
μισοπονηρεῖν   (§35)
περικαταρρεῖν   (§22)
συστασιάζειν   (§11)
ἐπάν   (§33: ἐάν Contius)

Total, 7. Deducted: ἀναγραφεύς (§2), κύρβις (§17), νεώσοικος

(§22), νομοθεσία (§35), συγγραφή (§17), σύλη (§22), ὑπογραμματεύς (§27), ὑπογραμματεύειν (§29).

XXXI: ἀδυναμία (§16)
εὐτύχημα (§9)
ἑκούσιος (§10) *Erot.* 233c
ἐξοικεῖν (§9)
μεταπορεύεσθαι (§2)
συσκευάζειν (§9)
ταλαιπωρεῖν (§12)
ὑπερμισεῖν (§19)

Total, 8. Deducted: ὁπλίζειν (§15), συντιμᾶν (§31).

XXXII: διοίκισις (§14)
πτωχεία (§10)
παμπληθής (§22)
ἀναπέμπειν (§8)
ἀποστέλλειν (§25) Isok. x.27, xi.7
διοικίζειν (§14)
διπλασιάζειν (§12)
φθέγγεσθαι (§18) Isok. x.13, xi.48

Total, 8. Deducted: ἀνυπόδητος (§16), ἀρνίον (§21), ἀρρηφορία (§5), ὁλκάς (§25), παιδαγωγός (§28), στρῶμα (§16), ὑπόδημα (§20).

If we possessed the first quarter of XII only, and calculated from this how many non-forensic words we should find in it (after the necessary deductions) if we had the whole speech, the answer would be 36; from the first half, 28; and from the first three quarters, 20. Since the actual number is 24, it is obvious that the number of non-forensic words in a speech much less than half the length of XII does not afford a firm basis of comparison unless it is a remarkably large number. It appears from the following table that the speeches which differ significantly from XII in respect of non-forensic vocabulary (on VI, a special case, see p. 80) are I, IV, VII, VIII, IX, X, XVII and XXIV, and (for its paucity of such words) XVIII.

A few speeches are characterised by the prominence of certain

126 Lysias and the *Corpus Lysiacum*

Speech	Length as proportion of XII	Number of non-forensic words	Projection to scale of XII	Ratio of non-forensic vocabulary to that of XII
I	0.47	24	51	2.1
III	0.44	17	31	1.3
IV	0.18	10	56	2.3
V	0.05	0	0	0
VII	0.4	19	48	2
VIII	0.2	10	50	2.1
IX	0.18	13	72	3
X	0.27	11	41	1.7
XIII	1	24	24	1
XIV	0.49	13	27	1.3
XVI	0.24	5	21	0.9
XVII	0.12	7	67	2.8
XVIII	0.28	2	7	0.3
XIX	0.62	16	26	1.2
XX	0.36	10	28	1.3
XXI	0.26	6	23	1
XXII	0.23	5	22	0.9
XXIII	0.16	2	13	0.5
XXIV	0.28	12	43	1.8
XXV	0.42	6	14	0.6
XXVI	0.28	9	32	1.3
XXVII	0.15	4	27	1.1
XXVIII	0.19	4	21	0.9
XXIX	0.14	0	0	0
XXX	0.39	7	16	0.7
XXXI	0.35	8	23	1
XXXII	0.35	8	23	1

types of word, which may be explained as "caprice" of the type described on p. 88:

VII contains an exceptionally high proportion of rare adjectives, four of which end in -τος (cf. X.3 ἐξαίρετος and X.28 σύμφυτος), which are not exemplified in the non-forensic vocabulary of XII.

XIII not only contains ἐντευθενί and τοιουτοσί, but has sixteen examples of οὑτοσί, which occurs only twice in XII (§§ 26, 79) and 22 times in the rest of the corpus.

XIV has two adjectives in -ής: ἀναφανής and ἐπιφανής.

XXIV has three adjectives in -μων: ἐλεήμων, πολυπράγμων and φιλαπεχθήμων.

Word order

Lexical rules of order require a division of Greek words into "prepositives," which never (or only under limited and strictly defined conditions) end a clause; "postpositives," which never begin a clause; and "mobiles," which are not subject to either limitation.[1] Any attempt to formulate general rules about postpositives in early Attic oratory will lead us into a morass, because no two of the commoner postpositives can be comprehended under the same set of rules; for example, ἄν is attracted by the simple negative, whereas αὐτόν is repelled, and the history of καί μοι ... is not the same as the history of καὶ αὐτῷ ... [2] I therefore confine myself to two postpositives, and treat them separately: ἄν, and anaphoric αὐτόν in all oblique cases.

Logical generalisations about word order require the classification of the mobiles of any actual sentence as "nuclei" and "concomitants," in the light of the relation of that sentence to its context.[3] Four words nearly always have concomitant status:

(1, 2) εἶναι and γίγνεσθαι with an adjectival predicate. The test of concomitant status is the possibility of omission without impairment of communication, and this criterion is easily satisfied in the case of εἶναι, by confrontation of similar passages, as—

XIX.13: ὅτι δ' οὐ χρημάτων ἕνεκα, ῥᾴδιον γνῶναι ἐκ τοῦ βίου παντός

~ XXXI.20: ἐξ ὧν δέ ... διεπράξατο τεκμαιρομένοις ῥᾴδιόν ἐστιν ὑμῖν γνῶναι.

I include γίγνεσθαι with εἶναι not because we should expect them to behave alike in respect of order but because it is observable that they do. There is room for disagreement and hesitation on the definition of "adjectival predicate," and I have made some decisions which may be regarded as arbitrary; I have included

[1] Cf. p. 62, n. 5.
[2] I owe this (and much other) information on postpositives to Mr. M. H. B. Marshall (University of Glasgow).
[3] Cf. p. 107.

participles, the word εἰκός, the adverb ἐμποδών ("felt," if I may say so, as an adjective), φίλος and ἐχθρός, but have excluded such words as φονεύς and μηνυτής and predicates in which an adjective and a substantive are combined (e.g., ἀνὴρ ἀγαθός) while accepting those in which a substantive depends on an adjective (e.g., ἄξιος πολλοῦ).

An example from another author will show the kind of thing we may expect to find. The opening section of the first *Tetralogy* of Antiphon (ii.α.1) reads:

ὁπόσα μὲν τῶν πραγμάτων ὑπὸ τῶν ἐπιτυχόντων ἐπιβουλεύεται, οὐ χαλεπὰ ἐλέγχεσθαί ἐστιν· ἂν δ' οἱ ἱκανῶς μὲν πεφυκότες, ἔμπειροι δὲ τῶν πραγμάτων ὄντες, ἐν δὲ τούτῳ τῆς ἡλικίας καθεστηκότες, ἐν ᾧ κράτιστοι φρονεῖν αὐτῶν εἰσί, πράσσωσι, χαλεποὶ καὶ γνωσθῆναι καὶ ἐλεγχθῆναί εἰσιν.

We have here three examples of the verb εἶναι, a predicative adjective, and an infinitive dependent on the adjective, arranged in the order: adjective, infinitive, εἶναι. There are no less than seventeen examples of this arrangement in the *Tetralogies* (ii.α.1*ter*, β.2, 7, γ.1; iii.β.10, 11, γ.8*bis*, 10*bis*, δ.2; iv.β.2, 3, 7, δ.7), but in the rest of Antiphon there are none. If we list all the differences between the *Tetralogies* and Antiphon I–V–VI in respect of shape of sentence and type of word, differences among which hardly any one could be conceived as consequent on any other, the sum total of the passages cited may be contemptibly small in the eyes of the statistician, and yet they present as cogent evidence of separate authorship as we are ever likely to find in Greek literature.

(3) ἔχειν with an abstract object (especially γνώμη, συγγνώμη and words of similar meaning). The test of concomitant status here is the frequency with which ἔχειν immediately follows its object, almost as if converting the noun into a *verbum denominativum*. Cf. *Epit.* 64:

οὔτ' ἐλαττοῦσθαι δυνάμενοι οὔτ' αὐτοὶ πλέον ἔχειν δεόμενοι.

(4). The early orators make great use of ποιεῖσθαι. In Isokrates

Refined Stylometry 129

xx we find two examples of the arrangement: predicative adjective + ποιεῖσθαι + article and object:

§5: μείζους ποιοῦμαι τοὺς λόγους
§19: ἐλάττους ποιεῖσθαι τὰς τιμωρίας.

We do not find precisely this phrasing elsewhere in early oratory except in Isok. x, the epideictic *Encomium on Helen*:

§66: τοιαύτας ποιεῖσθαι τὰς ἀπαρχάς
§24: ὠφελιμωτέρους καὶ τοῖς Ἕλλησιν οἰκειοτέρους ποιήσασθαι τοὺς κινδύνους

and in Isok. xi, the epideictic *Busiris*:

§46: τοιαύτας ὑπὲρ τῶν ἄλλων ποιεῖσθαι τὰς ἀπολογίας.

If we rise one step from sub-species, and take in all sentences containing

$$\left.\begin{array}{r}\text{adjective}\\ \text{adverb}\\ \text{prepositional phrase}\end{array}\right\} + \text{ποιεῖσθαι} + \left\{\begin{array}{l}\text{noun}\\ \text{article} + \text{noun}\end{array}\right.$$

we find that the distribution of this type is extremely uneven. There are no examples in Antiphon, and only one in Andokides (i.10); 10 in the *corpus Lysiacum*, spread over eight speeches (2 each in XXII [§§1, 13] and the fragmentary V [§§3, 4], none in XII); 12 in Isokrates (i.10, 23; vii.43; viii.22, 40; x.24, 66; xi.20, 44, 46; xx.5, 19). This is a distribution with ragged edges, and in isolation its probative value for the problem of ascription is small; but when a number of equally ragged distributions are imposed upon the map of early Attic oratory we begin to see the same kind of concentrations as we see when we superimpose isoglosses on the map of a region.

I confine myself in the first instance to the forensic speeches of the corpus, and defer the epideictic speeches for separate consideration. I take XII as the standard, as before, and I seek to discover the extent to which each other speech resembles or differs from XII in respect of the limited number of criteria examined. What is of particular interest is the "odd man out"—the speech which shows a concentration of separate differences not only from XII but from the rest of the corpus and even (as may on occasion happen) from early Attic oratory as a whole.

In respect of word order, the classification made in some lexica to the orators, according to the tense and mood which ἄν accompanies,[4] is of no significance at all, except in that when ἄν occurs in a relative clause with the subjunctive it is invariably attached to the relative; examples of this usage are of no interest to us now, because they admit of no alternative. Our primary classification must be:

1. Clauses containing a negative
2. Clauses containing an interrogative
3. Clauses containing neither

I exclude elliptical expressions, such as ὥσπερ ἂν εἰ..., or πῶς γὰρ ἄν as a complete clause, where no alternative position is open; for the same reason I exclude clauses containing only one mobile.

(1) ἄν is attached to the negative throughout XII, with the exception of §37, as we have seen (p. 90).

(2) ἄν is attached to the interrogative in two passages of XII, as very commonly in Greek prose:

§34: θαυμάζω δὲ τί ἄν ποτ' ἐποίησας συνειπών
§82: τί γὰρ ἂν παθόντες δίκην τὴν ἀξίαν εἴησαν τῶν ἔργων δεδωκότες;

Of the two exceptions to the general usage, one is §52, εἰ γὰρ ὑπὲρ τῶν ἀδικουμένων ἐστασίαζον (sc., Eratosthenes and his associates in 404, as they allege) ποῦ κάλλιον ἂν ἦν ἀνδρὶ ἄρχοντι ἢ Θρασυβούλου Φυλὴν κατειληφότος, τότε ἐπιδείξασθαι τὴν αὐτοῦ εὔνοιαν, where ἄν was deleted by Baiter on grounds of sense, not syntax; but it is not absolutely precluded by the sense. Cf. §48, where the MS. has χρῆν ἂν πρῶτον μὲν μὴ παρανόμως ἄρχειν: ἄν is not normally found with χρῆν in the sense "it would have been right...," and Bekker emended it to αὐτόν. In the other exception, §83, πότερον

[4] Only Van Cleef's *Index Antiphonteus* (Ithaca, N.Y., 1895) records the position of ἄν within the clause.

Refined Stylometry

εἰ..., ἱκανὴν ἂν τοῦ φόνου δίκην λάβοιμεν, a subordinate clause intervenes immediately after the interrogative word.

(3, a) ἄν is not attached to a prepositive anywhere in XII. It does not occur in a positive relative clause except in §92 (see c below), where sense precludes its attachment to the relative. (b) The predominant position of ἄν in XII is after the first mobile of a clause, as in

§29: ἴσως ἂν εἰκότως αὐτῷ συγγνώμην εἴχετε
§54: ἡγούμενοι δικαίως ἄν ... μισεῖσθαι[5]
§63: καίτοι σφόδρ' ἂν αὐτὸν οἶμαι ... προσποιεῖσθαι
§98: αὐτοὶ μὲν ἂν δείσαντες ἐφεύγετε.

Compare §§30, 31, 50, 78, 83, 84, 92. (c) The remaining instances exhibit adaptation of this principle to clauses which are divided into "cola" by antithesis.[6]

§88: καίτοι οὗτοι μὲν ⋮ σωθέντες ⋮ πάλιν ἂν δύναιντο τὴν πόλιν ἀπολέσαι· | ἐκεῖνοι δέ, ⋮ οὕς ... ⋮ πέρα ἔχουσι (Ctr. §98 above).
§98: οἱ δὲ παῖδες ὑμῶν, ⋮ ὅσοι μὲν ἐνθάδε ἦσαν, ⋮ ὑπὸ τούτων ἂν ὑβρίζοντο, | οἱ δ' (⋮) ἐπὶ ξένης ⋮ μικρῶν ἂν ἕνεκα συμβολαίων ἐδούλευον.

Compare §§22, 47, 92, 93.

The sole example of postponement of ἄν not explicable on any of the principles considered here is §37 (cf. p. 90), ... δίκην δοῦναι δύναιντ' ἄν.

The speeches which show interesting differences from XII in respect of ἄν are:

I.1: οἱοίπερ ἂν ὑμῖν αὐτοῖς εἴητε.
Here ἄν follows the relative, as in IV.12, VIII.7, XIX.50, XX.23, XXV.2.

IV.12: ὅσον ἂν ἐγένετο σημεῖον.
Cf. I.1.

VIII.4: καὶ γὰρ ἂν ἀπολύοιμι τῆς αἰτίας ὑμᾶς.

---

[5] Not without occasional misgivings, I place a clause boundary after ἡγούμενος, ἐπιστάμενος, νομίσας, etc., in utterances of this type.

[6] Cf. p. 69, n. 10.

Attachment of ἄν to καί, as in XXIV.8, XXIX.9, XXXI.22; contrast XXVIII.3.

VIII.7: ὁπόθεν ἂν εἰκότως ὑπερείδετε τὴν ἐμὴν ὁμιλία
Cf. I.1.

X.12: οὐκ οὖν ἄτοπον ἂν εἴη.
Here ἄν does not immediately follow the negative, but there may be several determinants of its position: the common sequence ἂν εἴη, the emotive force of ἄτοπον (cf. VII.41, πάντων γὰρ ἀθλιώτατος ἂν γενοίμην, but ctr. XX.15), and the presence of οὖν.

XIII.28: ἔπειτα οὐ πατρίδ' ἂν σαυτοῦ ἀπέλιπες.

XIII.51: οὐδενὶ τρόπῳ δύναιτ' ἂν ἀποδεῖξαι.
In the last two examples the separation of ἄν from the negative is not easily explicable, unless in §51 the optative of δύνασθαι attracts ἄν (cf. XII.37).

XIII.3: καὶ ποιοῦσι ταῦτα νομίζω ἡμῖν καὶ παρὰ θεῶν καὶ παρ' ἀνθρώπων ἄμεινον ἂν γίγνεσθαι.

XIII.11: νομίζων, : εἰ ..., : ἀσμένως ὁποιαντινοῦν ἐθελῆσαι ἂν εἰρήνην ποιήσασθαι.

XIII.74: πότερον οὖν δοκοῦσιν ὑμῖν οἱ τριάκοντα ..., : οἵ ..., : ἀφεῖναι ἂν λαβόντες τὸν Φρύνιχον ἀποκτείναντα, ἢ κτλ.
Not one of these three examples is completely different in kind from XII.37; but there are three of them, in addition to the two abnormalities in negative clauses.

XVIII.3: ὧν καθ' ἓν ἕκαστον πολὺ ἂν ἔργον εἴη λέγειν.

XIX.30: ἀλλ' οὐδ' οἱ πάλαι πλούσιοι δοκοῦντες εἶναι ἄξια λόγου ἔχοιεν ἂν ἐξενεγκεῖν.

XIX.49: οὐ γὰρ ὑπό γ' ἐκείνων ἐξελεγχθεῖεν ἄν.

XIX.60: οὐδ' ἂν εἰς λάθοι πονηρὸς ὤν.
Cf. XXIV.24; ctr. οὐδεὶς ἄν in XVI.12 and XXII.17 and οὐδεμίαν ἄν in VII.20.

XIX.61: οὐδὲ (adverb) δύο τάλαντα λάβοιτ' ἄν.
Ctr. XXX.20, καὶ τρία τάλαντ' ἂν περιεγένετο τῇ πόλει.

XIX.30: ... τοιαῦτα ⟨ἃ⟩ κτησάμενοι εἰς τὸν λοιπὸν χρόνον ἡδονὴν ἂν παρέχοι.

XIX.50: οἷον ἂν ἐγένετο.
Cf. I.1.
As in the case of XIII, what matters is the accumulation of six passages in which XIX is unlike XII; there are five others (§§8, 24, 44, 60, 61) in which ἄν immediately follows a negative.

XX.9: ὥςτε οὐκ ἂν ῥᾳδίως μετέστη ἂν ὑμῖν ἡ πολιτεία.

XX.15: πῶς ἂν οὖν οὐκ ἂν δεινὰ πάσχοιμεν.
These are the only examples of the repetition of ἄν in the corpus.

XX.4: διὰ τὰ πρόσθεν ἁμαρτήματα αὐτοῦ ἕνεκ' ἂν ἔπραττε.
No division into two cola is imposed by any antithetical point.

XX.23: ὡς ἂν τῇ πόλει ὠφελιμώτατοι εἶμεν.
Cf. I.1.

XXII.17: νῦν δὲ πῶς οὐ δεινὰ ἂν δόξαιτε ποιεῖν, εἰ ...
Cf. on X.12.

XXII.18: καίτοι πῶς ἂν οὐ θαυμαστὸν εἴη, εἰ ...
Cf. XX.15.

XXIV.24: ἀλλ' οὐδ' ἂν εἷς ἀποδείξειεν.
Cf. XIX.60.

XXIV.8: καὶ γὰρ ἂν ἄτοπον εἴη, ὦ βουλή, εἰ ...
Cf. VIII.4.

XXIV.9: δοκεῖ δέ μοι τῆς πενίας τῆς ἐμῆς τὸ μέγεθος ὁ κατήγορος ἂν ἐπιδεῖξαι σαφέστατα μόνος ἀνθρώπων.

XXV.2: οἷόσπερ ἂν ἐγένετο.

XXV.12: ἀνθ' ἧστινος ἂν προθυμούμενος ... ἐπεθύμουν.

XXV.30: τούτων δ' ἄξιον θαυμάζειν, ὅτι ἂν ἐποίησεν, εἰ ...
Cf. I.1; but note that three examples of the attachment of ἄν to a relative occur in this one speech, XXV.

XXVI.17: ὁποῖοι δ' ἄν τινες ἐν ὀλιγαρχίᾳ γένοιντο.
Cf. I.1.

XXVIII.13: οὐδὲ (conjunction) ἀδίκως τούτοις φημὶ ἂν εἶναι ὑπόλογον τὴν ἐκείνων φυγήν.

XXIX.9: καὶ γὰρ ἂν καὶ δεινὸν εἴη[7].
Cf. VIII.4.

XXIX.11 = XXIX.9.[8]

XXXI.6: οὗτοι δηλοί εἰσιν ὅτι ἂν παρέντες τὸ τῆς πόλεως κοινὸν ἀγαθὸν ἐπὶ τὸ ἑαυτῷ ἴδιον κέρδος ἔλθοιεν.
Cf. I.1; but ἄν is nowhere else immediately attached to illative ὅτι; hence κἄν cj. Dryander.

XXXI.22: ἐνόμιζε τοῦτον κἂν ἀπὸ τεθνεώσης φέρειν ἑαυτῆς.
This is the only speech in the corpus to exhibit καί + ἄν (as distinct from καί + ἄν).

In fourth-century Attic oratory αὐτόν is rarely if ever attached to the simple negative, to connective ἤ, or to connective or adverbial ἀλλά, καί, οὐδέ, οὔτε, μηδέ or μήτε.[9] Accordingly no alternative positions are open in XII.82 καὶ τοὺς παῖδας αὐτῶν and §87 καὶ τοὺς συνάρχοντας αὐτοῦ, any more than in §47 κατεμαρτύρουν ἂν αὐτῶν or §65 καὶ ὁ μὲν πατὴρ αὐτοῦ : τῶν προβούλων ὢν : ταῦτ' ἔπραττεν.

(1) The earliest position which αὐτόν takes in XII is that in which it immediately follows a relative. There are four examples:

§7: ἵν' αὐτοῖς ᾖ
§27: ὡς αὐτῷ προσετάχθη
§29: ὑφ' ἧς αὐτῷ προσετάττετο
§81: καὶ μεθ' ὧν αὐτῷ ταῦτα πέπρακται.

(2, a) It does not, however, necessarily follow the relative, as we see from:

§2: ἥτις ἦν αὐτοῖς

[7] The remarkable combination καὶ γαρ (...) καί is found also in Dem. xix.267, but is not the subject of separate treatment by Denniston.

[8] Cf. p. 88 and the threefold occurrence of πάντων ἂν εἴη δεινότατον in Is. i (§§38, 43, 51), an expression absent from other speeches ascribed to Isaios.

[9] Cf. p. 127, n. 2.

Refined Stylometry 135

§16: ὅτι Ἐρατοσθένης αὐτόν ... λαβών
§34: ὡς οὐκ ἀπήγαγεν αὐτόν
§39: ἐπεὶ κελεύετ' αὐτὸν ἀποδεῖξαι
§50: ὅτι ἐκεῖνά τ' αὐτῷ ἤρεσκε
§72: ἵνα μήτε ῥήτωρ αὐτοῖς μηδεὶς ἐναντιοῖτο
§74: ὅτι οὐδὲν αὐτῷ μέλοι.

(2, *b*) Examples in which αὐτόν follows the leading mobile word of the clause number 18:

§1: τοιαῦτα αὐτοῖς τὸ μέγεθος καὶ τοσαῦτα τὸ πλῆθος εἴργασται
§§7: ἔδοξεν οὖν αὐτοῖς : δέκα συλλαβεῖν
§18: ἀλλὰ κλεισίον μισθωσάμενοι : προύθεντο αὐτόν.

Cf. §§11, 14, 24, 38, 48, 50, 56, 58, 63, 76, 78, 86 *bis*, 89, 100. The following may be regarded as approximating to these.

(3, *a*) Those in which the two leading words are closely linked with each other:

§29: ἴσως ἂν εἰκότως αὐτῷ συγγνώμην εἴχετε
§43: τὸν μὲν τοίνυν μεταξὺ βίον αὐτοῦ παρήσω
§52: καὶ μιᾷ ψήφῳ αὐτῶν ἁπάντων θάνατον κατεψηφίσατο
§77: πολλὰς πίστεις αὐτῷ ἔργῳ δεδωκώς
§80: μηδ' ὧν φασι μέλλειν πράξειν : πλείω χάριν αὐτοῖς ἴστε.

(3, *b*) Those in which the leading word is marked off as antithetical, so that αὐτόν follows the leading mobile of the second colon:

§22: ἐγὼ δ' : ἐβουλόμην ἂν αὐτοὺς ἀληθῆ λέγειν.
Cf. §23 (νῦν δέ).

(3, *c*) Two in which the leading element is separated from the rest of its own clause by a subordinate clause or its equivalent:

§53: οἱ μὲν γὰρ ἐκ Πειραιῶς : κρείττους ὄντες : εἴασαν αὐτοὺς ἀπελθεῖν.
Cf. §63.

In one passage αὐτῶν is partitive, and an early position would have been semantically confusing:

§86: ἀλλ' οὐχ ὑπὲρ ὑμῶν οὐδεὶς αὐτῶν οὐδὲ τὰ δίκαια πώποτε ἐπεχείρησεν εἰπεῖν.

(4, a) There remain six abnormalities:

§27: καὶ μὴν οὐδὲ τοῦτο εἰκὸς αὐτῷ πιστεύειν
§69: ὅμως ἐπετρέψατ' αὐτῷ πατρίδα
§89: οὐκ οἴονται χρῆναι αὐτὸν ἀπολέσθαι.

§27 and §89 may be influenced by χρῆν αὐτόν..., ἔδοξεν αὐτῷ... and similar expressions, and in §27 it is possible that οὐδὲ τοῦτο has affinities with (3, b). In §69 ὅμως may be a colon or, alternatively, may be treated as akin to such words as adverbial οὐδέ.

(4, b) No such explanation can be offered for the remaining three abnormalities:

(i) §34: εἰ καὶ ἀδελφοὶ ὄντες ἐτυγχάνετ' αὐτοῦ
(ii) §14: ἡγεῖτο γὰρ ἅπαν ποιήσειν αὐτόν
§62: πυνθάνομαι δὲ ταῦτ' ἀπολογήσεσθαι αὐτόν.

In those speeches which have at least half as many examples of αὐτόν as XII (and the total varies greatly according to the nature of the proceedings, not simply with the length of the speech) the ratio of those which belong to category (2, b) is much the same, viz.: XII, 17 out of 43; III, 12 out of 32; VI, 9 out of 24; XIII, 30 out of 63, XIV, 14 out of 35; XXVI, 9 out of 25; XXXII, 11 out of 33. Certain categories appear, however, which are not represented in XII, and certain others which are not entirely alien to XII appear in striking concentrations. In I there are four relative clauses in which αὐτόν is placed after the second (or a later) mobile:

§21: ἐπειδὴ δὲ πάντα εἴρητο αὐτῇ
§33: ἀνθ' ὧν ὁ τὸν νόμον τιθεὶς θάνατον αὐτοῖς ἐποίησε τὴν ζημίαν
§39: καὶ ἐπειδὴ καλῶς εἶχεν αὐτῷ
   (Ctr. §23 ἐπειδὴ δὲ καλῶς αὐτῷ εἶχεν)[10]
§46: εἴπερ ἀδίκως ἐπεθύμουν αὐτὸν ἀπολέσαι.

[10] It must be remembered that καὶ ἐπειδή and ἐπειδὴ δέ start off a clause, as it were, on different feet, and the placing of a postpositive is determined by the shape and rhythm of the clause as a whole, not by the meanings and syntactical functions of the individual words when the clause is artificially dismembered.

Refined Stylometry 137

IV.4 is unique in presenting αὐτόν before the article-participle complex which governs it: ὅτι ἡμεῖς ἦμεν αὐτὸν οἱ κριτὴν ἐμβαλόντες.

In VI.37 αὐτοῦ is divested of its normal postpositive character by its position immediately after a subordinate clause (cf. on VII.34 below):

οἴεται πολλοὺς ὑμῶν, δεδιότας μὴ λύσητε τὰς συνθήκας, αὐτοῦ ἀποψηφιεῖσθαι.

Possibly αὐτοῦ here = "him himself"—him as opposed to the "other Athenians," as in the opening sentence of the section.

VII.34 has an example of the same category, though less striking:

μάρτυρας γὰρ ἔχων αὐτῷ προσῆλθον.

(Ctr. I.12, 25; III.15, 22; VI.45; XIII.55. The choice is avoided in XII, but cf. §10 ὤμοσεν τὸ τάλαντον λαβὼν με σώσειν.)[11]

X is distinguished by the regularity with which αὐτόν is placed after a verbal phrase of which the second element is a concomitant, as in I.39, not (as in, for instance, I.23; XIII.4–9, 81, 82, 95; XXX.16) between nucleus and concomitant:

§2: συγγνώμην ἂν εἶχον αὐτῷ τῶν εἰρημένων
§22: ἐλάττονος δ' οὔσης αὐτῷ τῆς συμφορᾶς
§25: κρεῖττον δ' ἦν αὐτῷ τότε ἀποθανεῖν
§28: τί γὰρ ἂν τούτου ἀνιαρότερον γένοιτ' αὐτῷ;

XIII has four instances (as against one [§74] in XII) of αὐτόν immediately following οὐδείς (cf. I.36, III.26, XIV.9, XXVI.20 [οὐδέποτε]):

§15: οὐδεὶς γὰρ αὐτοῖς τούτων
§31: οὐδεμιᾶς αὐτῷ ἀνάγκης οὔσης
§33: καὶ οὐδ' ὑφ' ἑνὸς αὐτὸν προσήκει ἐλεεῖσθαι
§82: οὐδεὶς γὰρ αὐτῷ διελέγετο.
   Cf. §79: ἀλλ' ὥσπερ ἀλιτηρίῳ οὐδεὶς ἀνθρώπων αὐτῷ διελέγετο.

XIV is distinguished by an exceptionally high concentration of

[11] Cf. Dover, 15.

138   Lysias and the *Corpus Lysiacum*

examples of "postponed" αὐτόν for which the reasons adduced in (3) and (4, a) above do not account:

§1: οὐδὲν ἧττον προσήκει ἐκ τῶν ἄλλων ἐπιτηδευμάτων ἐχθρὸν αὐτὸν ἡγεῖσθαι

§2: πειράσομαι ὑπὲρ πάντων τῶν πεπραγμένων μεθ' ὑμῶν αὐτὸν τιμωρήσασθαι

§7: ἡγοῦμαι δέ, ὦ ἄνδρες δικασταί, ὅλῳ τῷ νόμῳ μόνον αὐτὸν ... ἔνοχον εἶναι

§8: ἐγὼ δ' ἡγοῦμαι διὰ τοῦθ' ὑμᾶς δικαίως ἂν αὐτῷ ὀργίζεσθαι

§16: ἡγοῦμαι δέ, ὦ ἄνδρες δικασταί, περὶ μὲν τοῦ νόμου καὶ αὐτοῦ τοῦ πράγματος οὐχ ἕξειν αὐτοὺς ὅτι λέξουσιν

§17: ἐπειδὴ δέ ..., διὰ τὸν πατέρα ἐλεεῖν αὐτὸν ἀξιώσετε

§35: ἀλλ' ὅμως τοσούτων συμφορῶν καὶ οὕτως αὐτῷ μεγάλων ὑπαρχουσῶν ...

It will be observed that §16 is divisible into cola, and §§1, 2, 4, 7, 8 and 17 treat an adverbial phrase as a colon.

XIX.6 resembles VII.34:

πεπαυμένοι γὰρ τῆς ὀργῆς αὐτῶν ἀκροᾶσθε.

XX.14 is unique in placing αὐτόν immediately after ἀλλά:

ἀλλ' αὐτὸν ἠνάγκαζον, ἐπιβολὰς ἐπιβάλλοντες.

It also differs from other speeches of the corpus in postponing partitive αὐτῶν and separating it from the antithetical element:

§1: οἱ μὲν γὰρ ἐπιβουλεύοντες ἦσαν αὐτῶν

§9: τοὺς μὲν γὰρ ἐξήλαυνον αὐτῶν, τοὺς δ' ἀπεκτίννυσαν.

These two clauses resemble in shape the type in which the first colon is antithetical and αὐτῶν follows the leading mobile of the second colon (XII.22, 23); but contrast XIII.63 οἱ δ' αὐτῶν περιγενόμενοι καὶ σωθέντες, οὓς κτλ and XIV.41 οὐχ οἱ μὲν πολλοὶ αὐτῶν ἡταιρήκασιν;

XXII.3 resembles VII.34:

ἀναστὰς αὐτῶν κατηγόρουν.

XXVI.16 is unique, but similar to XX.14:

καίτοι γ' αὐτὸν ἀκούω λέξειν.

(Ctr. XII.63: III.22, XIV.8, XXIX.7.)

Refined Stylometry

XXVI is also marked by the fact that out of six examples of αὐτόν in a relative protasis five are immediately attached to the relative:

§3: εἴ τις αὐτὸν ἐᾷ
§5: ὅτ' αὐτὸν οὐκ ἔξεστιν ἀσελγαίνειν
§6: ἐὰν αὐτὸν ἀποδοκιμάσητε
§13: ἐν οἷς αὐτῶν πολλοὶ ... ἀπήγοντο
§21: ὃς αὐτῷ ἀπολογήσεται.

Contrast only §24.

XXXII shows the opposite characteristic; there are eight instances of αὐτόν in a relative clause, and seven of the eight are separated by one mobile from the relative:

§4: ἥπερ ἦν αὐτῷ μόνη
§8: ὧν ὁ ἀνὴρ αὐτῆς ἔδωκεν
§9: ὅτι καταλίποι αὐτοῖς
§16: ἃ <ὁ> πατὴρ αὐτοῖς κατέλιπον
§22: ἵνα γράμματ' αὐτοῖς ... ἀποδείξειεν
§26: εἰ ὁ λόγος αὐτῷ εἴη
§27: περὶ ὧν οὐδεὶς αὐτῷ σύνοιδεν.

Contrast only §22.

εἶναι and γίγνεσθαι occur with a simple adjectival or participial predicate 64 times in XII. Except that they do not begin a clause, the shape of the clause as a whole and the number of mobiles in it are not relevant to their position. In no less than 50 instances the verb follows the predicate immediately, or is separated from it only by a postpositive. It makes no difference whether the predicate is positive or negative.

	Adjectives	Participles
Positive:	1, 9, 9, 14, 15, 15, 21, 24, 31, 32, 38, 44, 44, 48, 49, 50, 50, 53, 57, 58, 59, 59, 59, 63, 63, 65, 65, 67, 67, 70, 77, 78, 78, 79, 79, 86, 87, 90, 94, 97, 97	§§ 22, 27, 27, 38, 53, 64
Negative:	§§ 20, 45, 49, 84	

In a further eight examples the verb is separated from the adjective only by words which have concomitant status:

§14: ἐπιτήδειος μέν μοι τυγχάνεις ὤν
§36: οὐχ οἷοί τ' ἔφασαν εἶναι
§40: βεβαιοτέραν ἐνόμιζον εἶναι
§49: εὖνοί φασιν εἶναι
§51: ἐχθρὰν ἐνόμιζον εἶναι
§87: εὐήθεις νομίζοντες ὑμᾶς εἶναι
§89: πολὺ ῥᾷον ἡγοῦμαι εἶναι
§93: εὔνους ᾤοντο εἶναι.

In §66 the predicate is complex:

προτέρους αὐτοῦ γιγνομένους.

In §64 the separation is more elaborate:

πολλῶν ἀγαθῶν αἰτίου ἀλλ' οὐ μεγάλων κακῶν γεγενημένου.

We are left with four cases of inversion (out of 64):

(a) §15: εἰ Θέογνις εἴη πεπεισμένος
    §32: εἴπερ ἦσθα χρηστός
(b) §22: καὶ εἰς τοσοῦτόν εἰσι τόλμης ἀφιγμένοι
    §82: τί γὰρ ἂν παθόντες δίκην τὴν ἀξίαν εἴησαν τῶν ἔργων δεδωκότες;

In the other speeches the attachment of εἶναι and γιγνεσθαι to the adjectival predicate is normal, but the following concentrations of abnormality occur.

(1) Inversion:

I: 5 out of 34:

§7: πασῶν ἦν βελτίστη
§18: ὅτι ἐγὼ πάντα εἴην πεπυσμένος
§29: τόν ... νόμον ἠξίουν εἶναι κυριώτερον
§40: πότερον ἦν μοι κρεῖττον
§45: εἰ μὴ τὸ μέγιστον τῶν ἀδικημάτων ἢ ὑπ' αὐτοῦ ἠδικημένος.

III: 4 out of 31:

§5: εὖ ποιῶν αὐτὸν ἠξίουν εἶναί μοι φίλον
§22: εἴπερ ἦν ταῦτ' ἀληθῆ

§36: ἡγοῦμαι πᾶσιν εἶναι δῆλον
§41: τίς γὰρ οὕτως ἐστὶν εὐηθής;

VII: 4 out of 36:
   §5: εἰ γὰρ μὴ δι' ἡμᾶς εἰσιν ἠφανισμέναι
   §20: ἐν τούτῳ τῷ τρόπῳ ἦσθ' ἄν με τετιμωρημένος
   §24: πολὺ ἦν ἀσφαλέστερον
   (Cf. I.7, 18)
   §39: <οἱ> τοιοῦτοί εἰσιν ἐπαιτιώτατοι καὶ ἀπορώτατοι τῶν κινδύνων.

VIII: 3 out of 11:
   §2: τοὺς δοκοῦντας εἶναι φίλους
   §11: εἰ γάρ ... μηδὲν ἦν δίκαιον εἰπεῖν
   §16: ... προφασιζόμενοι τότε μὲν ἐκ τῆς ... συνουσίας ἐστὲ φανεροί.

XIV: 5 out of 47:
   §2: ὡς ἔσται τοῦ λοιποῦ βελτίων
   §10: οὕτω γὰρ ἦσαν παρεσκευασμένοι
   §12: οὐδεὶς ἔσται τῶν ἄλλων βελτίων
   §33: ὡς τῶν αὐτῶν ὄντας ἀξίους
   §35: βουλόμενος εἶναι πονηρός.

XIX: 6 out of 30:
   §13: γεγονότας τ' ἐπιεικεῖς
   §23: οὐχ ἃ ἦν δυνατὸς πάντα παρασχόντα
   §23: ὡς τοίνυν ταῦτ' ἐστὶν ἀληθῆ
   §32: ἥτις ἐστὶ μεγίστη τοῖς ἀνθρώποις
   §36: καὶ τὰ ἐκεῖ ὁμοίως σφίσιν εἶναι σᾶ   (Cobet: ἴσα cod.)
   §61: εἰ γὰρ μὴ ἦν τοιοῦτος.

XXV: 7 out of 33:
   §8: ὅτι οὐδείς ἐστιν ἀνθρώπων φύσει οὔτε ὀλιγαρχικὸς οὔτε δημοτικός
   §10: ὅπως ἦσαν ἐν τῇ δημοκρατίᾳ πεπολιτευμένοι
   §20: καὶ ἡ πόλις ἔσται μεγίστη
   §23: οὐδὲν γὰρ ἂν εἴη αὐτοῖς χαλεπώτερον τούτων
   §25: δημοσίᾳ δὲ ὄντας μεγίστων κακῶν αἰτίους

142 Lysias and the *Corpus Lysiacum*

§31: καὶ τοσούτων κακῶν καὶ ἑτέρων πολλῶν ὄντες αἴτιοι
§34: μὴ δοκοῦντες εἶναι πονηροί.

(2) Separation.

I include here only those passages which are comparable with XII.64, and exclude those, like XII.66, with a rudimentary type of complex predicate.

VI: 6 out of 41:

§3: ἀδύνατον δὲ καὶ ὑμῖν ἐστι
§21: καὶ εἴ τις τοιοῦτος ἕτερός ἐστιν
(τις ... ἕτερος is subject)
§31: ἡ δὲ οὐσία αὐτοῦ ἐλάττων ἐκ τῶν κινδύνων γίγνεται
§32: ἥμισυς ὁ βίος βιῶναι κρείττων ἀλύπως ἐστὶν ἢ διπλάσιος λυπουμένῳ
§53: ὡς ἐν τούτων οὗτός ἐστι
§54: ἵνα ... σωφρονέστεροι οἱ ἄλλοι ὦσιν.

XIII: 7 out of 53:

§23: ὁρῶντες τὰ πράγματα οὐχ οἷα βέλτιστα ἐν τῇ πόλει ὄντα
§33: ἁπάντων τῶν κακῶν αἴτιος τῇ πόλει ἐγένετο
§52: ὧν μὴ οἷόν τε γενέσθαι ἐστὶν ὑπερβολήν
§54: οὐκ ἄξιοι ἐδόκουν τοῖς τριάκοντα σωτηρίας εἶναι
§57: αἴτιος ἐκείνῳ ἐστὶ τοῦ θανάτου
§80: οὕτω τολμηρὸς καὶ ἐκεῖ ἐγένετο
§94: ὁμόψηφοι κατ' ἐκείνων τῶν ἀνδρῶν τοῖς τριάκοντα γενήσονται.

XXVI: 4 out of 22:

§2: αἴτιοι δὲ τούτων ὑμεῖς ἐστέ
§2: ὧν εἷς οὗτος ὢν (cf. VI. 53) οὐκ ἀγαπᾷ
§6: ἄθυτα τὰ πάτρια ἱερὰ γίγνεται
§6: ἡ γὰρ αὔριον ἡμέρα μόνη λοιπὴ τοῦ ἐνιαυτοῦ ἐστίν.

XXXI: 5 out of 37:

§5: μεγάλα τὰ διαφέροντά ἐστιν
§5: διὰ τὸ ἀναγκαῖον σφίσιν αὐτοῖς ἡγεῖσθαι εἶναι
§18: ἀδύνατοι τῇ πόλει βοηθεῖν ἦσαν
§24: δεινὸν γὰρ ἔγωγε δοκεῖ εἶναι
§30: ἵν' ἀγαθοὶ προθυμῶνται γίγνεσθαι.

Refined Stylometry 143

(3) XX deserves mention in that, although only a third the length of XII, it has almost as many (58) occurrences of εἶναι and γίγνεσθαι with adjectival predicates; their distribution in types is essentially the same as in XII, 47 being attached to the predicate.

(4) XXI also deserves mention in that, out of a total of 18 instances, there is only one abnormality, and that a passage of peculiar structure:

§15: εὔχεσθαι τοὺς ἄλλους εἶναι τοιούτους πολίτας ("... that my fellow-citizens should be of my character.")

When ἔχειν governs an abstract object in XII, it is normally attached directly to the object:

§20: μεγάλων ἀδικημάτων ὀργὴν ἔχοντες
§24: τοιαύτην γὰρ γνώμην ἔχω.
Cf. §§29, 31, 50, 53, 90.

The only exception is:

§35: τίνα γνώμην περὶ τούτων ἕξετε.

In the other speeches, when γνώμη, ἐλπίς or συγγνώμη is the object of ἔχειν, the verb is normally attached directly: I.36, 47; III.19; VI.14; VII.12, 23, 36; X.2, 21, 26, 30; XIV.11; XVI.5, 11, 17, 21; XVIII.20; XIX.56; XXI.19, 25; XXII,21; XXV.1, 1, 3, 15, 17, 21, 21, 22, 29, 35; XXVI.10, 16; XXVII.3; XXVIII.2, 12; XXIX.5; XXXI.11. Occasionally, as in XII.35, a dative or a prepositional phrase intervenes: I.1, III.21, XIII.46, XXII.19, XXVI.14, XXVII.7, XXVIII.3.

Different types of intervening element are found only in:

VI.5: καὶ τίνα γνώμην οἴεσθε ἕξειν τοὺς μύστας
XXVI.18: τὴν αὐτὴν γνώμην ἅπαντες ἔσχον.

VI.5 may be compared with sentences such as XII.36 (p. 140), and XXVI.18 with (for example) III.21 τὴν αὐτὴν γνώμην ἐμοὶ ἔχειν. A more important abnormality is inversion:

XXIV.14: τὴν αὐτὴν ἔχετε γνώμην.
Cf. §1 οὐκ ἔχων πρόφασιν, §21 τὴν αὐτὴν ἔχειν περὶ ἐμοῦ διάνοιαν (ctr. §3 ἐξ ἴσου ... τὴν διάνοιαν ἕξω and I.3 τὴν

αὐτὴν διάνοιαν ἔχειν), §27 ἔξω τὴν χάριν (ctr. §1 χάριν ἔχειν, XVI.1 χάριν εἶχον).

XXV.20: τὴν αὐτὴν κατελθόντες περὶ αὐτοῦ ἔχετε γνώμην

In XXV these uses of ἔχειν are more numerous than in any other speech, so that occasional variation of order is almost inevitable (cf. p. 131). I therefore regard only XXIV as significantly different from XII.

Expressions of the group περὶ πολλοῦ (πλείστου, οὐδενός, etc.) ποιεῖσθαι are more often than not undivided.

XII.7: λαμβάνειν δὲ χρήματα περὶ πολλοῦ ἐποιοῦντο.

So too: I.1; VI.16, 24; VII.25, 26; VIII.4; IX.16, 18; XIV.40; XVIII.13, 15; XXI.6, 25; XXIII.5; XXVIII.11; XXXI.7, 18; XXXII.2, 13.

The exceptions are:

I.26: ὃν ... περὶ ἐλάττονος τῶν ἡδονῶν ἐποιήσω
XXIX.3: τίνα δὲ Ἐργοκλῆς περὶ πλέονος Φιλοκράτους ἐποιεῖτο
IV.8: ἡ δὲ τοτὲ μὲν ἐμὲ περὶ πολλοῦ, τοτὲ δὲ τοῦτόν φησι ποιεῖσθαι
IV.17: πολὺ γὰρ περὶ πλέονος τοῦτον ἢ ἐμὲ φαίνεται ποιησαμένη.

The striking nature of the last two examples isolates IV not only from the rest of the corpus, but from early Attic oratory in general. The subject or object of ποιεῖσθαι intervenes in *Tetr.* iv.α.1, And. i.9, Isok. xvii.57, xix.46, and Is. v.30, but none of these is as complex as IV.8 and 17.

When ποιεῖσθαι governs an abstract object, it normally follows the objects immediately. In XII we find:

§2: τοὺς λόγους ποιοῦμαι
§30: ζήτησιν ποιούμενοι.
Cf. §§3, 16, 19, 100.

This is the only usage in XII, but elsewhere both postponement and inversion occur.

A. Separation.

I arrange these examples as nearly as possible in order of "weight" of the intervening mobiles.

(1) XXII.3: τοὺς λόγους τούτους ἐποιούμην
(2) XIII.16: εἰρήνην τῷ δήμῳ τῷ Ἀθηναίων ποιήσασθαι
XIII.47: οὐκ ἔφασαν ἐπιτρέψειν τὴν εἰρήνην, ὦ ἄνδρες Ἀθηναῖοι, ποιήσασθαι
XIV.21: ἐπίδειξιν μὲν τῆς ἑαυτοῦ δυνάμεως ποιούμενοι
(3) III.22: συνθήκας πρὸς αὐτὸν ποιησάμενος
XXV.10: κρίσιν περὶ αὐτῶν ποιοῖσθε
(4) III.26: οὐδὲ μνείαν περὶ τούτου οὐδεμίαν ποιεῖσθαι
(5) IV.2: τὴν μὲν ἀντίδοσιν δι᾽ ἐκείνην φανερός ἐστι ποιησάμενος
XXVI.1: ἡγούμενος ἀκριβῆ νῦν τὴν δοκιμασίαν αὐτοὺς διὰ τὸν χρόνον ποιήσεσθαι
(6) XXVI.12: ἀκριβεστέραν τὴν δοκιμασίαν ἢ περὶ τῶν ἄλλων ἀρχῶν ποιεῖσθαι.

B. Inversion.

In all the examples the verb immediately precedes its noun-object:

IV.12: ἐκ τῆς ἀνθρώπου ποιήσασθαι τὸν ἔλεγχον
XXII.13: τοιούτους ποιεῖσθαι λόγους.

Compare V.3, 4; XVI.8, 9; XXII.1; XXV.2; XXX.15; XXXI.2.

Inversion occurs also in: Is. viii.2 (ἀμφισβήτησις); And. i.10 (ἀπολογία); Isok. xix.12; Is. i.10, iv.14, viii.40 (διαθήκη); Isok. xviii.14 (διαλλαγή); Is. ii.40 (διάλυσις); Isok. xx.5; Is. vii.43, viii.27, xi.20, 44, 50 (λόγος); Is. vii.42 (πρόνοια); Is. i.23 (σπουδή); Is. xi.21 (συνθήκη); Isok. xx.19 (τιμωρία).

It remains to be seen whether any of the respects in which speeches differ from XII can be characterised as epideictic. Examination of the *Epitaphios* and the fragmentary *Olympikos* suggests that hardly any of them can. In respect of ἄν, αὐτόν, εἶναι, γίγνεσθαι and ποιεῖσθαι the *Epitaphios* has the same character as XII (with §16 καίπερ ὧν ἀγαθῶν πολλῶν αἴτιος, cf. XII.32). Its

146 Lysias and the *Corpus Lysiacum*

only resemblances to abnormalities in other forensic speeches are:

§29: ἀμφότερα δ' ἦν αὐτοὺς τὰ πείθοντα.
Cf. IV.4.

§13: ἀλλὰ τὴν αὐτὴν εἶχον γνώμην ἥνπερ πρότερον.
Cf. XXIV.1, 14, 21, 27; XXV.20; XXXIV.7, 9; but contrast *Epit.* 35, 45.

IV, XXIV, XXV and XXIV do not, however, exhibit to any conspicuous degree the parallelisms and poetic vocabulary so characteristic of the *Epitaphios*. It should also be noted that one example of εἶναι in the *Epitaphios* has no parallel in the forensic speeches:

§35: οὔσης καὶ τῆς αὐτῶν σωτηρίας ἀπίστου.

Nothing is gained, and a misleading impression may be given, by attempting to quantify the relation of each forensic speech to XII in respect of the postpositives and concomitants examined *exempli gratia*.[12] The summary which follows, drawing attention to the peculiarities of certain speeches, is the equivalent of what might elsewhere be a table of figures. It should be examined in conjunction with the data on vocabulary (p. 126) and other phenomena (p. 88).

I: postponement of αὐτ- in relative clauses; inversion of εἶναι.
III: inversion of εἶναι; postponement of ποιεῖσθαι.
IV: inversion of αὐτ-; postponement of ποιεῖσθαι.
V: inversion of ποιεῖσθαι.
VI: postponement of εἶναι.
VII: inversion of εἶναι.
VIII: inversion of εἶναι.
X: postponement of αὐτ-.
XIII: postponement of ἄν in negative and positive clauses; frequent juxtaposition of οὐδείς and αὐτ-; postponement of εἶναι; postponement of ποιεῖσθαι.
XIV: postponement of αὐτ-; inversion of εἶναι.

[12] Future investigation of Greek word order may well lie in the direction indicated by B. Gaya Nuño, *Sobre un giro de la lengua de Demostenes* (Madrid, 1959).

XVI: inversion of ποιεῖσθαι.
XIX: postponement of ἄν in negative and positive clauses; inversion of εἶναι.
XX: repetition of ἄν; postponement of αὐτ-; juxtaposition of prepositive and αὐτ-; great frequency of εἶναι with adjectival predicate.
XXIV: inversion of ἔχειν.
XXV: juxtaposition of relative and ἄν; inversion of εἶναι.
XXVI: juxtaposition of prepositive and αὐτ-; juxtaposition of relative and αὐτ-; postponement of εἶναι; postponement of ποιεῖσθαι.
XXIX: juxtaposition of prepositive and ἄν.
XXXI: juxtaposition of prepositive and ἄν; juxtaposition of relative and ἄν; postponement of εἶναι.
XXXII: postponement of αὐτ- in relative clauses.

VIII

Client and Consultant

IN THE last chapter I pointed out the location, within the corpus, of concentrations of elements which are "un-Lysian" when judged against XII, and I suggested that this was the nearest we could come to deciding problems of ascription on technical grounds. The assumption has so far been made, in respect of any given speech, that it was composed either by Lysias or by someone other than Lysias. This assumption I now propose to question.

Let us put ourselves in the position of Euphiletos. He has killed a certain Eratosthenes, his wife's secret lover. The family and friends of Eratosthenes have taken formal steps to prosecute Euphiletos for murder. They allege[1] that Euphiletos sent a message to Eratosthenes by a slave-girl (I.37), enticing him to the house; that when Eratosthenes arrived he was seized and brought indoors; and that he was killed when he had betaken himself to the hearth as a suppliant (§27). Euphiletos, on the contrary, alleges that the slave-girl informed him when Eratosthenes had stealthily entered the house (§23); that he himself then collected such friends as he could from the neighbourhood (§23); and that they all found Eratosthenes in bed with Euphiletos's wife (§24)—whereupon

---

[1] Wilamowitz, *Hermes* lviii (1923), 60 f., suggests that this allegation came as a surprise to the defendant in court; but his feeling that §§37–46 are an insertion *post eventum* into a prepared speech in which §47 followed §36 does not seem to me adequate grounds for this hypothesis.

Euphiletos took the revenge which the law allowed and killed the adulterer. Euphiletos has witnesses, but I would be surprised if Eratosthenes' relations do not have witnesses also. Whom will the court believe? Euphiletos is in trouble. He consults his friends. Among them, or among a friend's friends, or perhaps only among people known to one of his friends by repute, is a man to whom those in legal trouble turn for good advice, because his advice has so often proved effective.[2] This man, whom I will call the "consultant," is more or less in the position which the Clouds promise to Strepsiades, in exaggerated pictorial terms, if he successfully completes a course of rhetorical instruction under Sokrates (Ar. *Clouds* 462-475): "You will have the most enviable life imaginable ... So that there will always be a crowd sitting at your door, wanting to discuss and talk over with you troubles and lawsuits over enormous sums of money, in the hope of consulting you on problems to which it will be profitable for you to turn your intelligence." A comparison with Thucydides' description (viii.68.1) of Antiphon imposes itself: "Whoever consulted him, there was no single man who was so well able to assist those who were engaged in a forensic or political contest." If the consultant is a personal friend of the litigant, and also an Athenian citizen, he can, of course, come to court as a friend and actually speak in support of the litigant; and in that case he may carry the main burden of refuting the opposing case (e.g., Dem. xxxvi.1, Is. iv.1), leaving the litigant himself little more than a brief and, if possible, dignified statement. If everyone knows that he is not a friend of the litigant it may be unwise for him to pretend that he is, for reasons which we shall see (p. 155). If, however, he is active in public life and exercises some degree of δυναστεία, he may judge it advantageous to speak in person. He may offer a reason for doing so: that the litigant is his friend, or that the litigant's adversary is an enemy, or that the case involves an issue of right and wrong which

---

[2] I am surprised at Kennedy's statement (p. 139), "To refuse a client ... would be analogous to a refusal on the part of a magistrate to hear a defence." I can find nothing in the evidence to support this implied picture of a professional organisation with a rigid ethical code.

deeply concerns him. These explicit reasons are less important than the fact that by coming to speak he is displaying an interest in the litigant and informing the jury by implication that an adverse verdict will be a rebuff to him; he is, as it were, elevating the case to a higher political level, and we must never lose sight of the extent to which redistributions of political power and influence at Athens turned on the issue of cases decided in the courts (cf. p. 50). The politician-consultant must take the situation of the moment into consideration in weighing the gain or loss consequent on a personal appearance.

If the consultant is not an Athenian citizen, he cannot speak on the litigant's side in court, even if his friendship with the man is intimate, of long standing and well known.

Now, assuming that the consultant is not going to speak himself, he can do either of two things. He can compose a complete speech for the litigant. Alternatively, he can instruct the litigant in the presentation of the case, either in broad outline—with advice on the sequence of argument and on the emphasis or suppression of individual points—or in detail, with suggestions for the precise wording of whole sections of the speech. No one except the litigant and consultant themselves can know exactly how much has been written out in full.[3] There is a calculated imprecision in Dem. xlvi.1, καὶ οἱ γράφοντες καὶ οἱ συμβουλεύοντες ὑπὲρ Φορμίωνος πολλοί (cf. Dem. xxii.4, πλάττων ... λόγους ~ xxiv.158, συμπαρέσεσθαι ... καί ... λόγους ... ἐσκέφθαι). Whichever course the consultant adopts, according to the needs and abilities of the litigant and nature of the case, the litigant, unless he is unusually confident or unusually fluent in extemporisation, will rehearse the speech he is to deliver in court in much the same way as an actor rehearses his part.[4] Compare Aristophanes' *Knights*, 347–350, where the

[3] I recall, however, an occasion on which laywer P asserted with complete confidence that a letter ostensibly written by lawyer Q had been dictated by Q's client R and merely signed by Q; his grounds were: "Old Q could never have risen to language like this!"

[4] Alkidamas 15.11, 18, 21, 34, implies that when a speech had been written out it was learned by heart, not read from a text held in the hand during the proceedings. Cf. Lavency, 184. Naturally, anyone knows that he may have to face arguments other

Paphlagonian says contemptuously: "If, on some occasion, you succeeded in pleading a piddling lawsuit against a metic, talking away to yourself, on and on, in the streets at night, and drinking (*sc.* only) water [cf. Dem. xix.46)], and boring your friends by trying your speech on them, you thought you were a real orator!"

It is possible that on occasion a consultant was credited with rather more than his due, rather as Iophon lay under a suspicion of producing his father's work as his own (Ar., *Frogs* 73 ff.) and Euripides of borrowing ideas from Kephisophon (*ibid.* 1451 ff.).

But although the exact nature of the relation between consultant and litigant makes little difference to the preparedness of the litigant when he comes into court, it can make a considerable difference to publication. If the consultant has written out the speech in its entirety, he may give it to the litigant, or lend it to the litigant and recover it later, or allow the litigant to take a copy. In any of these cases at least one readable version of a speech composed by the consultant has come into existence and has acquired a chance of survival into the twentieth century A.D. If the consultant has only given oral advice, it may be that nothing readable is put into writing at all. On the other hand, it may be that the speech is subsequently put into readable form by the consultant, or by the litigant with or without further reference to the consultant, or by both independently.[5] In one of these eventualities, the only written version of the speech which exists is partly the work of the consultant, and his part in it may be anything from the bare framework to more than half the wording. In another of the set of eventualities there will be two different written versions of the same speech—one of them wholly the work of the consultant and the other only partly his work.

---

than what he expects, and only an unusually feckless speaker comes unprovided with alternatives; a friend of mine who recently had to reply to an after-dinner toast rehearsed two entirely different speeches and only made his final choice between them in the light of the speech proposing the toast.

[5] Wilamowitz, *Hermes* lviii (1923), 68, took the bull by the horns and raised (but did not investigate as deeply as we might have wished) the question by whom, how, when and why a speech was put into circulation in writing. Cf. also Kennedy, 128.

We have seen that the extant speeches of the *corpus Lysiacum* differ from XII in respect of technique (under which I include language) in varying degrees, and that there is no clear division between a group which is like XII and another group which is not. We have also seen that although some differences can be explained by reference to the personality, status and profession of the litigant there are other differences for which this explanation does not carry conviction. The only alternative explanation so far considered is that speeches which were composed by many different people were ascribed to Lysias, carelessly or fraudulently, by booksellers in the fourth century B.C. I now introduce a third possibility: that among the speeches ascribed to Lysias by the booksellers many, perhaps the majority, were to some degree or other his work, but not wholly his work. In support of this hypothesis I adduce some general considerations, an analogy from later times and a phenomenon observable in the speeches themselves.

When we speak of the "publication" of a modern book, we mean the simultaneous release, to booksellers, of many thousands of identical copies. At any given moment thereafter the publishers —that is to say, the people who have created these identical copies —can tell us how many copies have gone from them to the booksellers and, with a reasonable margin of error, how many copies have gone out from the booksellers to purchasers. Conditions in the Greek world differed so fundamentally from modern conditions that it should be seriously considered whether the terms "publish" and "publication" ought to be used with a Greek reference except in translating a Greek passage which contains ἐκδιδόναι or ἔκδοσις. Once the composer of a poem, speech, story or argument had uttered it aloud in the presence of another person, or had allowed another person to see a written copy of it, he had lost control of its distribution—and lost control not only of the number of copies which might be made, but also of their accuracy and integrity. Neither he nor anyone else would ever be in a position thereafter to estimate, except in the vaguest terms and on poor evidence, how many copies of the work were in existence. If we must speak of "publication," the moment of publication of a work was the moment when an author first communicated that work to someone else in some way or other.

This fact does not always or necessarily imply a high degree of corruption in the multiplication of copies and the transmission of the text. The reader wanted to know what a great author had really written. Motives for actually wanting to acquire a truncated, adapted or interpolated text of Euripides' *Hippolytus* or the memoirs of Ion of Chios can hardly have existed. Motives for wanting to circulate such a text, although they undoubtedly existed, were limited (I would imagine) to a few people and to special circumstances. I would include among these motives the desire to lend prestige to a political, religious or philosophical view by inducing others to believe that eminent writers had shared it, to diminish its prestige by concealing that they had shared it or, less reprehensibly, to improve the text (and incidentally enhance the writer's reputation) by judicious emendation. In the early fourth century restraint was imposed on deliberate alterations of this kind by the comparatively small number of people with an active interest in literature; they naturally wanted authentic texts and were capable of holding and defending opinions on authenticity; and the professional reputation of a bookseller may well have depended more on his ability to satisfy the people who knew and cared than on his marginal sales to those who did not.

But forensic speeches, as the outcome of a relationship between client and consultant, are, for the reasons which I have suggested, a special case, and this is where a useful analogy may be sought from Galen (cf. p. 25). There are many questions, notably in the fields of philosophy, religion and politics, on which it would be most perilous to argue analogically from the Antonine period to the Attic democracy, but in certain social, economic and technological aspects ancient Mediterranean civilization remained comparatively unchanged and it is safe to argue from one period to another. In his essay *On His Own Books* (= *Scr. min.* [Marquardt], ii.92 ff.) Galen says that many people have passed off as their own, with omissions, additions and changes, works which were originally written by him (92.4–8). He had given these works as ὑπομνήματα to individual friends or pupils at their request, not intending general circulation and therefore without putting his own name on them (χωρὶς ἐπιγραφῆς, ὡς ἂν οὐδὲν πρὸς ἔκδοσιν). Some of the possessors of these works died, and after their death were regarded as the authors of the works; others communicated them to friends, who passed them off as their own (92.13–20; cf. 98.5 f.). In the course of time people who knew Galen came upon copies of these works, observed that two copies of the same work might diverge widely, and brought them to him to ask him what was really his (92.20–24). The content and style of such works when they originally left his hands, says Galen, were adapted to the needs, experience and abilities of the recipients (92.25–93.4; cf. 112.19 f.). He did not necessarily keep a copy himself (94.4–17). Another category of works was composed by him not with individual recipients in mind, still less for general circulation, but solely for his own use; some of these, however, were filched by his slaves and given (that is to say, sold) to other people who did not scruple to circulate them (118.1 f., 119.2–9).[6]

For the problem of the *corpus Lysiacum* the most interesting point which emerges from Galen's essay is that it was impossible for him to control the distribution and alteration of works which he had intended for the use of specific individuals and had written in a variety of ways which differed from the way in which he wrote for general circulation. That others should claim his work as their own represents a difference between the world of Galen and the world of Lysias. The Roman Empire was a big place, and it must have been easy for a man in Paphlagonia to claim authorship of a work which he had obtained from Galen in Italy. In Athens, on the other hand, if a litigant created a written version of a speech which he had delivered or intended to deliver in court, the people to whom he would read it or lend it in the first instance would be his own circle of friends—precisely the people to whom he had originally communicated his troubles and who would know better than anyone else where he had been to see a consultant, and if so, which

[6] An interesting parallel is afforded by Benjamin Franklin's practice; cf. Max Farrand's edition of his *Memoirs* (Berkeley and Los Angeles, 1949), especially pp. xxiv f.

Client and Consultant 155

consultant, and how much of the speech could properly be credited to the litigant.

The motivation for alternative ascription is curiously complex. If the consultant had in fact composed all or most of the speech, the litigant had a strong motive for not claiming authorship: he would not want his friends to laugh at him behind his back. If the consultant's share in the composition of the speech had been comparatively small, the litigant had a motive for claiming authorship, while the consultant had one motive for claiming it and another motive for not claiming it. Whatever the respective shares of litigant and consultant, any third party who obtained a copy of the speech had a motive for ascribing it to the consultant.

This enigmatic and perhaps confusing statement rests on the fundamental and constant ambivalence of the Athenian attitude towards the composition of speeches by skilled consultants. One attitude, which is essential to the plot of Aristophanes' *Clouds*, is that the just man has no need of skill; if he is in the right his case speaks for itself, and it is only the man in the wrong who needs artifice. From this attitude stem the apologies of the litigant for subtlety, and his claims that only the unscrupulousness and practised skill of his adversaries compel him to depart from the congenial role of a simple, plain-spoken man. The point of the antithesis ἀληθῆ μέν, λεπτὰ δὲ καὶ ἀκριβῆ in Ant. iii.δ.2 is supported by the abusive ὑπὸ πονηρᾶς λόγων ἀκριβείας in iii.γ.3, the defensive ἐὰν ἀκριβέστερον ἢ ὡς σύνηθες ὑμῖν δόξω εἰπεῖν in iii.β.3, and, much later, by Alkidamas 15.13, 25, 33 f. on ἀκρίβεια.[7]

It was possible throughout the great period of Attic oratory to decry the composition of forensic speeches for others as an occupation which demeaned the composer. Antiphon had to contend with this διαβολή when on trial for his life (fr. 1a, col. I): "My accusers say that I composed pleas (συνέγραφον δίκας) for others and that I profited from this." Pl. *Phdr.* 257CD speaks of λογογράφος as an abusive word cast at Lysias.[8] A generation later Aischines vilified Demosthenes as λογογράφος: i.94, λογογράφος τις ... ὁ

[7] Cf. Lavency, 50, 71.
[8] Cf. *ibid.*, 36 f., 64.

μηχανώμενος αὐτῷ (sc. Τιμάρχῳ) τὴν ἀπολογίαν: i.170, ἄνθρωπος τεχνίτης λόγων: ii.280, τῷ λογογράφῳ καὶ Σκύθῃ: iii.173, ἐκ τριηράρχου λογογράφος ἀνεφάνη: iii.200, κακοῦργος ἄνθρωπος καὶ τεχνίτης λόγων. The term alternates, or is associated, with σοφιστής in ii.175, 275 and Dem. xviii.276 and xix.246, 250; and we find λογογράφος καὶ ἀγοραῖος in Hyper. iii.3. Diodoros in Dem. xxii makes a similar sneer against Androtion: "He cannot make any straightforward answer, but he will try to deceive you by the manufacture of misleading κακούργους λόγους. ἔστι γάρ, ὦ ἄνδρες Ἀθηναῖοι, τεχνίτης τοῦ λέγειν καὶ πάντα τὸν βίον ἑνὶ ἐσχόλακεν τούτῳ" (§4). The notion of Androtion's "leisure" recurs in xxiv.158, and awakens an echo of Aristophanes' representation of scientists, sophists and lyric poets as "idle" men (ἀργοί, *Clouds* 316, 331–334).

Because of this complex of attitudes, the litigant had a motive for suggesting, whenever the suggestion was a practical possibility, that he had composed his own plea without skilled assistance. If the successful outcome of the case had given him a high opinion of his own ability to impress a jury, he might even entertain the ambition that other people would in the future seek his advice on their own troubles, and this might induce him to take credit for the whole speech even when his friends knew better. The consultant, for his part, might find it preferable, on many occasions, not to incur such opprobrium as could be attached to the λογογράφος, but rather to become known by word of mouth as a man whom it was profitable to consult; he stood to gain more by exaggerated rumour than by a label on a written text.[9]

There is a remarkable passage in Demon's *Defence against Zenothemis* (Dem. xxxii.31 f.), in which the speaker has to deal with the expected argument that he trusts in the support of Demosthenes, who is ῥήτωρ καὶ γνώριμος. He asserts most vigorously that Demosthenes is a relative of his—"I swear by all the gods," he says, "that I will tell the truth"—and is helping him only because

---

[9] The statement of R. J. Bonner, *Lawyers and Litigants in Ancient Athens* (Chicago, 1927), 13, that "The Athenian lawyer did his work in silence and obscurity; success brought no personal publicity" rests on an anachronistic notion of publicity.

Client and Consultant 157

the tie of kinship compels him to do so. It is a pity that the end of the speech is mutilated and we do not have the whole of Demon's report of what Demosthenes said about this obviously tricky question (cf. *Rhet. ad Alex.* 1442^{b}12–16). Hypereides treats as exceptionally and admirably democratic the legal right of "anyone who wishes" (iv.11, cf. i.10) to speak on behalf of a defendant; but he finds it necessary to do this in an attempt to forestall criticism, and no doubt a man on whose side ὁ βουλόμενος spoke would be regarded by his opponent as ῥήτορας παρεσκευασμένος (cf. Is. i.7).

It would be interesting to know how much, or in what form, a consultant expected to be rewarded for his services. In the papyrus of Antiphon's *Defence* (fr. 1a) Nicole, the first editor, read (col. ii.19 f.) και|[τ]ϱεεκερδαινον, and interpreted this as "and I took 20 percent (ε = πέμπτον) as my fee"; but even his own photograph shows that the reading is και|ῳϲεκερδαινον, "and that I profited." Antiphon (or perhaps we should say cautiously "an Antiphon") was ridiculed for φιλαργυρία by Plato Comicus (fr. 103), according to *Vit. Or.* 833c, and this may refer to consultancy. Throughout the fourth century the allegation that a man appears in court on another's behalf in return for money is a charge made against an enemy (e.g., Dein. i.111, Lykurg. *Leocr.* 138 [where pay is contrasted with the claims of kinship and friendship]) comparable with a charge of political or diplomatic corruption, and something of the stain which lay on the pretence of being a litigant's friend will naturally have spread to the man who, without regard for the rights and wrongs of the case, did the litigant the service of composing a speech for him. A law cited in Dem. xlvi.26 provides for the prosecution (by γραφή) ἐάν τις ... συνήγορος ὢν λαμβάνῃ χρήματα ἐπὶ ταῖς δίκαις ταῖς ἰδίαις ἢ δημοσίαις. It is not surprising that we do not hear of any actual case brought under this law; even a plausible attempt to establish guilt must have seemed extremely difficult.

Some sophists, as is well known, were businesslike in stating their fees for courses of instruction; this was simply an extension to the intellectual sphere of a normal feature of Greek life, the training of an apprentice by a skilled workman on a strictly defined contractual basis. Yet even the payment of a sophist might have been disguised with a veneer of politeness, if we are to take Aristophanes' *Clouds* 1146 f. as parody of reality: Strepsiades, on coming to receive his son from Sokrates' school, says "But let me give you this first," χρὴ γὰρ ἐπιθαυμάζειν τι τὸν διδάσκαλον, and the scholia reasonably interpret ἐπιθαυμάζειν τι as a euphemism for "pay" (cf. English euphemisms of the type "for a consideration"). The consultant's "fee" may have been much more heavily disguised, for the sophist could at least mitigate opprobrium by pointing to the parallel case of the apprentice. It is doubtful whether Pindar or Bacchylides tendered an estimate to a patron before a victory ode was commissioned, but the relation between poet and patron was as much a stock subject of humour in Aristophanic comedy as allegations of mercenariness are a stock feature of διαβολή in the orators.

The conventional attitude of mistrust towards composers of speeches was counteracted by the intense interest of Athenians in oratory and their admiration of good speeches as works of art (cf. p. 179).[10] There is, of course, logical inconsistency in making it a point against an opponent that he writes speeches or has consulted a speech-writer and at the same time listening to speeches with the ear of a connoisseur;[11] but inconsistency between the principles which a man implies by his conduct and the popular prejudices which he exploits for his own convenience, or between the religious precepts to which he gives formal assent and the socially acceptable code to which he conforms when it is a question of applying a precept to an actual case, is more the rule than the exception. The most obvious and striking example of such inconsistency is the "double standard" of sexual morality, observable in ancient and modern communities alike.[12] If we ask ourselves whether the Athenian speech-writer was admired or despised, the answer, I suggest, is "both"; whether a man expressed admiration

---

[10] Cf. Pilz, 23, on the people in assembly as aesthetic arbiters; but he seems to treat Thuc. iii.40.3 as if it were a considered statement by the historian, not an ingredient in a speech.

[11] Cf. Lavency, 63 f.

[12] Cf. K. J. Dover, *BICS* xi (1964), 31 f.

or contempt depended on the purpose which expression was intended to serve.[13]

For litigant and consultant, therefore, motives for claiming or disowning a speech were conflicting. For any third person who acquired a copy of the speech the conflict was greatly diminished and often absent. It was interesting and important to possess a speech which was known or believed or suspected to have been composed, wholly or in part, by a famous consultant or rhetorician; it was much less interesting and important to possess a speech attributed to a man not known outside the circle of his own family and friends. Some of the people to whom Galen gave ὑπομνήματα claimed authorship themselves, and when they were dead their authorship was accepted in good faith by their heirs; but sooner or later other people, who were interested in Galen as a writer, scholar and scientist, took the trouble to restore his claim to authorship and obtain corrections from him.

What I imagine to have happened in the fourth century was something like this. Let us suppose that Euphiletos consulted Lysias, and that Lysias not only organised his plea for him but also —after a shrewd assessment of Euphiletos's actual personality and a calculation of how best to exploit that personality for the persuasion of a jury—suggested much of the wording. After the case one of Euphiletos's friends—Sostratos, let us say (§22)—created a copy of Euphiletos's speech. If Sostratos did not know how great Lysias's contribution had been, he would label his copy "Euphiletos, defence against a charge of murdering Eratosthenes." If another person took a copy from Sostratos, and did know the extent of Lysias's contribution, this person would either substitute Lysias's name for that of Euphiletos or add it. If he merely added it, I would expect the first bookseller who multiplied copies of the speech for sale to take the decisive step from addition to substitution. Who, after all, was Euphiletos?

In another case, let us say, the litigant made and kept a copy of his speech but did not communicate it to anyone else. His heirs inherited it with his books, and, although they were fairly sure

[13] Cf. Lavency, 98 ff., 107 ff.

that it was the work of a consultant, they could not be sure whose work it was. Information from some relatives and friends pointed in one direction, while information from others pointed in a different direction, and the opinions of connoisseurs of oratory could be invoked to support both. Circumstances of this kind could explain why the *Trapezitikos* was ascribed to Isokrates by (I presume) Kallimachos and thereafter (demonstrably) by Dionysios and Harpokration, but to Lysias by someone else whose decision is first apparent to us in the Lysian Corpus F; though this is not, in my view (p. 22), the easiest explanation.[14]

Perhaps on occasion the original consultant put into circulation only that part of a speech which he regarded as likely to interest the general reader. Isok. xvi begins, "On the subject of the pair of horses ... you have heard the evidence of the envoys from Argos and those other witnesses who know the facts," and xx begins, "That Lochites struck me and was the aggressor, all the witnesses present have testified." These speeches are not συνηγορίαι, for the litigant himself is the speaker. It is misleading to call them "mutilated" or to speak of "lacunae," for those words imply accidental damage. The more plausible explanation is that the strictly forensic element in each speech was not committed to writing at all, and what was written was in xvi a wide-ranging defence of the career of Alkibiades and in xx an essay on ὕβρις linked, but not confined, to the particular case of Lochites. At least one speech in the *corpus Lysiacum* belongs to this category: XXI, which is spoken by the defendant himself and begins περὶ μὲν τῶν κατηγορημένων ... ἱκανῶς ὑμῖν ἀποδέδεικται (Blass, i.497). The same may be true of XVIII (Blass, i.523 f.), in so far as it seems to presuppose the presentation of evidence. Sch. Patm. Dem. (*Lex. gr. min.* 160) comments that *Against Euthydemos* began with the word καί, but the citation (fr. 36a), καὶ ἐξ αὐτῶν τῶν μαρτυριῶν, ὦ ἄνδρες δικασταί, ἃς οὗτοι παρείχοντο, πειράσομαι ὑμῖν ἀποδεῖξαι

[14] Pollux vii.14 cites πλειστηριάζειν from Isaios ἐν τῷ πρὸς Ἀνδοκίδην, whereas Harp. 250.8 f. cites it from Lysias ἐν τῷ πρὸς Ἀνδοκίδην, εἰ γνήσιος. Since Harpokration elsewhere adds ἀποστασίου to the designation, it seems that we are not concerned here with that portion of VI which is missing in the Palatinus, but with another speech of disputed ascription.

⟨...⟩, permits the translation "even," and does not necessarily indicate a truncated speech; Blass's conclusion (i.369) that it was a "Bagatellrede" is unfortunate.[15]

Composite authorship must, I submit, be added to the list of factors which stand in the way of clear-cut decision on the ascription of speeches in the *corpus Lysiacum*.[16] If my theory is valid, some important consequences follow. At the end of chapter ii I left the Athenian bookseller under a cloud, an imputation of fraud; I drew attention to the possibility that Aphareus was simply lying in defence of Isokrates' reputation (as he conceived it); and some readers may feel that I did an injustice to Aristotle also by attributing to him an agnosticism so complete as to be almost perverse. If, however, alternative claims to the authorship of a forensic speech could exist from the time of the litigant's death and sometimes right from the time of the lawsuit itself, Aristotle's agnosticism was the product of intelligent observation, Aphareus's denial was what is sometimes called in politics "a question of semantics," and the booksellers, though possibly open to criticism by the standards of scholarship, acted on the whole in good faith.

It would be reasonable to demand better support for the theory of composite authorship than the exercise of historical imagination in which I have so far indulged. Such support can, I believe, be drawn from consideration of Demosthenes' speeches against Androtion (xxii) and Timokrates (xxiv). In both cases the prosecutor was a certain Diodoros (xxiv.64, 7 ∼ xxii.1 f.). Now, there are three possibilities:

(1) Demosthenes wrote every syllable of both speeches (always excepting the later interpolations from xxiv.172 and 182 into xxii.67 and 74), and his relation to Diodorus was the relation of playwright to actor.

---

[15] Francken, 38 ff., 64, treats IV and IX as "acephalous"; but cf. n.16.

[16] Francken, 64, regards XXII as originally by Lysias but "satis superque ab aliis reficta." It must be remembered, however, in appraising much of the work done on Lysian speeches in the middle and late nineteenth century, that application of stylistic criteria at that time was often arbitrary, self-confident and vehemently expressed to a degree not often paralleled among ancient critics.

(2) Demosthenes and Diodoros worked closely together, and Diodoros made significant contributions to the argument and wording of both speeches.

(3) Both speeches were composed by Diodoros, an admirer and imitator of Demosthenes, and their ascription to Demosthenes is wholly mistaken.

Refraining, with some difficulty, from asking "Which of these three possibilities should we really regard as the most likely?" and from pursuing *a priori* argument even further than I have already done, I offer two data which favour the second of the three.

Although Diodoros represents himself, in conventional style, as a quiet man who has become provoked by the relentless enmity of Androtion and been forced into political action by disinterested patriotism and indignation at the dishonest manoeuvres of Androtion and Timokrates (xxiv.1, 3, 6–16), his self-portrait is belied by his narrative. He was closely associated with Euktemon, his fellow-prosecutor in xxii (cf. 1, 3); before that prosecution Androtion had prosecuted Euktemon successfully (xxii.1 ~ xxiv.7) and had also prosecuted Diodoros's uncle (unsuccessfully) for impiety, alleging that Diodoros himself was a parricide (xxii.2 ~ xxiv.7). After the case against Androtion, but before the case against Timokrates, Euktemon attacked Androtion in the Assembly, and Androtion prosecuted Euktemon for making an illegal proposal (xxiv.11–15). It was only after Euktemon's proposal had been upheld as legal that Timokrates was prosecuted by Diodoros for making a proposal which, Diodoros alleges, was designed to protect Androtion (xxiv.15f.). Thus by the time that he came to deliver the speech against Timokrates Diodoros was deeply embroiled in political warfare; and even before he prosecuted Androtion, Androtion had judged it worthwhile to try to destroy his reputation. Diodoros may not have been numbered among οἱ πάνυ πολιτευόμενοι; but he was anything but insignificant. It is worth recalling an intelligent remark made by Dionysios in rejecting the ascription of two speeches in defence of Menesaichmos to Deinarchos: "The speaker"—who had considerable political standing and administrative experience—"is not likely to have been so lacking in ability in private and public lawsuits as to use the services of Deinarchos as speech-writer" (i.361.5–15).

The probability that Diodoros's contribution to the speeches against Androtion and Timokrates was significant is increased by a curious phenomenon in xxiv. Take the central portion of the speech, from §91 to §159, excluding quotations from documents, divide it into ten equal portions and note the incidence of hiatus (as defined on p. 68). Allowing a 10 percent margin for disagreement (hence "*c.*") on what prodelisions or synizeses comedy would or would not permit, it will be seen that the incidence of hiatus rises to a peak in §§118–137 and then falls off at approximately the same rate, thus:

§§91–98	*c.* 5
§§99–107 (λυμαίνει)	1
§§107 (οἱ καὶ ζῶντας)–112	13
§§113–118 (τοῦ ἠδικηκότος)	12
§§118 (χρῆσθαι)–124 (δικασταί)	19
§§124 (ὅσοι ἄν)–130	19
§§131–137	21
§§138–143	14
§§144–153 (τῶν δεινοτάτων)	10
§§153 (τί γὰρ κωλύει)–159	5

The steep rise begins just after §108, which introduces a summary of the argument up to that point; the steep fall comes after the reading of the heliastic oath and in the middle of the argument which is based on its wording. Although one possible explanation is that Demosthenes polished the speech very unevenly,[17] should we not give some consideration to the alternative explanation that in this central portion of the speech we have more of Diodoros and less of Demosthenes?

Within the *corpus Lysiacum* there is one phenomenon which may possibly have a bearing on this question. There are four

---

[17] So the Budé editors, Navarre and Orsini, 120, 165 n.; but they speak as if §§110–154 could be sharply marked off from the surrounding text.

basic formulae for the introduction of witnesses in early Attic oratory:

"I will produce witnesses"—a statement to the jury; its principal variant is "I will produce so-and-so as witness(es)"

"Call the witnesses," or "call so-and-so"—a command addressed to the clerk of the court

"Step up"—a command to the witness(es)

"Hear the witness(es)" or "hear so-and-so"—a command to the jury; this is confined to XXXI.14, 23

Two of the four can, of course, be combined. It cannot be suggested that the same speech-writer confined himself to one formula,[18] for three of the four occur in two passages of XII:

§43: καὶ τούτων μάρτυρας ὑμῖν παρέξομαι

§47: πρὸς μὲν οὖν τούτους τοσαῦτα λέγω, τοὺς δὲ μάρτυράς μοι κάλει. καὶ ὑμεῖς ἀνάβητε.

The third passage of XII (§61) shows an elaborate variation:

ταῦτα δ' ἐπίστασθε μὲν καὶ αὐτοί, καὶ ⟨οὐκ⟩ οἶδ' ὅτι δεῖ μάρτυρας παρασχέσθαι. ὅμως δέ, ἐγώ τε γὰρ δέομαι ἀναπαύσασθαι, ὑμῶν τ' ἐνίοις ἥδιον ὡς πλείστων τοὺς αὐτοὺς λόγους ἀκούειν.

Thus the rhetorician writing for his own delivery. Comparable variety is to be found in XIII.42, 64, 66, 68, 79, 81; XIX.23, 27, 41, 58, 59; XX.25, 26, 28, 29. Isokrates uses the second formula in xvii.12, 13, 16; combines the first and the third in §32; and uses the third alone in §§37 and 41. Andokides i favours variations on the third formula, but not exclusively:

§18: καί μοι κάλει Καλλίαν καὶ Στέφανον

§18: κάλει δὲ καὶ Φίλιππον καὶ Ἀλέξιππον ... βλέπετε εἰς τούτους καὶ μαρτυρεῖτε εἰ ἀληθῆ λέγω

§28: καί μοι κάλει τούτων τοὺc μάρτυρας

[18] J. Rea, on the anonymous speech *P. Oxy.* 2538, draws attention to its use of καί μοι ἀνάβητε μάρτυρες and remarks, "The usage characterises Lysias." This is true in so far as the formula occurs in seven Lysian speeches (including XX), but its significance is diminished by the fact that only two Isokratean speeches (xvii and xviii) have any witness formulae at all.

§46: εἶτα δέ μοι τοὺς πρυτάνεις κάλει
§69: σὺ δέ μοι αὐτοὺς κάλει τοὺς λυθέντας ... μέχρι τούτου ἀναβήσονται καὶ λέξουσιν ὑμῖν ἕως ἂν ἀκροᾶσθαι βούλησθε
§112: καί μοι κάλει αὐτόν. πρῶτα μὲν οὖν ταῦτα εἰ ἀληθῆ λέγω μαρτύρησον, Εὔκλεις
§123: ὡς δ' ἀληθῆ λέγω, κάλει μοι τοὺς μάρτυρας
§127: καί μοι τούτων ἁπάντων τοὺς μάρτυρας κάλει.

In Antiphon v the changes are rung on alternative wordings of the first formula, and then on the formulae themselves:

{ §20: τούτων δ' ὑμῖν τοὺς μάρτυρας παρέξομαι
§22: τούτων δ' ὑμῖν μάρτυρας παρέξομαι

{ §24: τούτων δ' ὑμῖν τοὺς μάρτυρας παρσχήσομαι (morphological variation)
§28: τούτων δ' ὑμῖν τοὺς μάρτυρας παρασχήσομαι

§30: παρέξομαι δὲ τούτων τοὺς μάρτυρας (reversal of order)
§35: τούτων δὲ μάρτυράς μοι κάλει
§56: καί μοι μάρτυρας τούτων κάλει (reversal of order)
§83: <? καί μοι ἀνάβητε (Stephanus)> τούτων μάρτυρες.

What is the explanation of speeches in which monotony rather than variety seems to be sought, as when the speaker of XXIII caps each summons to witnesses with the words "Stop the water clock" (§§4, 8, 11, 14, 15)? Or again, when at XIX.23 we encounter κάλει μοι Εὔνομον but later in the same speech (§59) καί μοι κάλει τὸν καὶ τόν? I would suggest the possibility, with some hesitation, that the written version of XXIII was put into circulation by the client, whose artistic sensitivity did not restrain him from monotony when he inserted the witness formulae, and that of XIX by the consultant, who knew the name of one relevant witness at §23 (cf. §19) but had forgotten the rest, including those who accompanied Eunomos (note τῶν μαρτύρων in §24) and those summoned at §59.

If either the consultant or the client could put the speech into circulation, it must have happened on occasion that two different versions came into existence simultaneously, and it would be surprising if the corpus of an orator's work collected at Alexandria did not contain some "doublets" of this kind. As we have seen (p. 14), Corpus F contained both X and XI, and we might infer by analogy that it contained XV as well as XIV. It would be exciting if we could trace both members of each pair back to the immediate aftermath of the lawsuits themselves. It is disappointing to have to admit that XI probably, and XV certainly, are précis made by people unaware of the facts at issue.[19] The argument of XIV, sustained by somewhat special pleading (§§ 5–8; the prosecution to which Dem. xxxix.17 refers may have been similar) is that the younger Alkibiades is liable to a charge not simply of failure to present himself when called up for service on an expedition but of a more discreditable offence, abandoning his place in the line through cowardice. The composer of XV was unaware of the distinction, and writes (§§ 1, 4) as if ἀστρατεία were the charge (Blass, i.495 f. misses the point).[20] In x.4 the speaker says (according to the Palatinus) "I am 30, and this is the 20th year from the date of your return"—that is, from the democratic restoration; "it is therefore obvious that I was 13 when my father was killed by the Thirty." X.27 adds that the father was killed at the age of 67. In XI.1 f. the same statement is made as in X.4, but with "32" instead of "30" for the speaker's present age. XI.9 adds that the father was 70 when he was killed. The discrepancies between "13" and "12" and between "67" and "70" were in the text of Corpus F, and are noted by *P. Oxy.* 2537 *recto* 9–15; the discrepancy between "30" and "32" is not noted. "Seventy" may well be a rounding of "67," but "30" cannot be a rounding of "32," because (*a*) it is not in the speaker's interest to reduce the gap between his present age and his age when his father was killed, and (*b*) it would be obvious even to a simple-minded juror that the arithmetical conclusion drawn in X.4 does not follow from the premisses. "Thirty" in X.4 must therefore be a textual corruption of "32". If the speaker had his 13th birthday during the reign of

---

[19] E. Stutzer, *Hermes* xiv (1879), 499 ff., argues that VIII, IX and XX are all précis; but cf. n.16.

[20] Conversely, "cavalry" (XIV. 6–11, XV.7 f.) becomes "mounted archers" in XV.6; if this was a true detail of the case, failure to exploit it in XIV is inexplicable.

the Thirty Tyrants, before the democratic restoration, and his 14th after the restoration, his 32nd birthday would fall before the 19th anniversary of the restoration, so that although his 33rd birthday would fall during the 20th year of the restored democracy the calculation which he offers is a natural and obvious one: the age of 32 is the 20th year, on inclusive reckoning, from the age of 13. The calculation in XI.1 f., on the other hand, is either simply an error —caused by forgetting that if a man's 33rd year of life, during which he calls himself "32", approximately coincides with the 20th year of a regime, the year of his life coinciding with the first year of the regime was his 14th, during which he was "13 years old"—or the result of a decision that if the Thirty Tyrants were in power in 404/403 and the democracy was restored in 403/402 a man must have been a year younger under the Thirty than at the time of the restoration.

XI and XV, therefore, cannot be ascribed either to the consultant or to his client.[21]

A litigant who is defending himself can on occasion speak as if until the speeches for the prosecution have been made he does not know the details of the charges against him. Thus, the speaker of VII says (§3) that his adversary's "plot" against him has been revealed to him at the same time as to the jury, and now he must do his best to rebut the charge at short notice. Nikobulos (Dem. xxxvii.45–47) paints a dramatic picture of his colleague Euergos unexpectedly confronted, in a lawsuit ostensibly concerned with mining, with a charge that he had behaved outrageously towards the womenfolk of Pantainetos's family. To the extent to which the picture of a defendant faced with a need (cf. Hyper. i.9) to extemporise is true, passages in defending speeches which refer to what the prosecutors have said cannot have been composed before the case, but must have been inserted before a written version of the

---

[21] συνοίδασιν = συνίσασιν in XI. 1 is not a negligible argument for late authorship, but it is far from conclusive; even if πάντες οἴδασιν in Xen. Oec. 20.14 is ruled out as corrupt or as one of Xenophon's Ionicisms (cf. οἴδαμεν in Ant. ii.α.3) the co-existence of Attic and Koine inflections is demonstrated by καθελόντωσαν as early as 352/351 (IG ii².204.47 f.).

speech was circulated. Needless to say, we are not compelled to adopt this view of all such passages without exception. The written charge may sometimes have been more detailed than we would have imagined; Pantainetos's charge against Nikobulos (Dem. xxxvii.22–29) is remarkably detailed—compare the εἰσαγγελία against Alkibiades cited in Plu. *Alc.* 22.3. In an indiscreet and gossipy society, it was no doubt possible to find out a great deal about the charges, relevant or irrelevant, which the prosecutor proposed to make, and an experienced consultant is likely to have been resourceful in discovery. Apart from the natural indiscretion or calculated treachery of the adversary's friends' friends, many a household slave will have known how to turn sharp ears to good account (cf. Ar. *Frogs* 750–753).[22] Moreover, it is possible to anticipate alternative modes of attack by rehearsing in advance alternative defensive tactics.

But an ounce of evidence is worth a sackful of speculation, and on the very few occasions which permit us to decide whether or not a reply to an attack was written before or after a lawsuit the context and wording suggest that it was written after. Such occasions arise in Aischines ii, the reply to Demosthenes xix, and in Demosthenes xviii, the reply to Aischines iii.

> Aischines ii.10: "He tried to liken me to Dionysios, the tyrant of Syracuse . . . and related the dream of the priestess in Sicily." Nothing of this is to be found in Dem. xix.
>
> §86: "He has gone so far as to say that I drove Kritobulos, the ambassador from Kersebleptes, away from the sacrifice . . ." Dem. xix contains no such statement.
>
> §124: "He alleges that I rowed down the river Loidias at night to see Philip and wrote from Philip the letter that was sent to you." Dem. xix.175 says that Aischines' nocturnal communication with Philip took place at Pherai.

---

[22] It is perhaps this fact of social life which makes it so easy for Aristophanes, after showing us how Euripides' relation was persuaded in Agathon's house to disguise himself as a woman, to represent Kleisthenes in *Thesm.* 577 ff. as saying, "I heard a very serious matter being talked about in public just now . . . They say Euripides has sent an old relation of his here . . ."

§156: "... praising Satyros the comic actor because he begged from Philip at dinner the release of friends of his who were digging, chained, in Philip's vineyard." Demosthenes actually says (xix.192–196) that Satyros begged the release of the daughters of Apollophanes of Pydna.

Similarly, Demosthenes xviii twice refers (§§95, 238) to Aischines' vilification of Euboia and Byzantion; but Aischines' speech contains no such passage.

The simple and obvious explanation is that Aischines ii and Demosthenes xviii reply to arguments which were used in court but deleted from the circulated version, or alternatively, that they reply to arguments which might have been used but were not used. In either case, a substantial gulf is opened between what was uttered and what was put in writing, and it must be emphasised that this gulf appears in the only cases which are open to our inspection. Nothing can be learned from confrontation of VI with Andokides i, and this is not surprising, for VI is only part (the beginning is lost) of the second or third of three speeches to which Andokides had to reply.[23] The rivalry between Aischines and Demosthenes is, of course, separated by a full generation from the majority of speeches in the *corpus Lysiacum*, and inference from one to the other is always subject to the proviso that practice may have changed. The reader should bear this proviso in mind in the arguments which follow.

One of the best-known phenomena in Attic oratory is anticipation of the adversary's arguments, and this is as prominent in the *corpus Lysiacum* as later: "I learn that he will say ...," "I hear that they propose to argue ...," and the like. This phenomenon, which was for a long time chained to the discussion of such problems as

---

[23] Lämmli subjects VI and And. i to very close scrutiny. He remarks (51 f., 55) that VI seems to envisage a defence different from what Andokides (i.10, 30–32, 58, 70) offered; but he overlooks the fact that in politics and the social penumbra of politics the refutation of an allegation does little to prevent its being repeated. Again, he remarks (26 f.) that because there is no reference in VI.23 to Andokides' alleged denunciation of his father, Andokides' defence on that score must have been successful; but VI.23 probably refers to the herms, and the allegation that Andokides denounced his father referred to the mysteries (cf., however, MacDowell, 177 ff.).

the formulation of the charge, the "preliminary hearing," arbitration and the deposition of testimony, is now recognised as falling as much in the province of the sociologist as in that of the jurist.[24] I have already mentioned the difficulty of keeping secrets in Athens, and I should add to this one further point. It is often profitable to state that the defendant will use an argument which in fact you have no reason to believe he intends to use. When he fails to use it, some of the jury may believe that he intended to do so but cannot because you have already exposed it as invalid; if he attempts to improvise arguments against the prosecutor's refutation, he will use up valuable time and his chance of escaping a trap which has been set at leisure by the prosecutor or by the prosecutor's consultant is small. Conceivably Aischines iii.228, where "He likens me to the Sirens..." is included in ὧν πυνθάνομαι Δημοσθένην λέξειν but does not occur in Dem. xviii, is a case in point. But at least equal weight should be given to the possibility that §228 was put into the written version because Demosthenes had in fact likened Aischines to the Sirens, while Demosthenes at the same time deleted the comparison from the written version of *his* speech. There are certainly two passages of Aischines iii which suggest subsequent insertion rather than advance knowledge or intelligent anticipation: in §189 he refers to the contrast with the boxer Philammon, whom we find in Dem. xviii.319, and in §225 he deals with the doctor who tells a man's family at the funeral what treatment would have saved the patient, an analogy used by Demosthenes in xviii.243.

We must remember that when a written version of a speech was put into circulation it was not designed for compilers of law reports or for historians and scholars, but for four categories of reader: the partisan, the floating voter, the would-be politician and the connoisseur.

The partisan—that is to say, the man actively committed to politics as an associate of one or other of the parties to a lawsuit—was no more devoted to truth or precision than his modern counterpart; he wanted to be encouraged and armed. Scholars

---

[24] Thanks in the main to A. P. Dorjahn, *TAPA* lxvi (1935), 274 ff.

who seriously believe that the reputation of a Greek orator would be diminished by the detection of inaccuracies and distortions in his published speeches must be singularly blind to the workings of the world in which they themselves live, and in particular to the fact that in political life it is so much more important to score off an opponent than to assess his conduct judiciously. Political partisans, like religious partisans, have capacities for belief, disbelief and exclusion which are alien to the scholar in his professional capacity, but familiar enough to him in personal, social, legal and political relationships, and he has only to draw upon one part of his life for the better understanding of problems which fall within the other part. When, however, the subject of his study is Greek forensic oratory he must in addition recognise that at Athens issues which he would separate into the legal and the political were intertwined, so that the movement of an individual up and down the scale of status, power and influence in the community was determined by the outcome of δίκαι as well as γραφαί.

What I have called the "floating voter" is the man, then as now, whose allegiance can be determined, at least temporarily, by the impact of rhetoric, and I see no reason to suppose that an orator's written version would be more scrupulous than the propaganda of a modern political party in its choice of means to win him over. The would-be politician—that is to say, at Athens, the young man (like Glaukon in Xen. *Mem.* iii.6.1) who knows that to become influential he must be a persuasive speaker, and that once he has begun to make his influence felt he will have to stand up to lawsuits brought or supported by opponents—naturally takes as a model a speech as it could be, not as it was. He knows that it is the business of a speaker to anticipate his opponents arguments by all means at his disposal and to the utmost of his ability. The connoisseur, the man who enjoys oratory as an art form, not unnaturally prefers a good speech to a bad one, and if the written version of a speech is superior to what the speaker was actually able to deliver in court, so much the better.

I therefore find it difficult to see that substantial alteration of a speech before it was put into circulation would seem to either the consultant or the litigant likely to diminish his political and artistic reputation in any significant respect.[25]

If this is taken to its logical conclusion, we should expect to find written versions of speeches which were never delivered at all. So far as symbuleutic speeches are concerned, this is a possibility which Dionysios takes in his stride; he says of the Lysian speech against the proposal of Phormisios," It is not known whether this speech was actually delivered" (i.49.11–13).[26] As for forensic speeches, Plutarch (*Dem.* 15.3) inclines towards the hypothesis that the case to which Aischines ii and Dem. xix ostensibly relate never came into court. The ground of this hypothesis was somewhat infirm: the absence of any mention of the case in Aischines iii or Dem. xviii. But it appears to me certain, as it has appeared to the majority of scholars from ancient times onwards,[27] that Demosthenes' speech against Meidias (xxi) was not delivered. The relevant data are:

> §154: "I am 32." But according to the narratives in his speeches against his guardians (xxvii.4, 19, 23, 29, 36; xxx.15, 17), Demosthenes was 34 or 35 at the time (§§ 162 f.) of Meidias's alleged offence and therefore 36 or 37 at the ostensible date of the lawsuit, two years after the offence (§ 13; cf. § 114 ~ Aischines ii.17, iii.62 f., 73).[28] Of course the figure can be corrupt—so can any reading—but, if so, the corruption was very early;[29] it is necessary to assume

[25] I do not know how Lavency, 190 ff., finds it possible to say, "Les vraisemblances plaident donc en faveur d'un texte definitif fidèle à l'original."

[26] Kennedy, 204, makes a slip in saying that the speech "was delivered by someone, according to Dionysios."

[27] The contrary view is argued by H. Erbse, *Hermes* lxxxiv (1956), 135 ff. Erbse offers an explanation (not always, in my view, plausible) of each difficulty separately, but no explanation of the fact that the difficulties coexist and point the same way.

[28] Users of King's edition should be warned that he misunderstands τρίτον ἔτος τουτί.

[29] Erbse dismisses the figure as corrupt, as if there were no more to be said. Of course corruption of figures could be very early—cf. Polybios, xii.4a.4–6 on a possible corruption in the text of Ephoros before the time of Timaios—and perhaps (for completeness' sake) we should take into account also the hypothesis that Demosthenes misstated his age, as Vico misstates his own date of birth in the opening sentence of his autobiography.

that it was the only reading known to Dionysios, if we are to account for the fact that Dionysios, by adding 32 years to the date of the alleged offence, overlooking (as we see from (i.261.21–262.2) the interval of two years between the offence and the ostensible lawsuit, and relying on this in preference to the data available in the speeches against the guardians (cf. [Plu.] *Vit. Or.* 845D), concluded that Demosthenes was born in 381/380 (i.260.6 f.) and composed the speech against Androtion at the age of 25 (ctr. "27 or 28," Plu. *Dem.* 15.2).[30]

§§ 70, 102, 118 (cf. 181 f.): Demosthenes demands the death penalty; but in § 152 he envisages a crippling fine as an alternative, and in §§ 211 f. he seems to take a fine for granted—an unusual drop in temperature in the last part of a speech.

§§ 205, 208, 213: Demosthenes makes at least two, and possibly three, alternative approaches to criticism of the men who will support Meidias.

§§ 100 f. and §§ 183–185: These two passages are treatments of the same τόπος, and the second is greatly superior to the first.

§ 23: The relation between this section and what precedes it takes us by surprise, to such an extent that I find it very difficult to believe that in actual delivery the sequence would have been possible.

§§ 77–157: Demosthenes describes his feud with Meidias, which was of more than ten years' standing at the Dionysia of 349/348, and, if his description bears any relation to the facts, he had had a continuous stimulus, for the whole of that period, to the meditation of diatribes against Meidias.

Finally, Aischines iii.52 alleges that "Demosthenes sold for 30 mnai" (i.e., accepted a settlement out of court) "the outrage which he had suffered and the vote which the Assembly had passed against Meidias in the sanctuary of Dionysos."

[30] R. Sealey, *REG* lxiii (1955), 77 ff., suggests that the variant readings in Dem. xxx.15 may have contributed towards Dionysios's conclusion.

The combination of these data incidates that Demosthenes put into circulation an attack on Meidias which contained both what he would have said if his lawsuit had come into court in 347/346 and also much which he would have said if he had brought a lawsuit on an earlier occasion. His contemporaries knew what the true situation was; he knew that they knew; and he did not judge that circulation of such a document would damage his reputation.

I have focussed attention on speeches which belong to the third quarter of the fourth century, for the simplest and soundest of reasons: if we want detailed evidence, we must go to where it is. How far inferences from this evidence may be applied to the beginning of the century turns upon the history of the oration as an art form.

IX

Orator, Rhetorician and Reader

To AVOID ambiguity, I begin with four definitions. By "oratory" I mean speaking to a group of people with the intention either of persuading them to take a decision, adopt a mode of thinking or pursue a course of action, or of evoking in them a favourable aesthetic reaction to one's own speaking. By "rhetoric" I mean what the Greeks meant by ῥητορική, the intellectual study of the procedures of oratory, with or without the communication of the results of this study to "pupils."[1] A failure to distinguish between oratory and rhetoric imposes on us, unnecessarily, difficulties such as the evolution of our language has imposed on us in respect of the word "history," which means both "the past" and "the study of the past." By "consultancy" I mean acting as a consultant (Greek λογογράφος) as that word was used in the last

[1] Cf. G. Kennedy, *AJP* lxxx (1959), 169 ff. and S. Wilcox, *HSPh* liii (1942), 121 ff., on the early history of rhetorical teaching. It is right to emphasise (as Wilcox does; cf. H. Ll. Hudson-Williams, *CQ* N.S. i [1951], 68 ff.) the difference in technique between forensic and symbuleutic oratory, but also necessary to remember (cf. p. 50) how much political success depended on the successful conduct of cases in the law courts. The promise made by the Chorus to Strepsiades in Ar. *Clouds* 431 f. is relevant here; they offer him more than he asks for, but what they offer is the logical conclusion of the course on which he seems ready to embark.

chapter. By "publication" I mean the putting into circulation of a written version of a speech.

It would be interesting to know the grounds on which Aristotle, if he is correctly reported by Diogenes Laertios (viii.57 = Arist. fr. 65), regarded Empedokles as the "inventor of rhetoric."[2] Probably he drew a tentative inference from the fact that Teisias and Korax, to whom were ascribed what were regarded in his time as the oldest known technical manuals of rhetoric (Cic. *Brut*.46 [= Arist. fr. 137]; cf. *Inv*. ii.6, Theophr. *Scr. min*. [Usener] i.191), were, like Empedokles, Sicilians, but—together with Gorgias (cf. Diog. Laert. viii.58)—a generation younger than Empedokles and therefore at the receiving end of a pupil-teacher relationship. Probably also Aristotle did not say anything as positive as Diogenes attributes to him; Sextus Empiricus (*Math.* vii.6) reports Aristotle as saying that Empedokles "was the first to set rhetoric in motion (κεκινηκέναι)," and Quintilian (iii.1.8) uses very similar language: "primus... mouisse aliqua circa rhetoricen Empedocles dicitur." Since the ancients knew of no speeches written for actual forensic or symbuleutic occasions which could be ascribed to anyone earlier than Antiphon (Quint. iii.1.11; cf. Diod. Sic. *ap.* Clem. Str. i.79.3), who was executed in 411, it seems that the first rhetorical manuals were at the very latest contemporary with the first circulated versions of forensic speeches, and may well have been a little earlier. The idea that Antiphon gave rhetorical instruction is first implied in Pl. *Mnx.* 236A.

It did not escape the notice of the ancients (cf. especially Quint. xii.10.64) that the Greeks of the fifth century did not have to wait for Teisias and Korax to rescue them from primitive incoherence. When Wrong in Aristophanes' *Clouds* 1055–1057 makes the point that if spending one's time in the agora were disreputable Homer would not have used the term ἀγορητής of Nestor and other heroes, he is exploiting the ambiguities of the word ἀγορά and its derivatives, but he is incidentally saying something which could

[2] Navarre, 9 f., makes a speculative jump from Empedokles' involvement in politics, such as it was (Diog. Laert. viii. 66 f.), to the teaching of oratory.

also be said seriously and honestly (cf. Blass, i.6). When we read in Homer (*Il.* iii.204-224) Antenor's description of Menelaos and Odysseus as he had seen and heard them when they came on an embassy to demand the return of Helen, we become aware that a connoisseur is speaking.[3] Menelaos, he says, spoke fluently, not at great length, but in a clear voice and without stumbling (οὐδ' ἀφαμαρτοεπής). Odysseus stood with his eyes downcast, holding his sceptre stiffly and not using it for gesticulation, so that he looked at first like an unskilled (ἄϊδρις) man; but when he spoke, with his strong voice, "words like a winter snowstorm," he was incomparable.

Lest anyone should think that Homer was perhaps using high-flown language to describe orators who would have been bewildered if they had had to speak before a fifth-century audience, consider the sensitivity and subtlety of observation shown by the poet in his description of what at first glance seems a savage brawl between Agamemnon and Achilles in *Iliad* i. When Agamemnon demands recompense for the loss of Chryseis, he is not so foolish as to say to Achilles, "I will take something of yours"; for if Achilles were then to refuse there would be no drawing back from a disastrous and possibly mortal confrontation. He says (137-139), "I will take a prize of yours, or from Ajax, or from Odysseus; and to whomsoever I come, he will be enraged." This is a probe to discover Achilles' reaction. The reaction is not an outright "You will take nothing from me!" but a complaint: "You threaten to take a prize away from me ... I always get a smaller share of booty than you do. Now I shall go back home to Phthia ..." (161, 166-171). Agamemnon now knows that he is on safe ground, and he makes his threat specific (184-186): "I will come to *your* hut and take Briseis, your prize, that you may recognise how much I am your superior." Achilles has left it too late to say, "You shall not." He contemplates violence, but changes his mind—or, as Homer puts it, Athena appears to him and persuades him to yield, foretelling future reward—and he turns to verbal violence instead,

---

[3] Cf. Pilz, 9 f., on the extent to which Homer takes it for granted that good speaking is an important accomplishment, and Kennedy (*Art of Persuasion*), 35 ff., 93.

with an oath that the Greeks will one day regret his withdrawal from the fight (233–244). Nestor, in thirty lines of verse (254–284) which contain many types of argument familiar to us from Demosthenes, tries to pacify Agamemnon and Achilles, but fails entirely. Agamemnon's answer to his plea is a plaintive vilification of Achilles (286–291), and Achilles' answer a more violent defiance of Agamemnon (293–296), ending significantly (297–303) with the declaration: "I won't fight you or anyone else about the girl . . . But you won't take any other possession of mine . . . And if you try to . . . your blood will flow." Now, Agamemnon has not committed himself to taking anything except Briseis, so that by ending on a formidably threatening note Achilles is saving his own face, and saving it without risk. Here, as elsewhere, Homer observes and portrays people as they are; when, for example, Thersites, described as ἔχθιστος Ἀχιλῆϊ (ii.220), praises Achilles for his valour in battle and self-restraint in face of Agamemnon's provocation and ends his speech by making his own words previously uttered by Achilles (ii.239 f., cf. i.232) he is acting precisely as we would expect him to act. People who believe that they can find in Homer, Aischylos and Sophokles pervasive religious and philosophical doctrines often arrive at findings which are vulnerable simply because they have not made enough allowance for accurate portrayal of the subtlety and irrationality of human beings as they really are.[4]

That Homer should have a keen eye and ear for the stance, gestures and voice of an orator and for the interplay of personalities in conflict before an audience[5] is no matter for surprise when we reflect that the same phenomena can occur in illiterate societies at a much lower level of material culture than archaic

[4] I have in mind especially the trial scene in Aischylos's *Eumenides*, where commentators sometimes look for moral philosophy, and accordingly try to explain away the irrelevance and dishonesty of the arguments which are used, instead of accepting the grandeur and drama inherent in Aischylos's quasi-historical reconstruction of the irrational interplay between men, heroes and gods.

[5] The structure of arguments (rational or emotional) in Homeric speeches has been analysed often enough; that is why I have concentrated on a neglected aspect of the matter, Homer's representation of the interplay of personalities.

Greece.[6] Sir Arthur Grimble, in his book *A Pattern of Islands* (London, 1952) describes in the following terms (chap. iv) how a native of the Gilbert Islands in the central Pacific would plead for a reduction in his tax. "The Gilbertese man in the street . . . was a humorist, a dramatist and an orator in his bones . . . The staging of an elaborate petition was pure joy for him. A man would begin to think over his piece and coach his witnesses for their parts months before the date of the great production. The rejection of his plea, qua plea, was of course a foregone conclusion . . ." But it was the aesthetic approbation of the audience which mattered. The magistrate would ask the assembled crowd whether the petitioner's statements were true, and they would reply, "He lies!" And so the magistrate would give judgment against the petitioner; but he would be careful to compliment him on the quality of his pleading, and if the crowd too voiced its approbation the petitioner's failure to obtain a reduction in his tax was outweighed; his face was saved, and his status was enhanced.

The point to which I have been leading by this roundabout route is that the orator's stance, gestures, quality of voice, fluency and subtlety fell within what one might call the "area of sensitivity" of the Greeks from a very early date, and their treatment of oratory as an art was a matter for comment in the fifth century; the idea that one argues rationally oneself, whereas one's adversary entertains the audience and thereby artfully leads them away from the point at issue, became itself a matter for rhetorical exploitation (e.g., Thuc. iii.38.4–7).[7] The earliest rhetorical teaching and manuals, although they probably affected the development of oratory by focussing attention more on some techniques than on others, represented an intellectual analysis and systematisation of existing practice. In this respect they differed radically from

[6] Cf. C. Fries, *RPh* lxvi (1940), 43 ff., on the esteem in which forceful oratory was held in Egypt and other ancient civilisations, and J. J. Bateman, *Phoenix* xvi (1962), 159, on the Greek "delight in argument for its own sake."

[7] Naturally I would not dream of pandering to an audience's taste for oratorical display; it is you who do that—just as I rise and speak, but you jump out and shout.

contemporary scientific speculation, which was trying to answer questions which had not been asked before, and they differed even more from artistic innovation or technological invention. They had more in common with the medical literature which was taking shape at the same time, with modern sexual manuals, and perhaps with modern sociology, which I have heard described (unjustly, in my view) as "the articulation of what we already know." This is a matter in which the onlooker—that is to say, the historian—sees the most of the game. During and after the generation which experienced this remarkable concentration of intellectual activity on the principles of oratory it was widely believed that democracy—the government of the state by a sovereign assembly comprising the entire citizen body, and the settlement of lawsuits by large juries drawn from that same body—was intimately connected with rhetoric and consultancy.[8] Antiphon on trial for his life turns to his own advantage the allegation that he wrote speeches for others, and argues that since this practice was open to him under a democracy but would not have been open under an oligarchy he had no motive to desire an oligarchic revolution (fr. 1a. col. II.21–col. III.11). How was it possible for him to argue in this way, as if there were no lucrative prospects for a consultant in a society in which the political and legal decisions were taken by a much more restricted body?

Since I have argued (p. 50) that we should accept as valid Thucydides' picture of the structure and working of Athenian politics, on the grounds that he was there and we were not, I feel rather vulnerable in making the suggestion that the Athenians themselves were mistaken in assuming an intimate connection between consultancy, rhetoric and democracy; I can only plead that Thucydides' portrayal of politics fits the rest of the evidence and Antiphon's implication does not.

[8] Cf. Pilz, *passim*, and Lavency, 86, n. 6. Pilz, 14, suggests that technically accomplished oratory "even in the time of Gorgias" was more at home in the assembly than in the courts, but Ar. *Acharnians* 679 f. tells against this. It should be noted that a dangerous misinterpretation of ῥήτωρ in *IG* i.²45.21 is adopted by G. Zuntz, *C & M* ii (1939), 142 ("subversive activity of rhetors"); the meaning is simply "⟨as a⟩ speaker ⟨in the assembly⟩."

There is, of course, no doubt that when a lawsuit is heard *in camera* by a single magistrate (cf. Arist. *Rhet.* 1414ᵃ11–14) or by a very small body of nobles acting in a judicial capacity exercise of the techniques of persuasion is seriously inhibited. In particular, a tyrant who operates outside and above a system of law might be presumed to decide a case in accordance with his desire to secure one litigant as a grateful ally in the future and his indifference to the future hostility of the other litigant. Consideration of this possibility may have led Aristotle (if correctly reported by Cic. *Brut.* 46 = Arist. fr. 137) to associate Teisias and Korax with the overthrow of the Sicilian tyrants and the consequent reversion of lawsuits to juries. But a tyrant so apprehensive, or so secure, that he decided lawsuits *in camera* or delegated their decision to trusted individuals, was an unusual phenomenon. More typical of archaic Greece is the famous scene on the shield of Achilles (*Il.* xviii.497–508) where the people (λαοί) are "in assembly" (εἰν ἀγορῇ) and two adversaries in a lawsuit make their pleas before "the elders" who sit in a circle, holding sceptres. The litigants are described as "expounding *to the people*" (δήμῳ πιφαύσκων), and the crowd (which is kept in order by heralds, like the assembled Greek army in *Il.* ii.96–98) cries out in support of both of them.[9] In a hearing of this kind (and the parallel with the presenting of a petition to a magistrate in the Gilbert Islands forces itself upon us) the litigant stakes not merely the property which is the subject of the lawsuit but his standing in the community; and at the same time those who give their decisions under so strong and searching a light (cf. *Il.* xvi.387, Hes. *Th.* 84–86) are likely to be affected by the noises of approval and hostility which rise from the uninhibited Greek crowd.

When the first step is taken from government by a small aristocracy to government by a democratic assembly (of which large juries are, as it were, executive committees)[10] the differences in

---

[9] Cf. H. J. Wolff, *Traditio* iv (1946), 34 ff., for a comparison with the practice of other early European societies.

[10] Cf. especially Dem. xxi.167, 174, where "you," addressed to the jury, means also "those who were sent on the expedition to Euboia."

what is demanded of the litigant are reduced almost to vanishing point. Oratory which makes an impact on a hundred jurors selected at random from the entire population is not different in kind from what makes an impact on a council for which only a hundred men qualify by virtue of their landed property. The Council under the Thirty Tyrants was picked for its servility (Xen. *HG.* ii.3.11 f.), but Xenophon's portrayal of the mortal contest between Kritias and Theramenes before it (3.24–46) does not suggest any difference of oratorical technique from what was employed by Euryptolemos in addressing an excited Assembly two years earlier (i.7.16–33); and even the servile council had the spirit to create an approving clamour (ii.3.50) at the end of Theramenes' speech, much to the consternation of Kritias. It did not occur to Thucydides to differentiate in technique between speeches addressed to meetings of representatives and those addressed to democratic assemblies.[11] It should be added in this connection that under the democracy secret sessions of the Council (e.g., And. ii.19) or Areopagus (cf. Dem. lix.80) were a rarity, and restriction on listening to the speeches made to a jury or assembly virtually unknown. Normally as many people as were interested and could get within earshot would do so, as we see from XII.35, "Many citizens and foreigners have come to find out what your verdict on these men will be." Compare Ant. vi.14, a particularly detailed reference to the throng round a homicide trial; Aischines ii.5, εἰ γάρ τις ἢ τῶν ἔξωθεν περιεστηκότων πέπεισται (σχεδὸν δ' οἱ πλεῖστοι τῶν πολιτῶν πάρεισιν) ἢ τῶν δικαζόντων ὑμῶν: iii.124, ὅσοι ξένοι περιέστασαν τὴν ἐκκλησίαν: Dem. xix.17 τὸ γὰρ βουλευτήριον μεστὸν ἦν ἰδιωτῶν.

Now if we are to say that the Greeks themselves were mistaken in associating the consolidation and extension of democracy with the formulation of rhetorical technique, systematic instruction in

[11] Xen. *Mem.* i.2.31 says that Kritias, in power in 404, forbade by law the teaching of λόγων τέχνη. If this is true, it was a gesture in keeping with the oligarchic belief in a link between rhetoric and democracy. Xenophon's preposterous claim that this law was intended to discriminate against Sokrates, and that no other way of attacking Sokrates was open to the Thirty Tyrants, shows the extremity to which he is driven by the thesis he unwisely attempts to sustain in *Mem.* i.2.12 ff.

this technique and the circulation of forensic speeches in written versions, we must at least offer a plausible explanation of their error, and I do not think that the explanations are either forced or fallacious.

In the first place, it must be remembered that by the time that the Athenian democracy had been established for three generations historically distorted notions of the relation between tyranny, oligarchy and democracy were widespread. Looking back on the panorama of history we can see how tyranny displaced oligarchy and democracy in turn displaced tyranny; but to the Athenians who in 415 clamoured that the mutilation of the herms was perpetrated in furtherance of "an oligarchical and tyrannical conspiracy" (Thuc. vi.60–1) there seemed to be a simple antithesis between the rule of law, under which issues are determined by the litigants' presentation of their cases, and arbitrary power (whether exercised by one man or several), in which law was overridden and issues prejudged in accordance with the interests of the powerful. Aischines iii.6 presents this antithesis straightforwardly (cf. iii.233). It was therefore easy for Antiphon, adopting a current standpoint which he judged to be strongly represented in the jury, to argue that under an oligarchy there was no place for the consultant.

Secondly, once property and lineage cease to be necessary qualifications for membership of the body which governs the community, power is potentially transferred to those who have learned to speak persuasively, even if they lack any of the traditional qualifications; Polos in Pl. *Grg.* 466 A–C enlarges dramatically on the power of the orator.[12] The gap between actual and potential transfer can, however, be considerable. Even in the last quarter of the fifth century possession of great wealth and descent from distinguished ancestors carried remarkable weight with the Athenian Assembly; the bitter satire of Aristophanes' *Knights* is meaningful only in a society which still takes aristocratic leadership very much for granted. Moreover, the potential gap opened

[12] Kennedy, 34, makes the point that awareness of the potentialities of the speaker in the fifth century gave the essential impetus to the study of oratory.

by oratory between influence and responsibility was not actualised to the extent which might be imagined. An Athenian could not easily evade election to offices if the Assembly chose to find out whether he could perform what he had promised or advocated, and the holding of office carried with it the possibility of formidable punishment for failure. Even the orator who appeared at the moment of his success to have exercised irresponsible power was not immune from retribution; penalties were attached to "failure to give the best advice" (Hyper. iv.8); five of the speakers who had brought about the condemnation of the generals after Arginusai were subsequently charged with "deceiving the Assembly" and were lucky to escape in the civil strife which followed the disaster at Aigospotamoi (Xen. *HG.* i.7.34). I am inclined to think that the spectre of Thersites dominated the imagination of those who regarded leadership as their birthright, and that they wished that they could deal with the Thersitai of their own day as Odysseus had dealt with his prototype (*Il.* ii.243–277). Thersites did not look like a gentleman, and it is always interesting to observe in politics how the same voter may react quite differently to the same train of reasoning according to whether it is expressed in a rasping voice and a local accent or in a cultivated voice and elegant diction.

Thirdly, some of the writers with whose political attitudes we are best acquainted, notably Thucydides, Plato and Aristotle, were disposed to regard the irrationalities and self-seeking of a crowd which included poor men less leniently than the irrationalities and self-seeking of men who had great possessions.[13] No doubt philosopher-kings would have pursued justice inflexibly, immune to the blandishments, evasions and paralogisms of orators. But there were no philosopher-kings, and the assumption that oligarchies had been in the past, and would be in the future, less fickle and less vulnerable to rhetorical exploitation was no more than the Greek manifestation of a recurrent tendency in human history, the tendency to regard virtue, rationality and impartiality

---

[13] Modern writers too (e.g., Lavency, 170) tend to assume that a large crowd is more fickle in its sentiments than a small group.

as functions of property (or, in other epochs and regions, of the lack of property). Television, by enabling us to see and hear the conferences of rival political parties within the same week, or even on the same day, has also enabled us to understand how and why different classes and categories of people can hold mistaken beliefs about themselves and about one another.

Fourthly, transparently incorrect generalisations about political regimes occur in various connections; for example, Isok. xxi.11–13 argues simultaneously that his client Nikias would not have been able to συκοφαντεῖν under the Thirty Tyrants, even if that had previously been his wont, and that Nikias was compelled, under the Thirty, to give away much of his money τοῖς συκοφαντοῦσιν. So too [Xen.] *Resp. Ath.* 2.14 assumes that the poor have nothing to lose by war and invasion; but even Thucydides (ii.65.3) shows some awareness that having little and losing it all is worth mention in the same breath as having much and losing most of it.

Systematic rhetoric and consultancy had this much in common with democracy: both of them were manifestations of the immense range of rapid innovations which distinguished Greek civilisation from the civilisations which had preceded it. So were vase painting, representational sculpture, philosophy, agnosticism, historiography and drama. Among these innovations the relationship of the last two with oratory was especially intimate and perhaps more complicated than has sometimes been acknowledged.

Much has been said about the influence of oratory on Euripides, and rather less about its influence on Aischylos and Sophokles—perhaps because Euripides was an inferior theatrical craftsman, applying rhetorical technique to passages which consequently detach themselves from their dramatic context and force themselves on our attention, and preferring a detached prologue to any attempt to emulate the artistry with which Sophokles introduces us to the dramatic situation in the opening scene of a play.[14]

[14] Cf. Navarre, 75 ff., on methodical exposition in Euripides, and 73 f., on Soph. *El.* 516 ff.

I wonder if we should not pay some attention to the influence of drama on oratory.[15]

A Greek tragedy puts before our eyes people whom most Greeks regarded as having lived at approximately definable dates in the past—usually the remote past (though not so remote that they could not be linked by continuous genealogies with contemporary families), but sometimes the recent past, as in Phrynichos's *Capture of Miletos* and Aischylos's *Persians*. No tragedian would have claimed that he knew the actual arguments brought to bear on Philoktetes or the actual reproaches uttered by Elektra against Klytaimestra. What Aischylos or Sophokles would have claimed was that they put into the mouths of gods, heroes, heroines, men and women words which they would have used if they, and the situations in which they were involved, had truly been as the playwright conceived them. Euripides would perhaps have claimed, if he had been forced to make any such claim explicit, that he put into their mouths what they would have said if their own capacity to argue, persuade and attack had been comparable with his own. I would suggest for consideration that the Athenian public's long habituation to the dramatisation of events which they regarded as historical contributed to their acceptance of a written speech which did not purport to be a verbatim record of what was said in court but rather represented an artistically sophisticated version of what could or should have been said in court.

The second, and perhaps more important, contribution to the same end was made by Herodotos and by whatever other historical works in the third quarter of the fifth century were comparable with Herodotos in technique. The proportion of direct speech incorporated in Herodotean narrative is, after all, remarkably high; and just as a continuous thread of literary technique runs from Homer (e.g., *Il.* i.318–430) through Herodotos (e.g., i.6–13) to the narratives in I.6–27 and XXXII.4–18, so too the existence in Herodotos of the debate which followed the killing of the

---

[15] And, indeed, the influence of earlier poetry; cf. Blass, i.66, and Hollingsworth, 18, on the importance of Hesiodic antithesis for early oratory.

Persian Pretender (iii.80–82), the speech by which Sosikles deterred Kleomenes' allies from attempting to restore Hippias (v.92) or Leotychidas's admonition to the Athenians (vi.86) created an incentive to the composition of speeches which might have been uttered on past occasions.[16]

Furthermore, the fact that drama was performed and enjoyed in the performance does nothing to diminish the importance of the fact that it was also read. However salutary it may be to remind ourselves at frequent intervals that Greek literature was designed as a sequence of sounds and not as a sequence of visual patterns, that the Greeks read aloud to one another in circumstances where we would simply lend a book (e.g., Pl. *Phdr.* 228DE, 230E, *Tht.* 143BC), that they memorised in circumstances where we would rely on reference and reading (e.g., Ar. *Clouds* 1354–1372) and that as late as Lysias's own lifetime it was possible to make jokes about the reading and ownership of books (Ar. fr. 490 and *Frogs* 1114), it is equally necessary to remember that Phaidros in Plato does not depend solely on memorisation for acquisition of Lysias's *Erotikos* but borrows the original script (*Phdr.* 228B.D), and that we do after all possess not only plays of Aischylos but fragments of early prose works and even ephemeral essays such as that of the "Old Oligarch," which antedates anything that Lysias could have put into circulation.

In respect of the relation between a speech and the event with which the speech purports to be connected, it is possible to make a threefold classification of speeches which can be dated, with varying degrees of probability, to the late fifth or early fourth century.

I. Speeches which purport to have been delivered by contemporaries before a jury or before the Council or Assembly. The great majority of speeches in the *corpus Lysiacum* belong to this category. Among them are three of which the content is such as to provoke suspicion that there is a certain gap between them and the events to which they are ostensibly related. In one of these

[16] Cf. Navarre, 72 f., and Kennedy, 44 ff.

three cases I believe the suspicion to be justified, in one partly justified and in the third unjustified.

(1) In I, *On the Killing of Eratosthenes*, the prosecutor appears to have alleged that Euphiletos enticed Eratosthenes to his house by sending a slave-woman to fetch him (§37); Euphiletos alleges that the slave's part was simply to wake him up and tell him when Eratosthenes had entered the house (§23). This is precisely the type of conflict for the "resolution" of which Attic law provided that slaves should be tortured. Did Euphiletos offer his slave for torture or not? If he did and the offer was accepted, what did she say, and why does he not either use her evidence (if favourable) or rebut it (if unfavourable)—for instance, by enlarging on the hostility of slaves towards their masters (cf. VII.16,35), a theme for which his narrative (§§18–21) would have given him a sound basis? If he offered her for torture, and the offer was refused, why does he not exploit this fact (cf. VII.34 f)? If he did not make the offer, why is there no explanation of his refusal or inability? Here it is rational to postulate one significant difference between the published speech and the defence offered in court. Naturally it is proper to ask "Why did the published version not deal with the question of the slave?" and I do not know the answer; but the impossibility of answering a question does not diminish the importance of the original question which provoked it.

(2) XXV, erroneously entitled δήμου καταλύσεως ἀπολογία in the Palatinus, is, as we have seen (p. 7), a plea belonging to a δοκιμασία. In this case the grounds for suspicion are the high level of generalisation maintained throughout the speech, the intellectual aloofness of the argument in §§8–11, and the assurance of the inimical tone adopted in §25 towards certain individuals prominent in the closing years of the war. No reference is made to the speaker's relations with any named persons or to his conduct on specified occasions. His summary (§12), "I have been a trierarch five times, taken part in four sea battles, paid many capital levies in wartime and performed my other liturgies as well as any other citizen," makes a striking contrast with XXI.1–10. The end of the speech is lost through the mutilation of the Palatinus, and may

have contained what we miss in the extant portion; subject to this reservation, I suggest that XXV is a hypothetical defence of a man against whom the charge is made at a δοκιμασία that he remained in the city during the rule of the Thirty Tyrants.

(3) Suspicion has been attached to XXIV,[17] the *Defence of the Cripple*, because it seems surprising that so trivial a matter as a cripple's receipt of a dole could have provided the occasion for so elegant a speech, and one naturally wonders from what source the consultant received adequate reward. These suspicions should not carry weight (cf. Blass, i.637). At least in the late fourth century εἰσαγγελίαι were brought on charges involving trivial sums of money; Hypereides v.26 speaks of a certain Konon who was fined a talent because he had drawn theoric payment on behalf of his son during his son's absence from Attica, and elsewhere (iv.3) he ridicules abuses of the εἰσαγγελτικὸς νόμος which have led to the prosecution of, for example, two men who paid flute-girls more than the maximum prescribed by law. If the situation was similar in the early fourth century, even an honest cripple might have been the victim of malicious εἰσαγγελία, and we have no idea whether the cripple of XXIV was honest;[18] it must also be remembered that the occasion may have been a δοκιμασία (cf. p. 7). Whatever the nature of the case, if what his accusers said about his association with wealthy friends was true (§5), he was able to call on the services of a consultant.

II. Speeches composed for purely hypothetical circumstances. The one unquestioned example of this category is the set of *Tetralogies* belonging to the *corpus Antiphonteum*, each containing two speeches for the prosecution and two for the defence in a case of homicide. The only argument for comparatively late dating of the *Tetralogies* is the fact that one speaker claims to have paid "many capital levies." If one believes (*a*) that the capital levy was peculiar to Athens, (*b*) that the writer has an Athenian ambience consistently in mind and (*c*) that when Thucydides (iii.19.1)

---

[17] E.g., Bruns, 461 ff., and Lämmli, 69 ff.
[18] U. Albini, *RM* xcv (1952), 335, rightly emphasises the impossibility of discovering the relation of the plea to the facts.

describes the Athenian levy of 427 as raised "then for the first time" he means not the first during the war but literally the first, then it follows that one must date the *Tetralogies* some years later than 427. Since, however, I see no reason whatever to believe the first of the three premisses, no good reason to believe the second and at least some grounds for questioning the third, I attach much more importance to the fact that the language of the *Tetralogies* is in part Ionic, the language which predominated in prose literature until the last quarter of the fifth century, and I accordingly regard the *Tetralogies* as earlier than anything in the *corpus Lysiacum*.[19] That is to say, the composition of speeches for hypothetical circumstances was a genre which Lysias inherited and took for granted.

III. Speeches composed when the occasions to which they relate are known, by writer and reader alike, to belong to the past. These may be subdivided (by us, even if the Greeks would not have made so sharp a distinction)[20] into the mythical and the historical.

The best-known example of the mythical category is the defence put by Gorgias into the mouth of Palamedes. The date of Gorgias's death was not known to later writers, and is not known to us; *Palamedes* may or may not be earlier than anything in the *corpus Lysiacum*. The close relation of this genre to enkomia such as Gorgias's *Helen* and Isokrates' *Helen* and *Busiris* is obvious.

In the historical category[21] we must include Polykrates' *Accusation of Sokrates* (Isok. xi.4), Plato's *Defence of Sokrates* and a *Defence of Sokrates* ascribed to Lysias. Whether Polykrates adopted an address to a jury as a literary form, we do not know for certain.

---

[19] Cf. K. J. Dover, *CQ* xliv (1950), 58 f. Blass's discussion (i.152 ff.) of this aspect of the *Tetralogies* is a little perfunctory.

[20] When Hdt. iii.122.2 distinguishes ἡ ἀνθρωπηίη λεγομένη γενεή (which includes Polykrates) from another γενεή which includes Minos, I take it that he assigns Minos to the heroic age described by Hes. *Op.* 156 ff.

[21] I would include in this category (but I find no examples in the early fourth century) the late composition—bordering on "forgery" in the true sense—of speeches under the name of orators whose work did not survive in writing. The speeches ascribed to Demades are the best example; see the edition by V. de Falco (2d ed. Naples, 1954).

Plato certainly did, and so did the Lysianic work, if the source of [Plu.] *Vit. Or.* 836B is right in calling it ἐστοχασμένη τῶν δικαστῶν.

We must include also the speech ostensibly delivered by Nikias before his Syracusan captors. This was attributed to Lysias by Theophrastos (Dion. Hal. i.23.16–25.7), to the indignant surprise of Dionysios; cf. p. 98.

Further, we must include Andokides iv, which purports to be delivered by a person who is one of three—the other two being Nikias and Alkibiades—who are threatened with ostracism. It is apparent from Plu. *Alc.* 13.2 that this speech (cf. 13.4; *Nic.* 11.7) was regarded by Plutarch's source for that passage as the work of Phaiax. This source does not seem to have been Theophrastos, for the speech (§ 2) names Nikias as one of the three in danger, and Theophrastos (fr. 139 = Plu. *Nic.* 11.10) thought that the three were Phaiax, Alkibiades and Hyperbolos, not Nikias;[22] nor was it the source used by Plutarch in *Nic.* 11.1–6, for he there treats Nikias and Alkibiades as being originally the only two in danger but persuading their respective factions to combine in ostracising Hyperbolos. I would hazard a guess that the speech was ascribed to Andokides in Kallimachos's catalogue but to Phaiax in the Pergamene catalogue (cf. p. 21), perhaps because Andokides cannot conceivably have been considered as a "candidate" for ostracism in 416/415, the ostensible date of the speech (§§ 22, 25 ~ Thuc. v.50.4, 106, vi.8.2, 16.2, 30.1), and the speaker had been, like Phaiax (Thuc. v.4.1) an envoy to Italy and Sicily (§ 41). Since, however, the speech cannot have been delivered in 416/415 in any case, for Alkibiades is said to have had a son by a woman whom he bought when the population of Melos was enslaved (§ 22; cf. Thuc. v.106.2–4), and it is highly doubtful whether there

---

[22] A. E. Raubitschek, *TAPA* lxxix (1948), 209, suggests that Theophrastos may simply have said, with And. iv in mind, that Phaiax opposed Alkibiades openly; but Plutarch's wording is, "I am not ignorant that Theophrastos says that Hyperbolos was ostracised Φαίακος, οὐ Νικίου, πρὸς Ἀλκιβιάδην ἐρίσαντος." The phrasing adopted by A. R. Burn, *CQ*, N.S. iv (1954), 138, may suggest to the reader that Plutarch in *Alc.* 10.4 (= Theophr. fr. 134) named Theophrastos as his authority for ascribing And. iv to Phaiax; but Plutarch says nothing there about ostracism—he simply cites Theophrastos's judgment on Alkibiades' qualities as an orator.

was ever an occasion on which an Athenian could address anybody and say (§2): "Either I or X or Y must necessarily be ostracised," it is obvious that the speech is a piece of historical fiction composed by someone who did not understand how ostracism worked and had no desire to be pedantic about the date of the capture of Melos.[23] I can find no good reason why the writer should not have been Andokides, drawing in part on anecdotes told by relations and friends and in part on the *Abuse of Alkibiades* circulated by Antiphon (frr. 66 f.) in or before 411. The imagined rival of Nikias and Alkibiades could be Andokides' own father, Leogoras, who, like the speaker (§41), had been an envoy to Macedonia (*IG* i².57.50 f.; cf. And. ii.11 on Archelaos as πατρικὸς ξένος) and had the best of reasons, after the summer of 415, for hating Alkibiades: he and his family, together with Nikias's brother and Alkibiades' enemy Taureas (And. i.47; cf. Dem. xxi.147), were victims of the false denunciations instigated by associates of Alkibiades (i.65)[24] as a riposte to the denunciations of Alkibiades for profanation of the mysteries.

The existence of a *Defence of Sokrates* ascribed to Lysias inevitably gave rise to a story, first known to us from Cic. *De Or.* i.231 (cf. Diog. Laert. ii.40 f.), that Lysias actually composed the speech before the trial and offered it (in vain) to Sokrates. Considering the antiquity of fictitious speeches as a literary genre, the normal absence of any evidence to indicate whether or not a speech was actually delivered (cf. Dion. Hal. i.49.11–13, on the speech against the proposal of Phormisios) and the readiness of Hellenistic writers to accept forensic or symbuleutic form as purely conventional, it is curious to see how these same writers can assume, when an anecdote, an argument or a telling sarcasm hangs upon the

---

[23] This does not mean that the speech is a very late fiction. For example, the statement in Lys. VI says that Andokides was imprisoned "almost a year" (§23) before he gave information—a statement impossible to reconcile with Thuc. vi.60, if it refers to the herms—is probably no more than a gross falsehood fifteen years after the event (see, however, MacDowell on And. i.28, 48 and pp. 178 ff.

[24] I base this expression on the facts that (*a*) one of the two men who induced Diokleides to make his false denunciation was named Alkibiades, and (*b*) one of those denounced was Nikias's brother (i.47).

assumption, that a speech must be written before the event and for a real event; so Dionysios (i.303.20–24) argues against the authenticity of speeches ascribed to Deinarchos but datable to the period of Deinarchos's exile at Chalkis by saying, "People would not have sailed to Chalkis to get speeches."

What I have been saying has a bearing above all on the *Epitaphios*. To ask "Would the Athenians have elected a metic to deliver a funeral speech?" or "Would an eminent politician, elected to deliver a funeral speech, have got his text from a rhetorician?" is, I suggest, to ask questions which do not deserve the time that has been spent on trying to answer them. A funeral speech, like any enkomion or panegyric, belongs to a genre naturally attractive to anyone interested and skilled in oratory, and a rhetorician must often have composed such a speech without even entertaining the possibility that he himself or anyone else would deliver it at a real state funeral (cf. Blass, i.437). Consequently I see no reason why Lysias should not have composed the *Epitaphios* (cf., on its language, pp. 59 ff.).

Let me now pull the threads together. This book has been addressed to the question: how far is it possible, and on what grounds, to isolate the work of the individual Lysias within the total body of work which has at any time been ascribed to him? Here now is my answer to this question.

(1) XII is the only speech which we can safely affirm to have been written in its entirety by Lysias and by him alone.

(2) If Dionysios correctly interpreted the historical references in the second speech for Iphikrates, it is extremely improbable that Lysias was still alive to write that speech.

(3) If Dionysios correctly interpreted the historical references in the first speech for Iphikrates, and if there were no speeches in the *corpus Lysiacum*, except the two speeches for Iphikrates, datable after 378, it is improbable that Lysias wrote the first speech for Iphikrates.

(4) Among all the remaining speeches, whether extant, fragmentary or known only from citations, there is not one which can

be denied to Lysias either on chronological grounds or on grounds of ideological standpoint or (with the possible exception of VI [cf. p. 79]) political association.

(5) The known or presumed ascription of a speech to Lysias in the catalogue of Kallimachos is of value only because it implies ascription by booksellers at the end of the fourth century.

(6) Ascription of forensic and symbuleutic speeches to Lysias by the booksellers is of value in so far as it implies ascription in some cases by people acquainted, either directly or at an interval of one generation, with the speakers or with Lysias or with both. The speeches for Iphikrates warn us that we must not forget to say "in some cases." It might be—indeed, I think it would be—irrational to suppose that the majority of ascriptions received by the booksellers rested on error or were the product of deliberate falsification, but it is necessary to believe that some ascriptions rested on one or the other.

(7) Ascription of epideictic speeches received by the booksellers was less vulnerable to error or deceit, since the involvement of anyone but the author was rarer and smaller.

(8) So far, there are no technical criteria which help us to decide whether the ascription to Lysias of the *Epitaphios*, the *Olympikos*, the *Speech of Nikias* or the *Speech against the Proposal of Phormisios* was erroneous, or whether the *Erotikos* is authentic or a parody.

(9) There are so far no technical criteria which enable us to say that Lysias had no share in any given forensic speech ascribed to him, but there are technical criteria which enable us to assess, when there is no obstacle to the assumption that Lysias acted as consultant in the case, (*a*) how far he submerged his own "linguistic personality" in order to create an appropriate one for the speaker, and (*b*) the extent to which he went beyond the formulation of arguments and composed the actual wording of the speech.

(10) We very rarely have any grounds for entertaining an opinion on whether the speaker in a forensic speech is in the right or in the wrong.

(11) We never have reason to affirm that the speech which we

read is a faithful reproduction of what was said in court, and the only evidence available suggests that it is not.

(12) Although it would be perverse to suppose that a majority of speeches were composed for hypothetical cases or for cases settled out of court, there is not one speech ascribed to Lysias, with the virtually certain exception of XXVIII, of which we can positively assert, on independent evidence, that the case was heard.

A recent writer, commenting on an attempt to distinguish between Lysias's concept of law and alternative Attic concepts, expresses the opinion that, if some consistency of legal and political concepts cannot be discerned in the Lysian speeches, "one must admit that the speeches are artificial" and that "any search for Lysias himself in them is fruitless," adding: "I myself hesitate to make such an admission. It would make nonsense of a great deal of classical scholarship."[25] My first reaction to this opinion is, I fear, a little impatient. Of course forensic speeches are "artificial" —why should anyone ever have thought that they were not? We have only to remind ourselves of current legal and political behaviour, to observe how people argue when their lives or careers or property are at stake and to bring our knowledge of the world to bear upon the study of antiquity. My second reaction is pedantic: it is not the case that a "great deal" of classical scholarship has been devoted to the Attic orators. The proportion of the whole devoted to the study of Lysias is negligible compared with what has been devoted, say, to Plato or Homer. My third reaction is that although anyone is free to say that I have tried, with or without success, to "make nonsense" of such work as has been done on Lysias, I have not thought of my argument in those terms, nor would I make so extravagant a claim for my conclusions. There is, so far as I know, only one way of making nonsense of scholarship: to give habit the status of authority and thus allow it to suffocate radical curiosity. We have become accustomed to treat oratory as if it were philosophy, history, poetry or technical

---

[25] J. J. Bateman, *TAPA* lxxxix (1958), 277, in a critique of Erik Wolf, *Griechisches Rechtsdenken*.

literature, and to perpend the ascription of a speech as if we were somehow entitled to an answer "yes" or "no." We have tended, often unconsciously, to assume the absolute correctness of an ascription, unless we happen to learn, from the critical and lexicographical works which fortune has preserved, that its ascription was questioned in antiquity; and we have not reflected enough on the historical circumstances which created the possibility of disputed ascription in the first place. In short, we have got into a rather bad habit; and I suggest we get out of it.

In most circumstances I would be the last person to welcome the disappearance of a personality into the anonymity of a period or a community, but I do not find anything uncongenial or disturbing in the conclusions to which study of the *corpus Lysiacum* has led me. I gladly trade what I once believed to be my knowledge of Lysias's beliefs and principles for what I now believe to be a substantially correct picture of the relations between litigant, consultant, rhetorician, reader and bookseller.

Index

Aesthetics of oratory, 94 f., 158, 171, 178 f.
ἀγορά, 176
Aischines ii and iii, 111–114, 155 f., 172 f.
Aischylos, *Eumenides*, 178 n. 1; *Seven against Thebes*, 96
ἀκριβής, 155
Alkibiades (son of Alkibiades), 44, 53 f., 166
Alkibiades (son of Kleinias), 32, 43–45, 52–55, 191 f.
Alkidamas, *On Written Speeches*, 150 n. 4, 155
Alphabetical order of speeches, 3–6, 12
Alternative versions of speeches, 165 f.
ἄν, 89 f., 130–134, 146 f.
Andokides, 74 f., 84–86; i, 78–80, 169; iv, 19, 189 f., 191 f.
Anticipation of arguments, 169 f.
Antiphon, 6, 74 f.; ii–iv (Tetralogies), 106, 128, 189 f.; v, 165; fr. 1a, 157, 186
Aorist. *See* Aspect
ἀπαγωγή, 9
Apollodoros (litigant), 34–38, 51
Aristocracy, 183
Aristophanes, 68 n. 9, 83–88, 92; *Clouds*, 24, 149, 155, 158, 175 n. 1; *Knights*, 73 f., 150 f.; *Thesmophoriazusai*, 168 n. 22
Aristophanes of Byzantion, 21 n. 20
Aristotle, *Rhetoric*, 25 f., 59 f., 78; fr. 65, 176; fr. 140, 25, 161
Article, definite, 88 f., 105, 112
Ascription of speeches, 13–27, 45–87, 91 f., 155, 193–196

Aspect of verbs, 106, 113
Assonance, 60–64, 82, 91, 101
Asyndeton, 89, 98
αὐτόν, 134–139, 146 f.

Biography, 38, 42
Booksellers, 25 f., 153, 161, 194. *See also* Publication

Caecilius of Kale Akte, 15, 20, 23, 94
Caricature, 73. *See also* Parody
Chronological order of speeches, 3–6, 12 f.
Clausulae, 102 n. 6
Colloquial language, 83–85
Colometry of prose, 69, 90, 135, 138
Comic style, 83–86
Composite authorship, 151 f., 159, 161–163
Computers, 100–102
Consultancy, 140–171, 175
Cumulative sum ('cusum') graphs, 109 f.

δέ, 86, 105, 112 f.
Deinarchos, 12, 16–22, 26
Demades, 190 n. 21
Demetrios, *On Style*, 89 f.
Democracy, 47–51, 181–185
Demosthenes, 51, 150, 155 f.; i–xiii, 7, 13 n. 12; vii, 4 f., 7, 16, 46, 96 f.; xiii–xvii, 9 n. 11; xviii and xix, 111–114, 168 f.; xxi, 71, 172–174; xxii and xxiv, 104–106, 161–163; xxxii, 156 f.; xxxvii, 167 f.; xl, 16; lviii, 17 f., 23; lix, 10, 28, 34–40

198 Index

διδασκαλίαι, 24
Didymos, 7, 15 n. 14
Dionysios of Halikarnassos, 15, 38, 59; on Deinarchos, 4, 12, 16–20, 26, 192 f.; on Demosthenes, 16–21, 23, 173; on Isaios, 38, 104; on Isokrates, 16, 25, 60, 77, 104 f.; on Lysias, 6, 15, 19–23, 25 f., 38 f., 42 f., 45 f., 59, 76 f., 94 f., 98, 104, 193
Documents in speeches, 4 n. 3, 36 f.
δοκιμασία, 5, 7–9, 189
Dramatic dates, 31 f., 41–43
δυναστεία, 49 f.

εἰκός, 57
εἶναι, 127 f., 139–143, 146 f.
εἰσαγγελία, 189
εἶτα and ἔπειτα, 84 f.
ἔχειν, 128, 143 f., 146 f.
Empedokles, 176
Epideictic style, 59–69, 77, 104, 145 f.
ἦθος, 76–78, 82 f.
Euripides, 85
εὔθυναι, 8, 44

Fees. *See* Payment
Forensic style, 59, 83–86, 104, 175 n. 1
Forgery, 4 n. 3, 190 n. 21
Formulae, 106 f., 164 f.

Galen, *On his own Books*, 25, 153 f., 159
Generalisation, 35 f., 74–76, 107, 185
Genre, 57–71
γίγνεσθαι, 127 f., 139–143, 146 f.
Gilbert Islands, 179, 181
Gorgias, 58, 74 f., 90 f., 190

Harpokration, 13–22
Herodas, 68 n. 9
Herodotos, 186 f.
ἑταῖραι, 35 f.
Hiatus, 68 f., 89, 163
Homer, *Iliad* i. 121–303, 177 f.; ii. 220, 178; iii. 204–224, 177; xviii. 497–508, 181
Homicide, 8
Hypereides, 12

Imitation, 91–93
Improvisation, 150 n. 4, 167 f.
Inscriptiones Graecae i².45.21, 180 n. 8
Ionicisms, 167
Iphikrates, 35, 45
Isaios, 6 f., 89 n. 39; iii, 5
Isokrates, 33, 84–86, 106; xvi, 160; xvii, 14 f., 22, 60, 77, 104, 160; xx, 160

Juries, 54, 71, 77, 181 f.

καί, 58, 85, 88, 105, 112
Kallimachos, 8 n. 8, 20 f., 23–27, 160, 194
Kephalos, 29 f., 38 f., 41 f., 51 f.
Korax, 176

Leogoras, 192
λογογράφος, 155 f., 175 f.
λοιδορία, 9
Lysias, I (*On the Killing of Eratosthenes*), 2, 86, 88 n. 36, 116 f., 125 f., 131, 136, 140, 144, 146, 148 f., 159, 188; II (*Epitaphios*), 2, 25 f., 55 f., 59, 61–67, 69, 97, 145 f., 193 f.; III (*Defence against Simon*), 7, 76, 86, 117, 140 f., 145 f.; IV (*Defence against a charge of Malicious Wounding*), 7, 58 f., 117 f., 125 f., 131, 137, 144–146; V (*Defence of Kallias*), 7, 19, 118, 145 f.; VI (*Prosecution of Andokides*), 7, 18, 56, 78–83, 90, 137, 142 f., 146, 169, 192 n. 23, 194; VII (*On the Sacred Enclosure*), 7, 18, 88 n. 36, 118, 125 f., 137, 141, 146; VIII (*Against Associates*), 8 f., 11 f., 36 n. 6, 51, 89, 118 f., 125 f., 131 f., 141, 146, IX (*Defence of the Soldier*), 8 f., 11 f., 14, 18, 49, 119, 125 f.; X (*Prosecution of Theomnestos*), 7 f., 11–14, 18, 44, 119, 125 f., 132, 137, 146, 166; XI (précis of X), 7, 11 f., 14, 166 f.; XII (*Prosecution of Eratosthenes*), 8, 19, 28–30, 39, 44, 47, 51, 61–65, 67–69, 78, 82 f., 85 f., 88–90, 110–116, 129–131, 134–136, 139 f., 143 f., 164, 193; XIII (*Prosecution of Agoratos*), 5 n. 6, 8 f., 54, 57 n. 1, 61–63, 88, 110–114,

120, 126, 132, 137, 142, 145 f.; XIV (*Prosecution of Alkibiades*), 7–10, 18, 53, 55, 73, 120 f., 126, 137 f., 141, 145 f., 166 f.; XV (précis of XIV), 7, 11, 166 f.; XVI (*Defence of Mantitheos*), 9 f., 89, 121, 145, 147; XVII (*On the Estate of Eraton*), 4, 7, 121, 125 f.; XVIII (*On the Estate of Eukrates*), 5, 7, 121, 125 f., 132, 160; XIX (*On the Estate of Aristophanes*), 7, 54 f., 61, 64, 73, 121 f., 132 f., 138, 141, 147, 165; XX (*Defence of Polystratos*), 9, 19, 44, 56, 122, 133, 138, 143, 147; XXI (*Defence on a charge of Taking Bribes*), 9, 54, 73 f., 122, 143, 160; XXII (*Prosecution of the Grain-dealers*), 8, 10, 45 n. 11, 123, 133, 138, 145 f., XXIII (*On the Status of Pankleon*), 10, 123, 165; XXIV (*Defence of the Cripple*), 8, 19, 123, 125 f., 133, 143 f., 147, 189; XXV (defence of unidentified person), 7, 49 f., 56, 76, 78, 123, 133, 141 f., 144 f., 147; XXVI (*Scrutiny of Euandros*), 7, 44, 124, 134, 138 f., 142 f., 145, 147; XXVII (*Prosecution of Epikrates*), 7, 73, 124; XXVIII (*Prosecution of Ergokles*), 7, 124, 134, 195; XXIX (*Prosecution of Philokrates*), 7, 57, 72, 124, 134, 144, 147; XXX (*Prosecution of Nikomachos*), 8, 19, 54, 73, 124 f., 145; XXXI (*Scrutiny of Philon*), 9, 88 f., 125, 134, 142, 145, 147; XXXII (*Prosecution of Diogeiton*), 125, 139, 147; XXXIII (*Olympikos*), 60–65, 69, 194; XXXIV (*On the Proposal of Phormisios*), 172; XXXV (*Erotikos*), 69–71, 90 f., 194; frr. V and Va (*Defences against Alkibiades*), 53 f.; fr. XLVII (*On his own Benefactions*), 40 f.; fr. XLVIII (*Defence of Euthydemos*), 160 f.; fr. LXV (*Defences of Iphikrates*), 45 f., 193; fr. XCIX (*Speech of Nikias at Syracuse*), 97 f., 191, 194; fr. C (*Prosecution of Nikides*), 3, 19; fr. CXIII (*Defence of Sokrates*), 56, 192; fr. CXX (*On the Estate of Androkleidas*), 46, 58 n. 2; *Defence of Eryximachos* (*P.Ryl.* 489), 5, 56; *Defence against Hippotherses* (*P.Oxy.* 1606), 34, 40 f.; *Speech* (?) *against Alkibiades*, 53; *Trapezitikos*, 22, 160

Magistrates, 181
Manuscripts: Burneianus 95, 2, 6; Palatinus 88, 1–9, 19, 22, 27, 44; Parisinus Graecus 2934, 7, 10, 36 f.
Meletos, 78–80
Menander, 84
Metics, 30, 34, 41, 48

Names of litigants, 4
Narrative, 83–86, 88, 107
Neaira, 34–38
Nikias, 191 f.
Numbering of speeches, 3

Oligarchy, 47–51, 181–183

παιγνίον, 59, 69–71
Papyri: *P.Lit.Lond.*132, 12; *P.Oxy.*1606, 6, 28, 40; *P.Oxy.*2537, 4 n. 2, 11–14, 16, 22, 27; *P.Oxy.*2538, 164 n. 18; *P.Ryl.*489, 5
παραγραφή, 10
Parallelism. *See* Symmetry
Parody, 69 f., 90–92
Participles, 86, 105 f., 113
Party, political, 50 f.
Paulos of Mysia, 22 n. 23
Payment, 157 f.
Peiraieus, 30
Pergamene scholars, 21, 191
Perikles, 29, 39, 42, 51
Phaiax, 191
Phaidros, 29, 32
Pindar, 8 n. 8, 10, 12 f., 24
Plato, 31 f., 41–43, 102 n. 6; *Apology*, 78, 80 n. 30; *Euthyphro*, 78–80; *Phaedrus*, 28 f., 32 f., 41–43, 53, 68 f., 90 f.; *Protagoras*, 52; *Republic*, 29–31, 39, 42 f., 52 f.; *Symposium*, 52, 90 f.
[Plutarch], *Lives of the Ten Orators*, 39 f.
Poetic colouring, 79
ποιεῖσθαι, 128 f., 144–147
Polemarchos, 29 f., 32 f.

Index

Politics, 47–51, 55, 149 f., 170 f., 175 n. 1, 180, 183 f.
Polykrates (sophist), 190 f.
Prejudice against oratory, 155 f.
Probability, argument from, 57
Publication, 151–154, 168–174

Reading, 187
Rhetoric, 175 f., 179, 182

Samples, size of, 110, 114
Sentence-length, 107 f.
Sentence-structure, 60–64, 79
Slaves, 154, 168, 188
Sokrates, 29, 31–33, 78–80, 192 f.
Statistics, 95 n. 1, 98–103, 128
Stichometry, 36 f.
Stylistic caprice, 126, 134 n. 8
Stylometry, 57 f., 87–90, 94–147
Subjective judgment, 94–96
Supplementum Epigraphicum Graecum: x.64, 31 n. 3; xiii.17.112, 32
Symbuleutic style, 59, 175 n. 1
Symmetry, 60–64, 82

Syracuse, 38, 40–43

Teisias, 176
Thematic connection, 5, 9–11, 20
Theophrastos, 191
Thirty Tyrants, 29 f., 32 f., 47 f., 51, 182
Thrasymachos, 52 f.
Thucydides, 43, 50, 74, 106 f.
Thurioi, 51, 38 f., 42 f.
Titles of speeches, 4 f., 16 f., 20, 159
Torture, 188
Tragedy, 185 f.

ὕβρις, 12

Variation, stylistic, 59, 104, 106 f.
Vocabulary, 64–68, 79–82, 115–126

Word-frequency, 105, 112–114
Word order, 89 f., 104, 107, 127–147
Word-play, 98

ξενία, 11 f.
Xenophon, 108

www.ingramcontent.com/pod-product-compliance
Lightning Source LLC
Chambersburg PA
CBHW021707230426
43668CB00008B/753